wines

Rhône Valley

the 90 greatest

Rhône Valley

« Grandeur Nature » Collection

Collection based on an idea
by Marc Walter
© Marc Walter and Archipel
concept, 1999

Editor
Jean-Jacques Brisebarre

Art director
Marc Walter

Editorial assistant
Jeffrey Levy

Layout
Archipel concept

Creation and production
Archipel concept
9, rue de la Collégiale
75005 Paris

Printed in Italy by Milanostampa
september 2000

First edition
Vallée du Rhône Grandeur Nature
Editions E.P.A. -
Hachette-Livre, 1999

© for this edition
2000 - Hachette-Livre
Dépôt légal : 3787
september 2000
ISBN : 2.85120.568.4
65/0828/7-01

JAMES TURNBULL

the 90 greatest wines

Photographs by
Daniel Czap

HACHETTE
Livre

Contents

Note

Practical information concerning the estates and firms featured in this book—their addresses and telephone numbers, directions for visiting them, and an indication of the price of their wine and where to buy it—is given in the address list on page 190.

So strong is worldwide demand, some of the estates have little if any wine to sell to the passing visitor, who should instead call on the retail outlets in order to purchase bottles. Most estates may be visited, in which case common courtesy demands a telephone call in order to make an appointment before arriving.

Introduction

At last they have been 'rediscovered'. Consumers, tiring of bland New World wines, unaffordable Bordeaux and unavailable Burgundy, have discovered in the Rhône Valley a range of remarkably good wines, sold at very reasonable prices and packed with excitingly different flavours. Their interest has triggered a veritable renaissance up and down the Rhône Valley, and the return to prosperity has brought renewed confidence in the future. Historical vineyards which were stagnating, such as Côte-Rôtie, or even on the point of disappearing, such as that of the inimitable Condrieu (of which no more than 8 hectares remained in 1965) are once again the scene of much activity. In a conclusive demonstration of admiration, growers in many foreign countries are supplanting plots of Cabernet and Chardonnay with Viognier, Syrah, Grenache, Mourvèdre and the other grape varieties which make these intriguing, spicily-flavoured and generous wines.

Their reemergence over recent years has been accompanied by a revolution in wine-making methods. Many young growers nowadays take a course at a wine school, and follow it with work experience in another wine region or even country, enabling them to set out with a better idea of what is possible and what is being achieved elsewhere than their fathers probably ever had. Respect for soil, vine and microclimate is the order of the day, and many growers in the top appellations cultivate their vines organically, or biologically. Some such as Maison Chapoutier and Domaine de Marcoux have even put their vineyards under a biodynamic regime.

In the vatroom and cellars the faults which frequently marred yesterday's wines—rusticity, dried-out fruit, oxidation, lack of acidity...—have been largely eliminated, enabling the wines to hold their heads high alongside technically irreproachable products from elsewhere; today ripeness, freshness, aromatic purity, harmony and typicity are qualities towards which the young *vigneron* strives. The Rhône Valley is fortunate in having a handful of high-profile wine-makers such as Gérard Chave, Marcel Guigal, Auguste Clape and the Perrin brothers, who consistently attain extremely high standards, setting a splendid example for the region's youth. One relative newcomer who can also claim a degree of the credit is the consulting oenologist Jean-Luc Colombo, who from the mid-1980s started criticizing the sloppy wine-making which was responsible for many of the common defects, and for which the easy excuse of 'tradition' was regularly leaned on. There is unfortunately still a lot of mediocre wine, made from badly-sited vineyards by people who care more for quantity than quality... yet there is now very much more, from ordinary Côtes-du-Rhône upwards, which is well made and delicious.

The Rhône Valley's viticultural zone is second only to Bordeaux in size and production. It covers some 72,300 hectares, and is made up of two parts, each having distinctly different climatic and geological characteristics. The northern section, which runs from south of Vienne down to Saint-Péray, has a continental climate. A single black grape, the mighty Syrah, is responsible for all of its great red wines—Côte-Rôtie, Hermitage, Crozes-Hermitage, Saint-Joseph and Cornas. Planted on terraces or slopes mostly composed of clay, limestone, granite or sand, its wine is wonderfully expressive. Growers around the world, having tasted these wines, have been inspired to plant some Syrah; in many countries it is known as Shiraz. Three white grapes are to be found: the rare and capricious Viognier, parent of the perfumed Condrieu and Château-Grillet wines, and Marsanne and Roussanne, which together or alone produce white Hermitage, Saint-Joseph, Crozes-Hermitage and Saint-Péray.

South of Saint-Péray there is a 50-kilometre dearth of vineyards, until one passes Montélimar. From then on down to Avignon and beyond vast tracts of vineyard occupy the arid land. The climate is Mediterranean, and cypress and olive decorate the scenery. The principal wines are Châteauneuf-du-Pape, Gigondas, Vacqueyras, Lirac and Tavel, followed by Côtes-du-Rhône-Villages. The finest villages—there are 16 of them: Cairanne, Séguret, Sablet, Rasteau, Beaumes-de-Venise, and also Chusclan, Laudun, Roaix, Rochegude, Rousset-les-Vignes, Saint-Gervais, Saint-Maurice-sur-Eygues, Saint-Pantaléon-les-Vignes, Valréas, Vinsobres and Visan—are authorised to include their names on labels. The wine best known to the average consumer in and outside France however is ordinary Côtes-du-Rhône, an appellation accorded to vineyards in both northern and southern Rhône which lie outside the better areas. Five other areas, the source of more modest wines, also form part of the Rhône Valley: Costières de Nîmes, Côtes du Ventoux, Coteaux du Tricastin, Côtes du Vivarais and the Diois. Grenache Noir is the dominant black grape variety of the southern Rhône, yet it tends to lack structure and ageing potential when used on its own and is mixed with many subsidiary varieties. Châteauneuf-du-Pape may be made from no less than thirteen (Grenache included): Syrah, Mourvèdre, Cinsault, Vaccarèse, Counoise, Terret Noir and Muscardin (black grapes) and Clairette, Roussanne, Bourboulenc, Picpoul and Picardan (white grapes); other crus each have their list of authorised varieties among these and others.

The Rhône Valley has 7,000 wine-making estates, as well as some 70 cooperatives and many négociant businesses. Since there are numerous different bottles bearing the name of each appellation (Château-Grillet excepted) the grower's name is the most important piece of information on any label. Let no consumer forget it, nor be duped by a prestigious name: there are thoroughly mediocre versions of the greatest appellations just as there are magnificent if humbly-titled Côtes-du-Rhônes.

Who then are the finest wine-makers? Who are those who are incessantly experimenting, and those who faithfully adhere to time-honoured family traditions? What are the histories of their estates? Which grape varieties go to make their wines? Who are the 'modernists' who rear their wines in new oak, and the 'traditionalists' who remain faithful to the *foudre* and *demi-muid*? This book presents the men and women who make the finest wines, and reviews their growing and wine-making techniques, and the styles of wine achieved. By buying a bottle of their wine the consumer is highly likely to be delighted with its quality. The selection was made on the basis of two criteria, quality and regularity, assessed over many comparative tastings. The northern Rhône appellations precede their southern counterparts, and within each appellation the estates are listed by alphabetical order (name and surname).

U p in the hills above Ampuis, Bernard Burgaud goes about the numerous tasks that have made up the *vigneron*'s year since the first century A.D., when Pliny the Younger, Martial and Plutarch praised the wines of these hills. His 4-hectare estate is of average size for a Côte-Rôtie grower, and fortunately, with the wine selling at over 100 francs per bottle, the small production of his single cuvée enables him to live comfortably. Burgaud is one of the more highly rated small growers, and that is only justice.

A valuable insurance policy He started learning the trade young at his father Roger's side, and joined him full-time in 1980. Roger Burgaud had initially simply grown the grapes on his 2 hectares and sold them off to the *négoce*, before starting to make his own wine, which he proceeded to sell off in bulk. On Bernard's arrival the two men started bottling part of the crop. His early experience, completed by a course at the Beaune viticultural lycée, gave the son the necessary means to carry on after his father's sudden death in 1986.

Over the intervening years Burgaud has doubled his holding, often at the price of back-breaking work clearing vineyard terraces unused since the passage of Phylloxera a century ago, and now has land in the Le Champin, Leyat, Les Moutonnes, Côte-Blonde, Fongeant and La Brosse *lieux-dits*. This fragmentation is commonplace at Côte-Rôtie, and a definite insurance policy in Burgaud's opinion, for vines in different microclimates have different qualities and different faults. His are situated on terraces, on high slopes and on the plateau near his house.

Crafted for a long, distinguished life Burgaud sets out each year to make a wine which is rich, well-coloured and structured with the finest tannin for a long, distinguished life. To that end he ferments his fruit at a high 34°, having destalked the entire crop in order to avoid adding the harsher stalk tannin. During fermentation he forces the cap of solids down into the liquid (*pigeage*) up to 8 times a day for maximum extraction of colour, tannin and aroma from the skins. As soon as the fermentation is over the wines are transferred from the open enamel-lined concrete vats into large tuns, in which they undergo their second, malolactic fermentation. When this is over, they are racked into 228-litre casks for some 15 months' ageing, before being bottled with neither fining nor filtration. Burgaud reckons the influence of new oak on maturing wine is beneficial to a limited extent, and replaces one fifth of his casks every year.

Côte-Rôtie Bernard Burgaud's Côte-Rôtie may be enjoyed, he says, in its first 3 years, for its "power and fruit"... as long as it is decanted. Otherwise there is no point in opening it before its 10th birthday, and the best vintages will repay a far lengthier sojourn in the cellar. It is a superbly complex, fleshy wine, with a powerful bouquet of animal, leather, spice, *garrigue*... Intense on the palate, and long on the finish, its strong personality gets on very well with game dishes, red meats in sauce, and fairly spicy dishes.

- Owner:
Bernard Burgaud
- Wine-maker:
Bernard Burgaud
- Vineyard size:
4 hectares
- Grape Variety: Syrah
- Average vine age:
25 years
- Soil type: Schist
- Production:
15,000 bottles
- Exports: 50%
- Take-away sales: Yes
- Visits: By appointment

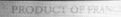

1996

PRODUCT OF FRANCE

Fructus Vitis Et Laboris Hominum

CÔTE RÔTIE

APPELLATION CÔTE - RÔTIE CONTRÔLÉE
MIS EN BOUTEILLE PAR BERNARD BURGAUD
VITICULTEUR - LE CHAMPIN, 69420 AMPUIS FRANCE

12,5% vol.

750 ml

DOMAINE CLUSEL-ROCH

Ampuis might be the historic heartland of Côte-Rôtie production, yet there are growers making excellent wines on the outlying slopes north and south of the town. One such is Domaine Clusel-Roch, based at Verenay. From promising beginnings the work of Gilbert Clusel and his wife Brigitte Roch has regularly improved, gaining them an ever-increasing reputation. Today their Côte-Rôties are among the finest.

Reverting to traditional practices Like many other small growers, René Clusel used to sell his crop to the *négoce*. His son Gilbert joined him after studying wine-making at Beaune, and in 1980 the decision was taken to start making and bottling their own wine, for consumers' interest in Côte-Rôtie and demand for the wine was growing rapidly. René then retired, and before long his son was teamed up with his wife Brigitte.

The couple now own or rent 3,5 hectares of vines, of which 50 ares lie on the Coteau de Chéry in Condrieu, making them 1500 bottles a year of magnificent white wine, the remainder being in Côte-Rôtie. There they have 1,5 hectares in La Viaillère and 80 ares in Le Champon with which they produce their 'classic' Côte-Rôtie, and 70 ares of old vines in Les Grandes Places, which since 1988 they have kept apart in the best years and made as a special cuvée.

Like many up-and-coming growers in the Rhône Valley, Clusel and Roch have reverted to 'traditional' vineyard practices: there is no mechanisation—the 45° angle of the slopes itself dictates manual labour anyway—, and since 1984 no insecticide, weedkiller or chemical fertilizer has been used, and spray treatments are only used as a last resort against fungal outbreaks such as mildew and oidium.

Vinification 'à l'ancienne' The Côte-Rôties are made very much in the ancestral fashion, by fermentation on their stalks by their own yeast in concrete vats for some 15 days. For extraction of colour, tannin and aroma there is lots of *pigeage* in the first days of vatting, and the liquid is subsequently pumped up and sprayed over the floating cap of solids (*remontage*) regularly to increase this. After the alcoholic fermentation the free-run wine is run off and the solid matter pressed by means of an old vertical wooden press. This press wine is then reincorporated after the free-run has undergone its malolactic fermentation, and the wine is then reared in oak barrels for 2 years before bottling, fined but unfiltered.

Côte-Rôtie Les Grandes Places What sets the domaine's top cuvée apart from the regular one is the greater age of the vines, the absence of any Viognier in the blend (there is some 4% in the regular wine, which softens up the Syrah somewhat) and the higher proportion (50%) of new oak in which the wine is reared. These factors all contribute to shaping a wine which is more powerful and structured and therefore less approachable in its youth; a wine which is destined for greater things, over a longer time scale. When after 8-10 years it is approaching maturity, one may envisage serving Les Grandes Places with a haunch of venison.

- Other red wine: Côte-Rôtie
- White wine: Condrieu
- Owners: Gilbert Clusel & Brigitte Roch
- Wine-makers: Gilbert Clusel & Brigitte Roch
- Combined vineyards: 3.5 hectares
- Production: 17,000 bottles
- Exports: 45%
- Take-away sales: Mon.-Sat., by appointment
- Visits: By appointment

Wine selected:
Côte-Rôtie
Les Grandes Places

- Grape Variety: Syrah
- Average vine age: 65 years
- Vineyard size: 0.7 hectares
- Soil type: Schist
- Average production: 2,000 bottles

1996

CÔTE - ROTIE

Appellation Côte-Rôtie Contrôlée

Les Grandes Places

DOMAINE CLUSEL-ROCH
Viticulteurs

12% Vol.   750 ml

Verenay . 69420 Ampuis - France

MISE EN BOUTEILLE A LA PROPRIÉTÉ   LGP96

MAISON E. GUIGAL

S ome 40% of all Côte-Rôtie is made by the Guigal family of Ampuis. Through the exceptional quality of their wines they have been responsible for putting the appellation on the map for numerous wine-lovers around the world, creating a demand which has brought a degree of prosperity to all its growers and resulted in much-improved general standards. Maison Guigal is today a large and thriving business, where quantity and quality manage to go hand in hand.

A young man makes good The firm was founded in 1946 when Etienne Guigal, who as a young man had started off as a cellar-hand and worked his way up at the famous Ampuis firm Vidal-Fleury, left to set up his own business. For 15 years things prospered, then in 1961 he was suddenly struck blind, and his 17-year-old son Marcel was summoned to help out. Blessed with an innate feeling for making wine, rigorous, methodical and perfectionist, and having a flair for public relations which many a company boss would envy, by the end of the 1970s Marcel Guigal's wines were being praised by critics and connoisseurs far and wide.

Grower and négociant Over the years the Guigals have painstakingly acquired prime parcels of land. The jewels in the crown are their 3 Côte-Rôtie *crus*, La Mouline, La Landonne and La Turque, for which there is much too little supply to meet the ferocious demand. In 1994 a prestige Condrieu named La Doriane was inaugurated, and the following year, the year Guigal's son Philippe first participated in the wine-making, the Côte-Rôtie Château d'Ampuis was launched.
Besides these, the products of Guigal's own 12 hectares, the firm produces a range of northern- and southern-Rhône wines from grapes bought from over 70 growers. The range encompasses all the important appellations, and all the wines are of very good if not excellent quality.

Top-quality fruit and protracted vinification The quality of Guigal wines derives from faultless raw material and perfectionism in the vatroom and cellars. Guigal vineyards are worked organically, the vines' production is ruthlessly limited, and the grapes are harvested at optimum ripeness, and these same criteria are demanded of the firm's supplying growers. Arriving fruit undergoes rigorous examination before admission to the vatroom, where it is carefully vinified in the most suitable manner, taking into account its origin and the quality of the vintage.
The top red wines are aged in nothing but new oak barrels—a fact which initially earned much criticism—and this treatment lasts no less than 42 months… yet the wines are so rich that after several years in bottle the oak influence is barely detectable. During this time they are racked no more than 6 times, and eventually bottled unfined and unfiltered. After such protracted treatment, their longevity is no surprise…

Côte-Rôtie La Turque Lying in between the two côtes, La Turque has both the virility typical of the Côte Brune and the feminine subtlety of the Côte Blonde. Very dark, rich, spicy and complex, with a red-fruit character when young, its intensity on the nose and palate is breathtaking, and its potential is underlined by an exceptionally long and complex finish. A haunch of venison is called for here!

- Other red wines:
Côte-Rôtie La Mouline,
Côte-Rôtie La Landonne,
Côte-Rôtie Château
d'Ampuis, Côte-Rôtie
Brune et Blonde,
Hermitage, Châteauneuf-
du-Pape, Gigondas,
Côtes-du-Rhône
- White wines:
Condrieu La Doriane,
Condrieu, Hermitage,
Côtes-du-Rhône
- Owner: E. Guigal S.A.
- Chairman & Managing
Director: Marcel Guigal
- Oenologist:
Philippe Guigal
- Combined vineyards:
12 hectares
- Exports: 60%
- Take-away sales: Yes
- Visits: By appointment

Wine selected:
Côte-Rôtie La Turque

- Grape Varieties:
Syrah 93%, Viognier 7%
- Average vine age:
20 years
- Vineyard size:
0.9 hectares
- Soil type:
Siliceous limestone with
iron oxide
- Average production:
4,000 bottles

1995

• LA TURQUE •
CÔTE BRUNE

Côte-
Rôtie

APPELLATION CÔTE-RÔTIE CONTRÔLÉE

RÉCOLTÉ VINIFIÉ ÉLEVÉ ET MIS EN BOUTEILLE PAR

E. GUIGAL

CHATEAU D'AMPUIS (RHÔNE) FRANCE

13% vol.   PRODUIT DE FRANCE

DOMAINE GILLES BARGE

Among the surprisingly numerous small growers at Côte-Rôtie—there were 44 of them declaring a harvest in 1995, in an area covering just 191 hectares—Gilles Barge is well-known to French and foreign Rhône-wine lovers for the quality of his wine. He is neither a traditionalist nor an out-and-out modernist, but reassesses his methods regularly, to its greater benefit.

Protecting Côte-Rôtie standards Barge started working alongside his father Pierre in 1979, and took over on the latter's retirement in 1993. Gradually the exploitation has grown over recent years, with acquisitions and farming contracts bringing the total holding up to 7.5 hectares. As if that were not enough to keep him busy he has also been President of the Côte-Rôtie growers' union since 1989. That has been a position of great responsibility, for with the increasing popularity of Côte-Rôtie since the early 1980s has come a flood of requests for planting rights; if accorded, they would inevitably herald a drop in the general standard of the wines, for less suitable land would probably find its way inside the appellation boundaries, and the market would also be flooded with a significant quantity of young-vine wine for a good number of years. Fortunately, in a praiseworthy show of self-discipline, the union's committee members have decided that in the near future not more than 5 hectares of new plantings should be allowed per year.

Vinifying for the long term Despite having a small percentage of Viognier, which adds delicacy and softness to Syrah wine, in the blend—the origins of this practice lie in the fact that different varieties used to grow side by side on the terraces, making it unfeasible to harvest varieties separately—Barge's wines need a fair amount of ageing in bottle, and rarely afford much pleasure before their sixth birthday. Hardly surprising, for he vinifies his crushed grapes on their stalks, in closed stainless steel vats with an internal design which prevents the cap of solids from rising to the surface, ensuring maximum extraction of colour, tannin and aroma. This is fine is good years, but can be detrimental to balance in years when the grapes ripen unevenly.
After 3 weeks the wines are run into barrel and *foudre* for 2 years' ageing, then bottled in one fell swoop with neither fining nor filtering—a welcome recent change of policy, to eliminate the gross discrepancies which used to occur in the wine as a result of many bottlings over a long period. Confusingly for the consumer, until his father retired there were regularly two versions of each vintage, one sold under the father's name, the other under the son's.

Côte-Rôtie Côte Brune The deep, dark purple colour prepares one for a rich, firm mouthful, and a waft of heady, peppery black fruit aromas leads on to the wonderfully intense flavour of the Côte Brune in the mouth. Even young and closed, this wine's pedigree is evident… yet, of course, time enables it to develop its glorious perfume, and to digest its tannic structure sufficiently and hone its seductive powers. Then, served alongside a simple fillet of beef, it does not fail to send all present into raptures!

- Other red wines:
Côte-Rôtie Cuvée du Plessy, Saint-Joseph Clos des Martinets
- White wines:
Condrieu, Saint-Joseph La Ribaudy
- Owner: Gilles Barge
- Wine-maker:
Gilles Barge
- Oenologist:
Michel Laurent
- Combined vineyards:
7.5 hectares
- Production:
40,000 bottles
- Exports: 30%
- Take-away sales: Yes
- Visits: Yes

Wine selected:
Côte-Rôtie Côte Brune

- Grape Varieties:
Syrah 95%, Viognier 5%
- Average vine age:
35 years
- Vineyard size:
1.5 hectares
- Soil type:
Micaschist and gneiss
- Average production:
5,000 bottles

DOMAINE J. VIDAL-FLEURY

The Rhône Valley wine industry owes much to Joseph Vidal and his successors, who for two centuries produced wines which were standard-bearers for the region. Since 1985 the firm has been in the ownership of the renowned Guigal family, which has been thoroughly beneficial for it: the Vidal-Fleury Côte-Rôties in particular are remarkable!

A vineyard worker makes good The Vidals were originally vineyard workers. In 1781 Joseph Vidal bought a vineyard plot on the steep slopes overlooking Ampuis, which he tended in the rare moments which were not taken up in the service of his employer, M. d'Harenc, the Lord of Ampuis. He soon started selling his wine in Lyon, yet this brought him into direct competition with d'Harenc, and he soon found himself without a job. There was only one course open to him, so Vidal sought out other vineyard plots to rent in order to be able to make a living as his own master.
During the Revolution he became mayor of Ampuis, and when his former employer chose to flee he had the satisfaction of acquiring his vineyards. Vidal went on to live his life to the full, as grower, wine-maker and mayor, until his death in 1848.

Saved from approaching decline Successive generations built on his legacy, acquiring further land on the Côte Blonde, consolidating the firm's reputation for fine wines, and eventually battling their way through the terrible hardship caused by the Phylloxera invasion. After the Great War Joseph Vidal-Fleury inherited the firm, and he too devoted his life to it, investing in vineyards and cellars and producing wines of great quality. However he died without heir in 1979, and the rudderless company's standards started slipping.
Its salvation was to come from Etienne Guigal, who had learnt his trade during 15 years under the patriarch Joseph before leaving to set up his own business in 1946. In 1985 he and his son Marcel fulfilled what must have been a lifetime dream, for Vidal-Fleury owned some of the finest parcels of Côte-Rôtie, and its acquisition gave them control of a very large share of the production of that appellation.

An inspired choice The Guigals handed responsibilities for their new acquisition to Jean-Pierre Rochias, who had previously been with the Bordeaux firm Cordier, and he has proved an inspired choice, for the renaissance at Vidal-Fleury has been rapid and unmistakable. As well as producing Côte-Rôties from its own estate, the firm matures and markets a range of wines covering the whole length of the Rhône valley from bought-in wine. Vinifications take place in Guigal's recently-built state-of-the-art winery, but apart from that the two firms theoretically remain totally independent.

Côte-Rôtie La Châtillonne Vidal-Fleury's finest wine, from a parcel named La Châtillonne on the Côte Blonde, is an exquisitely suave, perfumed and complex brew, black of colour, which at a half-dozen years of age bewitches the taster with its heady bouquet of violets, liquorice and roasted coffee. This remarkable blend of power and finesse is naturally well-suited to all manner of game dishes, yet its qualities are equally entranced by the simplicity of a fillet of top-quality beef.

- Other red wines: Côte-Rôtie Brune et Blonde, Côte-Rôtie, Hermitage, Crozes-Hermitage, Cornas, Saint-Joseph, Châteauneuf-du-Pape, Gigondas, Vacqueyras, Cairanne, Côtes-du-Rhône-Villages, Côtes-du-Rhône, Côtes-du-Ventoux
- White wines: Condrieu, Saint-Joseph, Crozes-Hermitage, Châteauneuf-du-Pape, Côtes-du-Rhône, Muscat de Beaumes-de-Venise
- Rosé wines: Tavel, Côtes-du-Rhône
- Manager: Jean-Pierre Rochias
- Wine-maker: Jean-Pierre Rochias
- Combined vineyards: 10 hectares
- Exports: 60%
- Take-away sales: Weekdays only
- Visits: No

Wine selected:
**Côte-Rôtie
La Châtillonne**

- Grape Varieties: Syrah 85%, Viognier 15%
- Average vine age: 56 years
- Vineyard size: 1 hectare
- Soil type: Granite and sand
- Average production: 3,400 bottles

U p in the hills away from Ampuis and the busy RN86 the Jamet brothers craft their single wine, a Côte-Rôtie, with all the devotion and attention to detail of the master wine-maker, and each new vintage demonstrates just how high are the standards they set themselves. Jean-Paul and Jean-Luc Jamet can be counted without any hesitation among the élite of the young generation of Côte-Rôtie growers.

From difficult times to prosperity The estate was founded by Joseph Jamet in the early 1950s. Economic circumstances at the time were difficult for wine-makers, and for a long while he grew apricots, peaches and nectarines on his plateau land, for Côte-Rôtie sold too cheaply. Gradually little parcels were added to the initial 35 ares, and as the appellation started to enjoy a revival he found an outlet for his produce with the major *négociants* Jaboulet, Chapoutier and Delas. He did not start bottling until 1976, but his wines were soon recognized for their quality.

Having trained his sons he handed over responsibilities to them in the mid-1980s and retired. Since then, by dint of hard work and talent, some notable vintages have been notched up—1988, 1989, 1991 and 1995 are all remarkable, and the lesser years are generally excellent within their context—and the family holdings have been further expanded. Today they cover 7 hectares, and are spread fairly widely, principally on the Côte Brune.

Every step is aimed at eventual perfection The viticultural cycle always starts with severe pruning, and this is followed later on by a careful debudding operation, for yield reduction is naturally at the core of vineyard policy. Leaf-stripping is a handy measure to improve aeration and ripening, and if yields are still higher than required a 'green harvest' around the end of July is necessary.

The brothers always hold on until the grapes are as ripe as possible before beginning the harvest, and then proceed with the wine-making in their own fashion. They never destem the fruit, but lightly crush it and then ferment it in stainless steel by the action of the fruit's own yeast. Daily *remontages* help to extract the colour, tannin and aroma, and temperature control preserves the wine's purity and finesse. The period of fermentation and maceration lasts some 18-20 days, at the end of which the wine, stiffened by the addition of the press-wine, is run into *foudres* and casks for its malolactic fermentation and subsequent *élevage*. One fifth of the casks are renewed each year. Finally the wine is bottled without filtration.

Côte-Rôtie In style the Jamet Côte-Rôtie is medium-bodied, well-balanced and harmonious. Its fruit is always very pure, ripe and well-defined, its structure never excessive nor aggressive, and it is always remarkably elegant. These qualities enable it to develop well in bottle over a good 15-20 years in the better vintages, and it is guaranteed to delight the taster with its sumptuous bouquet of bilberry, liquorice and spice, which often has a smoky aspect and takes on nuances of truffle, leather and wood as it ages. Rabbit fricassee or fillet of beef *en brioche* make very suitable table companions for this great wine.

- Owners: Jean-Paul & Jean-Luc Jamet
- Wine-makers: Jean-Paul & Jean-Luc Jamet
- Oenology: Chambre d'Agriculture de la Drôme
- Vineyard size: 7 hectares
- Grape Variety: Syrah
- Average vine age: 20 years
- Soil type: Schist
- Production: 33,000 bottles
- Exports: 40%
- Take-away sales: Yes
- Visits: By appointment

Côte-Rôtie | Ampuis

Côte Rôtie

Appellation Côte-Rôtie Contrôlée

75 cl

mis en bouteille à la propriété

G.A.E.C. Jamet, Jean-Paul et Jean-Luc

Viticulteurs - 'Le Vallin', Ampuis (Rhône) - France

Product of France

The Jasmin family is well known to French, American and British lovers of Côte-Rôtie thanks to many a vintage of traditionally-crafted, fragrant wine. Jasmin Côte-Rôtie has its own style, it is a genuine 'grower' wine, with all the flaws and flashes of genius that are part and parcel of that category, as opposed to its impeccably-vinified yet frequently standardised 'œnologue' counterpart.

A change of climate   It was a job as cook at the Château d'Ampuis which brought the first Jasmin from Champagne down to the Rhône Valley. Cooks then as today being frequently drawn to wine-making—Alain Senderens, Marc Meneau and Michel Lorain, to name but three, will not deny that!—Jasmin was soon interested in the precarious terraced slopes above Ampuis and their inimitable, perfumed nectar, and purchased a hectare of vines.

In time, his grandson Georges inherited the estate, to which he added a half hectare. Then from 1960 onwards, over almost four decades Robert Jasmin exercised his increasingly sure talents making Côte-Rôtie which gained the small family exploitation an international reputation. A tragic accident deprived the Jasmin family of this warm-hearted man in 1999, and put the responsibility of continuity firmly on the shoulders of his son Patrick, who had fortunately already benefited from 15 years' working alongside him.

A little modernity in a haven of tradition   There is but one Jasmin wine, a Côte-Rôtie produced with grapes from several different parcels spread over the appellation's 191 hectares. The geological variation between the different parcels, which total 4 hectares today, and the fact that they are all on slopes and not on flat land, are factors which explain the wine's quality and aromatic complexity. The family owns 2 hectares on the Côte Brune above the northern end of Ampuis, in the Les Moutonnes and Côte Bodin *climats*, one hectare in the *lieu-dit* Les Baleyats and one hectare on the Côte Blonde.

Until recently Robert Jasmin, thoroughly traditional in his ways, never destemmed his grapes and fermented in cement vats with little regard for temperature control. However a little stainless steel has recently found its way onto the premises, and if the raw material demands it there may be 50% or even 100% destemming. Likewise bottling, which to many foreign clients' frustration was carried out in three or four sessions, is now accomplished in just two. The growing influence of the younger generation?

Côte-Rôtie   Never the darkest of Côte-Rôties, the Jasmins' wine is always beautifully perfumed and harmoniously balanced, with an elegance which has often led to it being described as the most 'Burgundian' of its ilk. Delicate strawberry aromas seasoned with a little pepper rise from the swirled wine, which subsequently surprises the taster by its fullness of flavour on the palate, and its very apparent breed. It may be appreciated relatively young, yet great vintages can live two decades or more. At the moment of truth, a noble red meat is called for: this Côte-Rôtie proves highly eloquent alongside a truffled fillet of beef.

- Owner: Patrick Jasmin
- Wine-maker: Patrick Jasmin
- Combined vineyards: 4 hectares
- Grape Varieties: Syrah 95%, Viognier 5%
- Average vine age: 25 years
- Soil type: Clay and limestone
- Production: 20,000 bottles
- Exports: 40%
- Take-away sales: 9-12 a.m., 2-4 p.m., by appt.
- Visits: By appointment, maximum 15 people

Côte-Rôtie | Ampuis

DOMAINE JEAN-MICHEL GERIN

I n a short period of time Jean-Michel Gerin has forcefully inscribed his credentials alongside those of the other star producers of Côte-Rôtie and Condrieu, with wines eminently capable of satisfying the most exacting oenophiles. Gerin is a man who has seen tradition at work, compared it with some of the more modern options, and made up his own mind. His wines are well worth seeking out.

A young man goes it alone Gerin's family is well-known in the area, for his father Alfred was local Senator and Mayor of Ampuis, and the instigator of a planting programme in the 1960s which gave birth to the Domaine de Bonserine, a Franco-American enterprise which was eventually sold in 1988 to the Beaujolais merchant Maison Georges Duboeuf. Gerin Junior started out on his own in 1990 with 5 hectares of vines, to which 3 more have since been added. Besides a small amount of the La Landome slope, his estate now comprises 1.3 hectares in Les Grandes Places, above Verenay, 4 hectares on the Champin plateau above Ampuis, and 2 hectares of Viognier at Condrieu, on the Coteau de la Loye.
Being of the same outlook as many other thinking growers of his generation, his vineyards are cultivated with the greatest respect for soil, vine and environment, for only by respecting the soil can the *terroir* express itself. To protect the soil's micro-organic life vineyard maintenance tasks such as weeding are therefore carried out manually, and no synthetic insecticides or fertilizers are used.

Selection and rejection Perfect ripeness being considered essential for quality wine, Gerin never rushes to harvest, and when his pickers start work they not only cut off the bunches but also examine them and reject all that is not fit for vinification. The fruit is placed in shallow crates of a capacity of 25 kgs in order to avoid any of it getting crushed, and is then rushed off to the cellars.
Since his early days Gerin has taken the advice of the oenologist Jean-Luc Colombo for the wine-making. Grapes are entirely destalked and then receive 25-30 days' *cuvaison* in stainless steel vats with narrow tops, with lots of *pigeage* to extract as much colour, tannin and aroma as possible. To that end also temperatures in the vat are allowed to rise higher than many others would countenance. In years of rain dilution a *saignée* is carried out to increase the ratio of solid matter to liquid, for greater concentration.
After fermentation comes *élevage*. Here Gerin is revealed in his true modernist colours, for there is not a *foudre* nor a *demi-muid* in sight in his cellars. His Condrieu is fermented and reared in 228-litre barrels and his two Côte-Rôties also make close acquaintance with small oak for their *élevage*. He opts for barrels with a heavy 'toast'.

Côte-Rôtie Les Grandes Places Gerin's single-parcel Les Grandes Places is reared in nothing but new oak for 2 years, and is a remarkably elegant, balanced and harmonious example of Côte-Rôtie. Soft on the palate, rich and refined, its subtlety of structure makes it very different to that of Clusel-Roch, for example. That this bottle gives tasters pleasure and incites them to conviviality, that is Gerin's hope; at table it has the necessary manners to look a Châteaubriand maître d'hôtel in the eye.

- Other red wines: Côte-Rôtie Champin Le Seigneur, Côte-Rôtie La Landonne
- White wine: Condrieu Coteau de la Loye
- Owner: Jean-Michel Gerin
- Wine-maker: Jean-Michel Gerin
- Oenologist: Jean-Luc Colombo
- Combined vineyards: 8 hectares
- Production: 40,000 bottles
- Exports: 30%
- Take-away sales: 9-12 a.m., 2-6 p.m.
- Visits: No

Wine selected:
Côte-Rôtie
Les Grandes Places

- Grape Variety: Syrah
- Average vine age: 10 and 60 years
- Vineyard size: 1.3 hectares
- Soil type: Mica-schist
- Average production: 5,000 bottles

Côte-Rôtie | Vérenay

CÔTE
RÔTIE
Appellation Côte-Rôtie contrôlée
Les Grandes Places
1996
Jean-Michel Gerin
Mis en bouteille à la Propriété
Ampuis 69420 France
Red Rhône Wine
750 ml - Alc by vol 12,5%
Produce of France
L5611

For a half-century Emile Champet has produced Côte-Rôtie packed with character, like the man himself, which progressively reveals its aromatic depth as the years go by. In the latter half of the 1980s he started easing up and handed over most of his vines to his son Joël, who learnt the trade at his side. These days the Joël Champet Côte-Rôtie is among the finest of the appellation… but it is unfortunately made in very limited quantities.

A year in the vineyard The diminutive and youthful Emile passed on all the finer points of producing top-quality Syrah grapes to his son, who is now regularly to be seen on the steep, stony slopes of La Viaillère carrying out the various operations which make up the vine's year. Every month sees activity of some sort in the vineyard: during the vine's period of dormancy between November and March the essential operation of pruning is carried out, and the soil is turned and manured—although growers on the steeper slopes prefer to let the soil become compact, to lessen the risk of it sliding downhill during the rains; between April and August the Syrah undergoes prolific growth and must be restrained in order to achieve good balance between leaf and fruit, by cutting off excess shoots and attaching those retained; also, although relatively disease-resistant, it must be protected by (limited) spraying; around the end of July excess bunches are lopped off when they change colour to keep yields down to the required level, and the month of August sees the grapes ripen, a process lasting about 100 days; finally in September and October the moment of truth arrives, as the crop is harvested and brought in for transformation into wine…

Vinification in the traditional family manner The wine-making process has always been as traditional as one could wish chez Champet, with all the good and bad points that that entails. Made in Emile's time under the family house down near the river in Ampuis, it is now produced in Joël's premises in the middle of the vines outside Verenay, 2 kilometres north of Ampuis. Grapes are never destemmed, and are fermented and macerated for 3 weeks in open concrete vats, with regular *pigeage* by wooden grill. The wine is then aged in cask and *foudre* for 15-18 months, and eventually bottled without filtration. Bottling is carried out by hand over a 15-month period, with the result that bottle variation is not unknown.

Côte-Rôtie La Viallière Champet's wine, produced in the splendid Viaillère vineyard north of Ampuis, is the colour of black cherries, and indeed has an appealing nose of morello cherry and plum. It is nicely concentrated on the palate, with spiciness and an earthy aspect, and great elegance. In difficult years it does occasionally lack balance or display bitter stalk tannin—that is the price of unwavering adherence to vinification *à l'ancienne*—yet when the going's good, La Viallière (as Champet calls it) is great. It has been described as the most 'Burgundian' of Côte-Rôties by certain writers, and indeed served blind could trip up an experienced taster. Venison and wild boar are the meats for this wine, preferably prepared *en civet*.

- Owner: Joël Champet
- Wine-maker: Joël Champet
- Vineyard size: 2.3 hectares
- Grape Varieties: Syrah 92%, Viognier 8%
- Average vine age: 20 years
- Soil type: Stony
- Production: 11,000 bottles
- Exports: 2%
- Take-away sales: Yes
- Visits: By appointment

Côte-Rôtie | Ampuis

Few growers in Ampuis have as fine a selection of Côte-Rôtie vineyards at their disposal as René Rostaing, and it is therefore satisfying to note that few put what they have to as good a use. Rostaing seems to have an innate understanding of his vines and a talent for extracting their very finest qualities, to make Côte-Rôties of great purity and harmony. His wines are without doubt some of the appellation's finest.

Marriage and a new vocation Rostaing is unusual in being a businessman who came to wine by marriage, an outsider who has wholeheartedly embraced a new occupation. Most of his professional life has been spent building up a successful estate agency and property-management business in Condrieu, yet when he married the daughter of Albert Dervieux, one of the finest old-school Côte-Rôtie growers, a new world was opened up to him. Advised by his father-in-law he started making small quantities of wine, which very rapidly earned critical acclaim.

A fine portfolio is pieced together It was only natural that he should want to increase his vineyard holdings, yet acquiring Côte-Rôtie vineyards is a difficult affair—the appellation covers less than some 200 hectares, which are exploited by a good 40 growers. However luck has definitely been on his side. When Dervieux retired in 1990 Rostaing was offered the tenancy of his superbly-sited vineyards on a *fermage* basis, and 3 years later Marius Gentaz-Dervieux also retired, offering the young man his on the same basis. He now makes 3 different Côte-Rôties, as well as a tiny amount of Condrieu.

Vinification tailored to the vintage Rostaing makes his wines in a new winery down by the 'port' of Ampuis. As one might expect from an outsider who has not been subjected to family tradition since youth, he reflects a great deal each year on how to make the best use of what Nature has given him, and this is no doubt a great strength. Some years there is more destalking than others, and while the generic cuvée is generally entirely destalked, the top wines are only partially so. Stainless steel vats with automatic *pigeage* equipment stand ready, in which the Côte-Rôties are vinified for some 3 weeks at relatively high temperatures, before maturation in a mix of 225-litre *pièces* and 600-litre *demi-muids*, roughly one third of which are replaced each year. After 2 years the wines are bottled, with neither fining nor filtration if their condition permits it.

Côte-Rôtie Côte Blonde The exquisite Côte Blonde is without doubt one of the most seductive and elegant wines of the appellation, yet it nevertheless has all the richness, concentration, colour and tannin of a top-quality Syrah wine. In general its bouquet is perfectly developed after 6-8 years, with the formidable intensity and definition of very low yields and very old vines. Any chance of acquiring a bottle should not be missed, for this wine provides a sublimely hedonistic tasting experience! Winged game suit it perfectly, with the general rule that the older the wine, the longer the bird should be hung.

- Other red wines:
Côte-Rôtie La Landonne,
Côte-Rôtie
- White wine: Condrieu
- Owner: René Rostaing
- Wine-maker:
René Rostaing
- Combined vineyards:
8 hectares
- Production:
33,000 bottles
- Exports: 90%
- Take-away sales:
By appointment
- Visits: By appointment

Wine selected:
Côte-Rôtie Côte Blonde

- Grape Variety: Syrah
- Average vine age:
60 years
- Vineyard size:
1.2 hectares
- Soil type: Mica-schist
- Average production:
4,000 bottles

Produit Français

« Ce vin du Viennois   à odeur de violette »
(Pline le Jeune)

Côte-Rôtie

COTE BLONDE

APPELLATION CÔTE-RÔTIE CONTRÔLÉE

R. ROSTAING, Propriétaire à Ampuis (Rhône) FRANCE

Mis en bouteille à la propriété

DOMAINE ANDRÉ PERRET

Condrieu's unique and highly-prized wines are made exclusively with the Viognier grape, on terraces of granitic soil looking down on the Rhône. There are few really good producers of Condrieu, for Viognier is notoriously difficult to grow, yet the most talented handful maintain standards with zeal, passion and devotion. One of the foremost is the young André Perret, who produces wines which invariably display the quintessential qualities which make this wine so sought-after.

Different soils for different wines Perret took over from his father in 1982, and has enlarged the estate from the half-hectare that was exploited at the time—in those days fruit was the mainstay of the family business—to 10 hectares. No less than 4 of these lie in the Condrieu appellation, while the remainder produce red and white Saint-Joseph and red Côtes-du-Rhône.

Perret produces his Condrieus from two vineyards which have different soils, and thus give wines which have distinctly different characters. The Coteau de Chéry, lying over a bend in the Rhône between Condrieu and Vérin, has a layer of arzelle, a powdery soil of granite, mica and schist; this is one of Condrieu's finest slopes, and this soil is reckoned by many to give body and power to its wines. A few kilometres further south, looking down on Chavanay, lies Clos Chanson, whose soil has a higher clay content, and gives a wine which is perhaps less demanding of the taster, yet is redolent of the exquisite floral aromas which characterise Viognier wines.

Limited yields and barrel fermentation There are many essentials which can not be ignored if one is to produce quality fruit with this variety. Yields must be kept very low and fruit must be allowed to ripen fully before harvesting; Perret is never reluctant to prune, and the high average age of his vines also works against large yields, and makes for really top-quality juice. Insecticides are not used, manure is organic, and all viticultural operations are based on *lutte raisonnée*.

Coteau de Chéry and Clos Chanson are both fermented and matured exclusively in barrels, while the third, young-vine Condrieu knows stainless steel as well as wood. Malolactic fermentations are systematically encouraged, taking place in barrel for the two main wines, and the Burgundian technique of stirring up the lees is used to increase flavour and texture. After 12 months the wines are ready for bottling.

Condrieu Coteau de Chéry Starting out—as do many Condrieus—a fine yellow gold colour, the Coteau de Chéry is more marked initially by its terroir than the wines of most other slopes, and requires 3-5 years for the varietal characteristics to come into their own, by which time (atypically for a white wine) the colour will have lightened up somewhat. At a half-dozen years of age André Perret's Coteau de Chéry brilliantly combines power, richness and fascinating aromatic complexity, with a delicious and original bouquet of herbs and violets. At that age, suggests Perret, it is the perfect partner for shrimps' tail gratin.

- Other white wines:
Condrieu Clos Chanson,
Condrieu, Saint-Joseph
- Red wines:
Saint-Joseph, Côtes-du-Rhône
- Owner: André Perret
- Wine-maker:
André Perret
- Combined vineyards:
10 hectares
- Production:
40,000 bottles
- Exports: 40%
- Take-away sales: Yes
- Visits: By appointment

Wine selected:
Condrieu
Coteau de Chéry

- Grape Variety: Viognier
- Average vine age:
35 years
- Vineyard size:
3 hectares
- Soil type: Granite
- Average production:
8,000 bottles

Condrieu | Verlieu

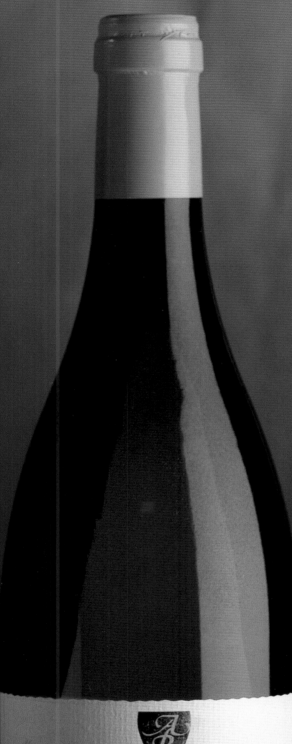

1997

COTEAU DE CHERY

Condrieu

APPELLATION CONDRIEU CONTRÔLÉE

ANDRE PERRET

PROPRIETAIRE VITICULTEUR À CHAVANAY 42410 FRANCE
PRODUCE OF FRANCE

DOMAINE FRANÇOIS VILLARD

No line-up of good Condrieu would be complete without one or two of François Villard's wines, about which it is easy to be too liberal with the superlatives. Powerful, intensely aromatic and impeccably balanced, they show just how magnificent the Viognier grape is, and how at home it is in the decomposed granite and mica-schist of Condrieu's terraces... and they show just what a gulf there is between Condrieu and wines made elsewhere from the Viognier.

A change of job Villard's rise to prominence has been as remarkable as it has been meteoric, since he does not come from a wine-making background. The young man was a hospital cook until giving up that job at the start of 1988 to make wine. Knowing nothing more about the subject than the average wine-loving man in the street he signed up to do a sommellerie course in Tain l'Hermitage, and followed that with a viticulture course at the Macon Davayé *lycée agricole*.
He started off with one hectare of land, planting it in 1989, and in the intervening years has progressively added to his portfolio, which in spring 1999 covered 7 hectares. Since each new acquisition has had to be planted, the age of his vines is still very low... yet that in no way compromises the richness and complexity of his wines!

Noble rot and late harvest Low yields for the red wines, and over-ripeness for the whites, these are the cornerstones of Villard's wine-making. In the vineyards all is as natural as possible, with organic soil-enriching and manual weeding; however he is considering leaving the grass to grow on his terraced vineyards in order to anchor the topsoil, the better to protect it from being washed down the slope during rainy spells.
Every year Villard hopes that his Viognier will be attacked by botrytis, which does happen often, but even failing the fungus's appearance the fruit is left on the vine for long enough to develop very concentrated, sweet juice, which explains the intense, powerful aroma of his Condrieus. If only some of the other, early-picking growers would follow his example! He makes four different wines from 3 different sites, fermenting them in cask at a low temperature and then ageing them in cask for the best part of a year, with *weekly bâtonnage* for the first 8 months. They are not racked during the year, in order to preserve their fragrance.

Condrieu Coteaux de Poncins Villard's 10-year-old vines on the splendid Poncins slopes, lying opposite Château-Grillet, give birth to a wine of sublime intensity and fragrance, with an overt peach, dried-apricot and vanilla character, which is equally remarkable for the juxtaposition of its thick, opulent flesh, significant alcohol and impeccable acidity; here is a Condrieu which, unlike most, might acquire some interesting characteristics over a decade or so in the cellar. In its youth it has sufficient flavour to look some foie gras *de canard* in the eye, and enough breeding to charm some scallops in *crème d'artichauts*.

- Other white wines: Condrieu Les Terrasses du Palat, Condrieu Le Grand Vallon, Condrieu Quintessence, Saint-Joseph Mairlant
- Red wines: Côte-Rôtie La Brocarde, Saint-Joseph Reflet
- Owner: François Villard
- Wine-maker: François Villard
- Combined vineyards: 7 hectares
- Production: 26,000 bottles
- Exports: 55%
- Take-away sales: Yes
- Visits: By appointment

Wine selected:
**Condrieu
Coteaux de Poncins**

- Grape Variety: Viognier
- Average vine age: 10 years
- Vineyard size: 1 hectare
- Soil type: Decomposed granite and mica
- Average production: 4,500 bottles

DOMAINE GEORGES VERNAY

Since setting up on his own in 1953 with 1.5 hectares of vines, Georges Vernay has become a repository of all there is to know of the fickle Viognier grape, and has forged himself a reputation second to none for his intensely perfumed Condrieu wines. They are quintessential examples of their appellation, eloquently proving that Condrieu is one of the great dry white wines of the world.

On the verge of extinction Wine-lovers owe Vernay a debt of gratitude not just for the quality of his wines but for Condrieu's very existence, for it was he who championed it when, unprofitable and unfashionable, the vineyard risked disappearing in the 1960s. By 1965 this historic wine region had been reduced to a pitiful 8 hectares. Gradually, thanks to several obstinate growers and above all Georges Vernay and his consistently excellent production, international interest slowly picked up, which had the effect of renewing confidence locally in the future. The terraces, abandoned or occupied by other fruit or vegetables, started to be reclaimed by the vine.

Vernay is now officially retired, and the domaine's wines are made by his daughter Christine, who learnt her trade following her father around from an early age, and his son Luc, who divides his time between the estate and his microlite school. However the patriarch is always around, ready to help his children and indeed other growers with generous advice and encouragement.

The terraces of hell The estate has been gradually enlarged whenever suitable land has come up for sale, to the point where it covers 16 hectares today, and produces red Syrah wines from Côte-Rôtie and Saint-Joseph as well as Viognier wines. Vernay has always produced two Condrieus, a generic and the Coteau de Vernon, however in response to a problem of excessive demand for the latter he introduced the evocatively-named Les Chaillées de l'Enfer ("the terraces of hell") in 1992, which lies between the other two in terms of quality, being a selection of fruit from the best slopes.

How then do the Vernays make such beautifully aromatic wines? Very dense plantation, old vines and low yields—18 hectolitres per hectare is not unheard-of in the case of the Coteau de Vernon—are the inescapable requisites in the vineyard. Fruit is harvested as late as possible for maximum aroma, even at the expense of acidity, and vinified at a cool 14-18° in stainless steel and *foudre*, or cask in the case of the Chaillées and the Vernon. Malolactic fermentations are generally encouraged.

Condrieu Coteau de Vernon The Vernays' top Condrieu is aged in oak barrels, one fifth of which are renewed each year, for 12-18 months, with periodic stirring of the lees to increase aromatic intensity. It could well be the quintessential expression of the Viognier grape: its intense flavour of apricot, peach and violets is absolutely irresistible, and it is fat and succulent on the palate, with just the right acidity for balance. It is delicious on its own, yet the Vernays recommend drinking it with lobster, langoustine or foie gras. Sublime!

- Other white wines: Condrieu, Condrieu Les Chaillées de l'Enfer, Vin de Pays des Collines Rhodaniennes
- Red wines: Côte-Rôtie, Saint-Joseph, Côtes-du-Rhône Sainte-Agathe, Vin de Pays des Collines Rhodaniennes
- Owner: Domaine Georges Vernay
- Wine-maker: Christine Vernay
- Combined vineyards: 16 hectares
- Production: 80,000 bottles
- Exports: 20%
- Take-away sales: By appointment
- Visits: No

Wine selected:
Condrieu Coteau de Vernon

- Grape Variety: Viognier
- Average vine age: 60 years
- Vineyard size: 1.5 hectares
- Soil type: Granite
- Average production: 5,000 bottles

PRODUIT DE FRANCE

Coteau de Vernon

CONDRIEU

Appellation Condrieu contrôlée

13,5% vol   1996   750ml

Mis en bouteille à la Propriété

EARL Georges VERNAY, Viticulteur à CONDRIEU (Rhône) FRANCE

DOMAINE ROBERT NIERO

As generation succeeds generation in the northern Rhône Valley's smaller appellations, some names disappear and some appear, while others are quite simply permanent fixtures! Condrieu has seen quite a lot of the first two cases in recent years, and among the new recruits has been one Robert Niero. This young man was not born into a wine-making family, but has shown great gifts for his new trade. His wines are well worth seeking out.

A change of occupation   Niero had already spent a number of years working in a Lyons bank when the option of making wine presented itself through his marriage to the daughter of the late Jean Pinchon, one of the best known Condrieu growers of his generation. Pinchon, who had taken over the tiny 1.5-hectare family estate after his father's death, had made himself a reputation for classic Condrieu, aged in old wood for longer than nearly all others, which was capable of improving in bottle over a decade; Pinchon it also was who had cultivated the vines and made the superb Coteau de Chéry wines of the Jurie des Camiers family until 1982.

Niero duly took on his new responsibilities in the mid-1980s, enabling his father-in-law to take well-earned retirement. With the latter's advice and by dint of much learning as he went along, he started refining his craft, and his name started to become known to Condrieu aficionados.

Traditional wine-making without gimmicks   It was necessary to find means of expanding his holdings in order to be able to earn a better living, and over a 10-year period Niero managed to double his holdings. These now include some Syrah vineyards in Côte-Rôtie and Côtes-du-Rhône, which have obliged their owner to learn the disciplines of red wine-making, which he does very credibly, even if they do not yet have the distinction of his Condrieu. The parcels of Viognier lie on the Côte Châtillon, Rozay and La Roncharde slopes as well as on the *très recherché* Coteau de Chéry; a high average age (many vines are over 60 years old) contributes to the significant intensity of flavour in the finished Condrieu wines.

Niero's wine-making is traditional with neither gimmick nor innovation, and the results vindicate his choice. His Viognier grapes are pressed and the must is then chilled (to avoid the use of SO2) and left to settle over 24 hours, giving the larger matter in suspension time to sink to the bottom of the vat. The alcoholic fermentation then proceeds at a maintained temperature of 18-20°, and is followed by the malolactic fermentation in the Spring. The wines are reared, as they are fermented, in a mix of used casks and stainless steel vats, and are fined and filtered before bottling.

Condrieu Coteau de Chéry   One of the finest wines made from this hallowed, terraced slope, Niero's offering has the same sort of character as had those of his father-in-law: thick, powerful and concentrated, with a sublimely rich flavour which takes several years to come out of its shell... This is a style which is made for drinking at table, and the possibilities are legion: grilled lobster, salmon *en feuilleté*, or even capon, stuffed with foie gras and cooked *en pot-au-feu*... Sublime!

- Other white wine: Condrieu
- Red wines: Côte-Rôtie, Côtes-du-Rhône
- Owner: Robert Niero
- Wine-maker: Robert Niero
- Oenologist: Michel Laurent
- Combined vineyards: 4 hectares
- Production: 18,000 bottles
- Exports: 25%
- Take-away sales: By appointment
- Visits: By appointment

Wine selected:
Condrieu
Coteau de Chéry

- Grape Variety: Viognier
- Average vine age: 15-60 years
- Vineyard size: 0.8 hectares
- Soil type: Granite
- Average production: 4,000 bottles max.

DOMAINE YVES CUILLERON

A mong the young generation of Condrieu wine-makers one particularly bright star has emerged, making wines of stunning purity, harmony and breeding. Yves Cuilleron is without doubt a master wine-maker, a young man who knows what he is aiming at and nurtures his vines, vats and casks in such a way as to get it.

A young man takes on a challenge The estate was previously exploited by Antoine Cuilleron, his uncle. There being no direct heir available to take over, an important question mark hung over its future, until the young nephew Yves Cuilleron persuaded the family to let him take on the challenge. After graduating at Macon's oenology school and gaining experience for a year at the Courbis estate, he started work in 1986.

Once he was in the driving seat, Cuilleron set about increasing the 4-hectare estate to give himself a variety and spread of vineyards on a level with his ambitions; today it covers 24 hectares, producing not only Condrieu but also Côte-Rôtie and red and white Saint-Joseph.

Far transcending general standards Method and attention to detail are the linchpins of Cuilleron's work, and the young man is fired by a strong will to surpass himself year after year. The Condrieus are magnificently perfumed, with exemplary definition and great balance—not the easiest thing with the fickle Viognier, which is low in acidity and high in alcohol—and the same goes for the white Saint-Josephs, which far transcend the standards generally achieved, and are stunningly rich and intense, indeed probably the finest expressions of pure Marsanne around today. Of his reds, the Saint-Joseph particularly is remarkably deep and rich for an appellation which is often the source of rather simple wines, given the potential of the magnificent Syrah.

The renaissance of a Roman vineyard Not content with what he has already achieved, Yves Cuilleron and fellow growers Pierre Gaillard and François Villard have replanted the abandoned slopes of Seyssuel, north of Vienne, which were first cultivated by the Romans and made highly-reputed wine, praised by Pliny the Elder and many others over the centuries, until their devastation by the Phylloxera bug. In view of their exceptional *terroir* and the talent of the three young men, the wines of the Domaine des Vins de Vienne will no doubt become highly prized as their vines grow older.

Condrieu Ayguets Another, more recent, tradition preserved by Cuilleron and one or two others is that of late-harvested Condrieu. When conditions are right some of his fruit is affected by *pourriture noble*, the famous 'noble rot' of Sauternes, and equally if the weather does not break fruit may sometimes be left on the vine until very late in the year, becoming progressively more shrivelled and concentrated. By visiting the vineyard half-a-dozen or more times to harvest grapes in these two conditions, Cuilleron makes a massive, sublimely unctuous, rich and perfumed wine which almost defies description, so unusual and so masterful it is. Any rare bottle found on sale should be snapped up and reserved for a very special occasion, to be sipped on its own or, as favoured by its maker, drunk with chocolate cake.

- Other white wines: Condrieu La Petite Cote, Condrieu Les Chaillets, Saint-Joseph Lyzeras, Saint-Joseph Le Lombard, Saint-Joseph Coteau Saint-Pierre
- Red wines: Côte-Rôtie Coteau de Bassenon, Saint-Joseph Les Pierres Sèches, Saint-Joseph L'Amarybelle, Saint-Joseph Les Serines
- Owner: Yves Cuilleron
- Wine-maker: Yves Cuilleron
- Oenologist: Jean-François Hebrard
- Combined vineyards: 24 hectares
- Production: 106,000 bottles
- Exports: 40%
- Take-away sales: Yes
- Visits: 9-12 a.m., 2-6 p.m.

Wine selected:
Condrieu Ayguets
(50 cl. bottle)

- Grape Variety: Viognier
- Average vine age: 30 years
- Vineyard size: 2 hectares
- Soil type: Granite and sand
- Average production: 4,000 bottles

T he distinctive brown bottle with its yellow capsule and sober label are little seen, for inside is one of France's most legendary and rare white wines. This is the celebrated Château-Grillet, a Viognier wine made on a site recognized as far back as Roman times for its quality. This is a one-off, an original.

A very special microclimate Château-Grillet is not only a wine and an estate, since 1936 it has been an *appellation contrôlée*, an enclave inside the Condrieu appellation, in recognition of the fact that its magnificent vineyard site is capable of producing a wine markedly different from the neighbouring Viognier wines. The vineyard lies in a south-facing amphitheatre with a soil of granitic sand, looking down onto the Rhône from its 165-250 metres. Sheltered from north winds, it is a veritable sun-trap in which the vines are cultivated on terraces, each containing two or three rows; the terrace walls, reflecting the heat, only increase the efficacy of the amphitheatre's microclimate, which brings the fruit to perfect ripeness.

Dry, perfumed and inimitable Lauded in past centuries by such connoisseurs as Thomas Jefferson and André Jullien, this wine has long been sought out by the world's gourmets. Over the years many itinerant oenophiles have written about it, and it appears to have been made as a sweet wine until around the end of the 19th century. Today it is dry, perfumed, and… inimitable.

It is also, unfortunately, much misunderstood. Many of the world's wine writers have criticized it in recent years as lacking in depth and aroma, and not being worth its price compared with the best of today's Condrieus. Unfortunately, tasting the latest vintage of these different wines side by side, they are not comparing like with like: Château-Grillet does not shine in the first flush of youth, but gradually develops its qualities over a dozen years or more in bottle, like good Burgundy. Conversely, rare is the Condrieu which is not on the decline after half that time. The Neyret-Gachet family, proprietors of Château-Grillet since the 1820s, and their descendants the Canets, have always recognized the potential of their *terroir* for making a *vin de garde*, and do not seek the fragrant primary aromas and vibrancy that cold fermentation gives; rather, they ferment in the traditional manner and then leave the wine to enrich itself on its lees until the spring, during which time it undergoes its malolactic fermentation. It is then aged in Burgundian barrels, mainly used, until winter the following year.

Château-Grillet Once past its tongue-tied first three years of life, Château-Grillet starts to display its elegance, richness and concentration, and blossoms best at 12-13°, aired in a decanter. Its *ampleur* places it unreservedly in the wine-for-food category (certainly not aperitifs!), and its superbly complex flavour—in which, depending on the year, nuances of honey, quince, peach, apricot, violets, even grilled almonds may be detected—marries very well with foie gras, freshwater fish and white meats. For a real feast, partner a Château-Grillet with a truffled capon in salt crust!

- Owners: Canet family
- Wine-maker: Isabelle Baratin-Canet
- Vineyard size: 3.4 hectares
- Average vine age: 40 and 80 years
- Soil type: Granitic sand
- Average production: 10,000 bottles
- Exports: 25%
- Take-away sales: Subject to availability
- Visits: By appointment

Château-Grillet | Vérin

For yardstick Hermitage, be it red or white, the wines of Bernard Faurie are difficult to better. Crafted with great sensibility, they provide consummate evidence of the suitability of the Syrah and Marsanne grapes to the granitic, sandy and limestone soils of the Hermitage hill, and of the talent of their maker. Any chance of acquiring a bottle or two should therefore not be missed, particularly in view of the fact that they are made in very limited quantities.

Limited production and uncompromising quality With only 4 hectares of vines, the temptation must be great, yet Faurie has never wanted to compromise on the quality of his production. It would be so easy to produce more, and sell it to uncomplaining buyers at the same price… The fourth generation of his family to make wine (and also to exploit 4 hectares of apricot trees), he worked in a factory after leaving school and took over his father's 56 ares of Hermitage vines in 1980. Since then the rest of his vines have come through purchase or rental from other family members. Faurie would willingly take on further vines, but the small grower is these days powerless against the financial muscle of the large *négociants*, who can pay exorbitant prices for all the good land that comes up for sale, and he is not alone in seeking vines to rent or work for others.

His wine-making career has followed a learning curve, as in the early days he received advice from different quarters and tried out various techniques, and the wines have become progressively finer over the years. Today Faurie knows exactly what sort of wine he wants to produce and how to produce it, and goes about his trade with unerring skill.

Vinification by traditional methods Tradition influences his methods to a great extent. Reduction of yields and perfect ripeness are his priorities in the vineyard, and once picked, the Syrah grapes are fermented without any destalking for 15-20 days, in open wooden vats. *Remontages* help extract colour, tannin and aroma, then the vats are covered over at the end of fermentation to preserve the latter. Once the vatting is finished the wine is aged in 600-litre *demi-muids* for 12-18 months, then bottled without filtration. The white wines are vinified in barrel traditionally, and undergo their malolactic fermentation if the vintage requires it. After some 12 months' *élevage* they are fined but not filtered and then bottled.

Hermitage Le Méal Faurie possesses small parcels in Les Greffieux, Le Méal and Les Bessards, and generally produces a *cuvée* Méal and a blended *cuvée*, although the Greffieux is also sometimes bottled on its own. None, confusingly, have the *lieu-dit* inscribed on the label, and all are very fine, but the finest is arguably Le Méal, a very dark wine which positively oozes thick black fruit when young, and has a fleshy, rich constitution which enfolds the important tannic structure, though not so much as to hide it totally. Harmony is another, welcome quality of this sweet, chewy masterpiece, which requires long keeping. Bottles are best broached with fellow Hermitage-lovers, perhaps over a saddle of hare.

- Other red wines: Hermitage Les Greffieux, Hermitage Cuvée Assemblage, Saint-Joseph
- White wines: Hermitage, Saint-Joseph
- Owner: Bernard Faurie
- Wine-maker: Bernard Faurie
- Combined vineyards: 4 hectares
- Production: 17,000 bottles
- Exports: 50%
- Take-away sales: By appointment
- Visits: By appointment, not more than 10 people

Wine selected:
Hermitage Le Méal

- Grape Variety: Syrah
- Average vine age: 40 years
- Vineyard size: 0.2 hectares
- Soil type: Stony limestone

1997

PRODUIT DE FRANCE

Hermitage

APPELLATION HERMITAGE CONTROLEE

13 % vol.   750 ml

MIS EN BOUTEILLE A LA PROPRIETE

BERNARD FAURIE

VITICULTEUR A TOURNON-SUR-RHONE (ARDÈCHE) FRANCE

Delas Frères is one of largest of the northern Rhône *négociant* houses, yet it maintains a low profile on the world wine stage, despite producing several exceptional wines from the most prestigious northern Rhône appellations. Its greatest strength lies in its Hermitages, home-grown wines of great individuality with all the complexity and depth one could wish for.

The original Rhône Valley vineyard The vast majority of its production, which encompasses all the Rhône appellations, comes from grapes and must which it buys in. However it owns 10 hectares of vineyards at Hermitage and 4 at Saint-Joseph, and farms another 8.5 in Condrieu and Côte-Rôtie belonging to Michel Delas. Its choicest land is that which lies on the Hermitage hill.

This awe-inspiring lump of granite, dominating the towns of Tain and, across the river, Tournon, is reckoned by historians to have been the original Rhône Valley vineyard, dating at least from Roman times, or in the view of locals from as far back even as 600 BC. Eight hectares of the Delas land are planted with Syrah, for red wine, and are situated mainly in the *climat* Les Bessards, as well as in l'Hermite and Le Sabot. The remaining two are planted with the white grapes Marsanne and Roussanne, principally in l'Hermite.

Geological nuances play their role Despite being composed predominantly of granite, the hill's different parcels each have their own geological nuances, which duly shape the character of their produce. Lying on the south-west slope of the hill, steep to the point of ruling out any mechanization, Les Bessards, with its loose soil of Gore (decomposed granite) produces some of the most structured and powerful of the hill's wines. Blended with the produce of the other *climats*, it can be refined, given more elegance, suppleness, aroma, and so forth. In 1990 Delas inaugurated a single-vineyard Les Bessards wine, which the firm only makes in the finest years; on a regular basis its best fruit makes up the excellent Marquise de la Tourette wine, and the rest composes Les Grands Chemins.

Hermitage Les Bessards For the prestige *cuvée* the oldest Bessards vines, yielding a niggardly 15-20 hectolitres per hectare, are vinified in small open wooden vats with a prolonged maceration with *pigeage* and *remontages*, so as to fully extract the *terroir* character. The finished wine is then aged in newish casks for 16-18 months during which it is racked every 4 months, and bottled after being fined with egg white.

A very dark purple to the eye, a young Bessards is powerful, dense and massively structured, with peppery aromas of blackcurrant and blackberry, and a suggestion of toasted oak. The nobility of the wine is stunning, and one can only try to imagine how it will enthrall the taster after 20 years' keeping or more. Jacques Puisais might have been thinking of this wine when he wrote in *Le Goût Juste*: "... It needs its freedom. It will revel in an escapade with a hare *à la dauphinoise*, lightly creamed, or an ascent at the side of a leg of *chamois grand veneur*. It will dominate the scene, serenely, and on the way back down will toy with a few wild mushrooms au gratin."

- Other red wines: Hermitage Marquise de la Tourette, Hermitage Les Grands Chemins, Côte-Rôtie Seigneur de Maugiron, Côte-Rôtie Les Ravines, Cornas Chante-Perdrix, Saint-Joseph François de Tournon, Saint-Joseph Les Challeys, Crozes-Hermitage Tour d'Albon, Châteauneuf-du-Pape Les Hautes Pierres, Châteauneuf-du-Pape Calcernier, Gigondas Les Reinages, Vacqueyras Domaine des Genêts
- White wines: Condrieu Clos Boucher, Condrieu, Hermitage Marquise de la Tourette, Crozes-Hermitage Les Launes, Saint-Joseph Les Challeys, Muscat de Beaumes-de-Venise
- Rosé wine: Tavel La Comballe
- Owner: S.A. Champagne Deutz
- Wine-maker: Jacques Grange
- Combined vineyards: 14 hectares
- Production: 1.350,000 bottles (domaine and négoce)
- Exports: 55%
- Take-away sales: Yes
- Visits: 9.30-12.00 a.m., 2.30-6.30 p.m.

Wine selected:
Hermitage Les Bessards

- Grape Variety: Syrah
- Average vine age: 60 years
- Vineyard size: 6 hectares
- Soil type: Decomposed granite
- Average production: 5,000 bottles

Very few wine-makers, not only in the Rhône Valley but all over France and further afield, are held in such high esteem as Gérard Chave, whose red and white Hermitage are masterpieces of complexity, elegance and harmony. These great wines take time to develop their personalities and blossom, yet with the passing of the years they reward the patient wine-lover with a nectar which has no equivalent. Indeed both red and white have exceptional longevity—a half-century for a good vintage, left in a good cellar, is perfectly possible!

500 years of direct succession Having looked after his own vines since the tender age of 17, Chave already had a wealth of practical experience when he succeeded his father Jean-Louis 18 years later, in 1970. Yet wine-making no doubt runs in the blood of this family, for the Chaves celebrated a remarkable 500 years of direct, uninterrupted succession in 1981. And the line is not about to peter out, for Gérard's son, named after grandfather Jean-Louis, has been thoroughly trained by his father and today plays an ever more important role in the family business.

Perfectionism and unrivalled intuition The Chaves own no less than 15 hectares on the Hermitage hill, which are spread over 9 different *climats*… and therein lies one factor explaining the quality of their wines. Yet to that one must add the even more important perfectionism of their makers, who with rare intelligence do nothing by routine. Having given their vines the best possible conditions for bearing excellent fruit—yields are kept well down, manual vineyard labour is preferred to herbicide, compost to artificial fertilizer, and fruit is never harvested before peak ripeness—they take each year's crop on its merits, vinify it accordingly, parcel by parcel, and age the different wines separately. Chave has tried new wood for ageing, and is not for it. Instead he prefers to use second-hand Burgundian *pièces*, with just the odd new cask being admitted to the cellar to replace those due for retirement.

Only when the *élevage* of the different wines is complete are they blended. In a demonstration of unrivalled intuition the Chaves look for affinity and complementarity between the wines of the different parcels, to make a harmonious whole which reflects the character of the vintage. All the wine is therefore not necessarily used every year, and that which is surplus to requirements is simply sold off in bulk to the *négoce*.

Hermitage Nothing is sadder than the sight of very young bottles of Chave Hermitage being opened and consumed, as so often happens in France's top restaurants, for these are wines which give little pleasure when young, yet undergo a veritable metamorphosis if left alone for 12-25 years. The red Hermitage, densely-coloured and with an earthy blackcurrant nose when young, gradually takes on a fascinating range of aromas of the smoked, roasted variety, with hints of tar, leather, cigar-box, prune, spice… which call for something special at table. Gérard Chave, a renowned gourmet, would no doubt approve of a saddle of hare.

• Other red wines:
Ermitage Cuvée Cathelin,
Saint-Joseph
• White wine: Hermitage
• Owners:
Gérard & Jean-Louis Chave
• Wine-makers:
Gérard & Jean-Louis Chave
• Combined vineyards:
17 hectares
• Production:
66,000 bottles
• Exports: 60%
• Take-away sales: No
• Visits: No

Wine selected:
Hermitage

• Grape Variety: Syrah
• Average vine age:
45 years
• Vineyard size:
10 hectares
• Soil type: Granite, loess
• Average production:
30,000 bottles

Hermitage | Mauves

Chapoutier, founded in 1808, is one of the most venerable names in the northern Rhône, a firm which has produced numerous great wines over the course of its long and illustrious existence. Yet following a change of generation the 1990s have seen it making what are perhaps more exciting wines than ever before... wines which are earning the praises of international experts and wine-lovers everywhere.

Areas for improvement This new lease of life is the result of a total re-evaluation of viticultural and vinification practices by the young brothers Marc and Michel Chapoutier. If the truth be known, the firm seemed to get in a rut in the 1970s and 1980s, continuing to produce the heavy, oxidized wines which had been popular in earlier times, whereas growers all around were focusing on *terroir* definition and vintage characteristics.

The major problems, as the brothers saw it, lay in the raw material, overproduced and thus giving wines of little identity, and the *élevage*, which took place in old chestnut barrels and lasted until sales necessitated bottling, which often resulted in excessive oxidation.

Adoption of biodynamic viticultural methods The quest for better raw material led the Chapoutiers to embrace biodynamic viticultural methods, which, they argue, are the most effective way of promoting the living, healthy soil essential to the health of vines and thus to the production of fine grapes. Weedkiller, pesticides and synthetic fertilizer have therefore been banished from the vineyards. Yields are rigorously controlled by severe pruning and the presence of old vines.

The firm buys large quantities of grapes as a supplement to the fruit of its own 80 hectares, in order to be able to provide a complete range of Rhône wines. To improve the quality of the bought-in grapes, Chapoutier now pays its growers by the size of their vineyard rather than the quantity they produce—relieving them of a difficult dilemma—and encourages them to work along biodynamic lines.

Changes in the wine-making Vinification is seen as merely the conclusion of the viticultural year. Nevertheless, here also there has been much change: use of indigenous yeast, not cooling excessively, ageing whites on their lees with *bâtonnage*, vatting periods for the reds of up to 6 weeks with *pigeage* and *remontage*... and new oak for ageing, with bottling as soon as tasting indicates that it is time—perfect grapes and perfectionist wine-making is the simple recipe which has changed everything. Even the labels, in an original and admirable initiative, are now printed in Braille.

Hermitage Chante-Alouette Selecting a single wine is difficult, so excellent are they all at their own levels... Take the magnificent white Hermitage from the *lieu-dit* Chante-Alouette: it transcends the usual dimensions of its kind, rewarding the taster with a thick, fleshy texture and concentrated, toasted flavour, with complex spicy and fruity highlights. Its firmness, good acidity and long finish promise a long, rewarding life, at the end of which it would want to find itself at table with a deserving companion: scallops cooked in saffron will get it talking!

• Other white wines: Ermitage de l'Orée, Condrieu, Saint-Joseph Deschants, Crozes-Hermitage Les Meysonniers, Châteauneuf-du-Pape La Bernardine
• Red wines: Ermitage Le Pavillon, Hermitage Monier de la Sizeranne, Côte-Rôtie La Mordorée, Côte-Rôtie, Saint-Joseph Deschants, Crozes-Hermitage Les Meysonniers, Châteauneuf-du-Pape Barbe-Rac, Châteauneuf-du-Pape La Bernardine.
• Wine-makers: Michel Chapoutier & Albéric Mazoyer
• Combined vineyards: 80+ hectares
• Exports: 60%
• Take-away sales: Yes. Telephone for opening hours
• Visits: By appointment

Wine selected:
Hermitage Chante-Alouette

• Grape Variety: Marsanne
• Average vine age: 40 years
• Soil type: Loess and alluvial limestone
• Average production: 20,000 bottles

M. CHAPOUTIER
1996

Chante-Alouette®

HERMITAGE

APPELLATION HERMITAGE CONTROLEE

mis en bouteille par

M. CHAPOUTIER

750 ml
VIN BLANC
WHITE WINE
PRODUIT DE FRANCE

26600 TAIN (FRANCE)

1996
75 cl

13,5 % alc./vol.

PRODUCE OF FRANCE

B esides the large *négociant* firms who own the lion's share of the Hermitage hill, there exist a few small growers who have plots here and there, making in some cases wine of remarkable quality, albeit in quantities so small that the wines are usually difficult to track down. Marc Sorrel is one such, a young man who makes both red and white Hermitage with equal, consummate talent.

A change of career Marc Sorrel's father Henri, from a family present in Tain l'Hermitage since at least the beginning of the 20th century, was the Tain *notaire*, and until the 1970s the fruit produced on his 3.4-hectare holding was sold to the *négoce*. Then half-way through that decade Henri Sorrel started making and bottling wine himself, producing in 1978 and 1979 two extremely successful vintages.

However he was suffering declining health, and his son Marc, who had embarked on his own professional career, returned in 1982 at Henri's request to help him with the estate. Marc applied himself to learning the business without losing any time. Two years later, after Henri had passed away, he found himself irrevocably cast in the role of *vigneron*.

Mastery of the two colours Sorrel inherited 2 hectares of Henri's vines, the remainder going to his brothers, and has since acquired further land on the Hermitage hill and in Crozes-Hermitage, as well as renting a half-hectare parcel of 50-year-old Marsanne at Larnage, which all in all has doubled to 4 hectares the land at his disposal. With that he produces three red and three white wines.

His two white Hermitages are fermented at some 18° in Burgundy barrels which have already been used a good half-dozen times; the essential differences between the two wines come from the age of the vines and the length of ageing prior to bottling. These are splendid examples of white Hermitage, which if really necessary may be enjoyed in their first few years, but should ideally be allowed to traverse their subsequent dumb period and then be consumed at 10-15 years of age. Sorrel's white Crozes-Hermitage is also praiseworthy. The red Hermitages, both the Classique and the Le Gréal, are never (or rarely) destalked, and are fermented in a mixture of stainless steel and open wooden vats for 18-20 days, then left to mature for 16-20 months before bottling unfined and unfiltered. There are generally 3 bottlings over a six-month period.

Hermitage Le Gréal Do not look for Le Gréal on a map of the Hermitage hill, for it is the name Sorrel has given to his blend of 1 hectare of old Le Méal vines and 20 ares of younger Les Greffieux plants. These two adjacent *lieux-dits* are composed respectively of limestone with stones and sandy clay and limestone, which goes a long way to explaining the nature of the Sorrel Le Gréal: rich and savoury on the palate, medium bodied and exquisitely aromatic—liquorice, blackcurrant and spice are generally the dominant aromas—it is unusually elegant. This Hermitage ranks among the greatest, and is naturally a wine which amply repays long cellaring, at the end of which it is ready to take its place at table opposite a duck and foie gras pie.

- Other red wines: Hermitage, Crozes-Hermitage
- White wines: Hermitage Les Rocoules, Hermitage, Crozes-Hermitage
- Owner: Marc Sorrel
- Wine-maker: Marc Sorrel
- Combined vineyards: 4 hectares
- Production: 20,000 bottles
- Exports: 60%
- Take-away sales: Yes
- Visits: By appointment

Wine selected:
Hermitage Le Gréal

- Grape Variety: Syrah
- Average vine age: 50 years
- Vineyard size: 1.2 hectares
- Soil type: Limestone
- Average production: 4,500 bottles

LE GRÉAL

Hermitage

APPELLATION CONTROLÉE

Mise en bouteilles à la propriété

M. SORREL

Tain l'Hermitage
(DRÔME)

PROPRIÉTAIRE
ALC. BY VOL. 12,8%
750 ML

Lot 1034

Which Rhône-wine admirer has not heard of Hermitage La Chapelle? Perhaps more than any other it has been this wine, a quintessential expression of the Syrah grown in an ideal location, which has opened the eyes of the world's wine-lovers to the delights of Rhône wines in recent years... and which has inspired many a grower, French or foreign, to buy some cuttings of Syrah (or Shiraz) and try to emulate them!

A family business of world-wide renown Despite its size, Paul Jaboulet Aîné has always been a family-run affair. Founded by Antoine Jaboulet in 1834, it was developed by his twin sons Paul and Henri and thereafter passed down Paul's side of the family. Today the third and fourth generations, Michel, Jacques, Philippe, Odile, Frédéric, Nicolas and Laurent look after the numerous tasks that occupy any firm which exports a large product range to 70 countries. The year 1997 was sadly marked by the untimely death of Jacques's brother Gérard, who had been the urbane, globe-trotting public face of the firm.

The comprehensive Rhône range As Rhône wines have gained in popularity, the Jaboulet range has been widened, and now includes just about all the major appellations of both the northern and the southern parts of the Rhône Valley. However popularity and growing demand is a two-edged sword, for growers are more reluctant to sell their best vats, preferring to bottle and sell them themselves; it can therefore be a problem for Jacques Jaboulet, in charge of purchasing and wine-making, to source material of sufficient quality.

The finest wines undoubtedly come from the northern section, from Jaboulet's own Hermitage, Crozes-Hermitage and Cornas vineyards, where rigorous viticulture and low yields guarantee a regular supply of top-quality raw material. The Domaine de Thalabert, the superb 1996 acquisition Domaine Raymond Roure, the 1993 Cornas acquisition Domaine de Saint-Pierre, and the firm's 5 hectares of white vines spread over the Hermitage hill which make the Chevalier de Stérimberg... all these provide a worthy escort to the firm's principal wine.

Hermitage La Chapelle The name La Chapelle refers not to a vineyard plot but to the tiny Saint-Christophe chapel near the top of the Hermitage hill, erected, as the legend would have it, by the knight Gaspard de Stérimberg in 1235. Wounded while on crusade, the returning knight fell in love with this spot and spent the rest of his days leading the life of a hermit there.

Besides owning the chapel since 1919, the Jaboulets have a magnificent 20-hectare holding spread over the various *climats* of Hermitage, and La Chapelle comes from their vines in the exceptional Bessards and Méal plots. Granite, associated with limestone and quartzite... and old Syrah vines. La Chapelle needs a dozen years to digest its tannic structure and start revealing its extraordinary richness and complexity, and thereafter develops sumptuous aromas of leather, truffle and undergrowth, so compelling that its remarkable harmony and finesse is often overlooked. The greatest vintages of this wine can live for a half-century! Decanted well before the service, a mature La Chapelle served alongside a haunch of venison or a saddle of hare provides a memorable experience.

- Other red wines: Hermitage Le Pied de la Côte, Crozes-Hermitage Domaine de Thalabert, Crozes-Hermitage Domaine Raymond Roure, Crozes-Hermitage Les Jalets, Côte-Rôtie Les Jumelles, Cornas Domaine de Saint-Pierre, Cornas, Saint-Joseph Le Grand Pompée, Châteauneuf-du-Pape Les Cèdres, Gigondas Pierre Aiguille, Vacqueyras, Côtes-du-Rhône-Villages, Côtes-du-Rhône Parallèle 45, Côtes-du-Ventoux Les Traverses
- White wines: Hermitage Le Chevalier de Stérimberg, Crozes-Hermitage Mule Blanche, Crozes-Hermitage Domaine Raymond Roure, Condrieu, Saint-Joseph Le Grand Pompée, Châteauneuf-du-Pape Les Cèdres, Côtes-du-Rhône Parallèle 45, Côtes-du-Ventoux Les Traverses, Muscat de Beaumes-de-Venise
- Rosé wines: Tavel L'Espiègle, Côtes-du-Ventoux Royal Rubis
- Owner: Paul Jaboulet Aîné
- Managing Director: Philippe Jaboulet
- Wine-maker: Jacques Jaboulet
- Oenologist: Jacques Jaboulet
- Combined vineyards: 82 hectares
- Production: 465,000 bottles (domaine wines)
- Exports: 70%
- Take-away sales: Yes
- Visits: Yes

Wine selected:
Hermitage La Chapelle

- Grape Variety: Syrah
- Average vine age: 30 and 70 years
- Vineyard size: 20 hectares
- Soil type: Granite, limestone and quartzite
- Average production: 94,000 bottles

A small *négociant* firm was set up in 1994 with the aim of buying wines in the best *crus* of the Rhône valley, north and south, and producing the purest, most natural and authentic examples possible of each wine. Tardieu-Laurent's success has been rapid and total, and such are the sensitivity and perfectionism which drive it, one can harbour few doubts about the firm's future pre-eminence in the Rhône wine world.

A meeting leads to a partnership The firm was set up by Michel Tardieu, a civil servant and dedicated oenophile, after a meeting with the highly talented *éleveur* of Burgundies, Dominique Laurent. As Thierry Gontier recounts it in *Le Rouge et le Blanc*, Tardieu, who out of hours was responsible for the wine list of the great Lourmarin restaurant La Fenière, was presenting Laurent's wines with the man himself, and the two got on so famously that the idea of a partnership was born.

It did not take much time to turn the idea into reality. Cold cellars—a rarity in that hot part of France—were not easy to find, but eventually Tardieu was able to rent the old vaulted chapel under the Château de Lourmarin, equip it with enough barrels for his needs and go out in search of suitable wines.

Non-interventionist wine-making The partners' aim was to treat the finest appellations of the Rhône valley in much the same manner as had made Laurent's reputation in Burgundy. First of all *vignerons* are persuaded to part with choice lots of their finest old-vine wines, those they do not really wish to sell. After blending them, Tardieu's and Laurent's role is then to transform the wines by slow cosseting in wood, the aim being to give them both a gentle yet thorough airing through the wood's pores and a deep oaking—contrary to imparting the oaky make-up which disfigures so many wines. The preparation of the oak, from 200-year-old Allier trees, is naturally of primary importance: new oak barrels are bought not with their inside surfaces burnt, for the *éleveurs* do not want any toasted flavours, but cooked, in order to eliminate the wood's natural flavours, which are not wanted either.

The partners' philosophy might be described as non-interventionist, for the wines are left to themselves to feed off their lees wherever possible, with a minimum of racking, for that usually involves a dose of SO2 on each occasion, not to mention much disturbance for the wine. When it is eventually necessary to separate the wine from its lees, the operation is done by gravity, never pumping. Wines are finally bottled after 2 years, all by hand, with neither fining nor filtration.

Hermitage Tardieu and Laurent source their Hermitage components in the cellars of several producers with land in the *climats* of Le Méal, Rocoules, Beaumes, Les Diognières, Les Greffieux and l'Hermite, giving their end-product great complexity indeed. Very dark in colour, it is a supremely elegant and harmonious example of its kind, demonstrating just why Hermitage has enjoyed such a long reputation for its *grands vins*. This eminent ambassador particularly enjoys the company of woodcock ragout.

- Other red wines: Côte-Rôtie, Cornas, Saint-Joseph, Crozes-Hermitage, Châteauneuf-du-Pape, Gigondas, Vacqueyras, Côtes-du-Rhône, Bandol
- White wines: Condrieu, Hermitage
- Owners: Michel Tardieu & Dominique Laurent
- Wine-maker: Michel Tardieu
- Production: 40,000 bottles
- Exports: 50%
- Take-away sales: No
- Visits: By appointment

Wine selected:
Hermitage

- Grape Variety: Syrah
- Average vine age: Very old!
- Soil type: Granite
- Average production: 4,000 bottles

Hermitage | Lauris

DOMAINE DE VALLOUIT

The name De Vallouit is rarely cited in guidebooks and wine reviews, yet the firm produces a large range of wines, both from bought-in raw material and from the produce of its own vines. While the former vary in quality, several of the latter, those wines known as Cuvées Spéciales which come from choice parcels of the firm's best vineyards in Côte-Rôtie, Hermitage, Cornas, Saint-Joseph and Crozes-Hermitage, are actually excellent and well worth tracking down…

The only wine-maker in town De Vallouit, founded in the 1920s, has its offices and cellars in the small town of Saint-Vallier, on the left bank of the Rhône some 15 kilometres north of Tain, a sort of vinous no-man's-land between Hermitage and Condrieu where it is the only wine-making establishment… which can hardly be an incentive to busy journalists and clients to visit! For many years the company has been run and its wines made by Louis de Vallouit and his wife Cécile, yet it would seem that they sold some of their equity in the company in the late 1990s, and while they are still involved in the firm's affairs, one of the new shareholders, Gilles Boyer, has taken over the day-to-day running.

Vinified to last The purchases of land started in the 1960s, and the firm's portfolio has gradually grown to 22 hectares, spread over all the best northern Rhône appellations. The best land though is in Côte-Rôtie, which provides the fruit for two wines which go by the names La Vonière and Les Roziers, and on the Hermitage hill, where the grapes for their Les Greffières originate. The vines are old, the yields are moderate, and the fruit is picked relatively late for maximum richness; there is also a double selection process, during harvest and before vatting, to ensure that nothing but perfectly healthy fruit finds its way into the vats.

These wines are destined to last, and are vinified accordingly. The fruit is not destemmed, and is given just a very light crushing prior to being loaded into the wooden fermentation vats. Over some 20 days the tannin, colour and aroma are extracted by both *pigeage* and *remontage*, and after *décuvage* the press-wine is reincorporated into the *vin de goutte*. There then follows protracted ageing in a variety of old wood of various sizes lasting between 24-36 months, and subsequently bottling with a light fining and filtration.

Hermitage Les Greffières A horse is still used to cultivate the Les Greffières vines, which are admirably sited and benefit from a topsoil of *galets roulés*, affording easy ripening and obliging the vines to bury their roots deeply to find sustenance. The splendid raw material is transformed by the ultra-traditional vinification into a densely-coloured, extremely concentrated wine with a remarkably intense bouquet, which in lighter years may suggest violets and spice, in greater years like the highly successful 1991 complex torrefied aromas. It is tannic, and certainly less user-friendly than some of the more modern-style Hermitages, but what magnificence! Nothing less than haunch of venison will do for this wine!

- Other red wines: Côte-Rôtie La Vonière, Côte-Rôtie Les Roziers, Côte-Rôtie, Hermitage, Cornas Les Médiévales, Cornas, Saint-Joseph Les Anges, Saint-Joseph, Crozes-Hermitage Comte de Larnage, Crozes-Hermitage
- White wines: Condrieu, Hermitage, Saint-Joseph, Crozes-Hermitage
- Owner: Société de Vallouit
- Manager: Gilles Boyer
- Wine-maker: Sylvain Pellegrinelli
- Oenologist: Michel Laurent
- Combined vineyards: 22 hectares
- Production: 106,000 bottles
- Exports: 40%
- Take-away sales: Yes
- Visits: 9-12 a.m.

Wine selected:
**Hermitage
Les Greffières**

- Grape Variety: Syrah
- Average vine age: 50 years
- Vineyard size: 1 hectare
- Soil type: Quartzite stones
- Average production: 3,500 bottles

Hermitage | Saint-Vallier

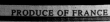

PRODUCE OF FRANCE

Domaine de Vallouit

LeS
GreffièreS
HERMITAGE
APPELLATION HERMITAGE CONTRÔLÉE

1991

MISE EN BOUTEILLES PAR
L. de VALLOUIT S.A. - 26240 ST-VALLIER S/RHÔNE - FRANCE

75cl

12.5% vol

DOMAINE ALAIN GRAILLOT

The appellation Crozes-Hermitage, which for long years lived off the reputation of Hermitage and was used to market numerous wines of dubious provenance, is now the source of some excellent bottles thanks to a new generation of wine-makers. The turning-point came around 1985, and its instigator was probably Alain Graillot. Proving that it is possible to produce good wine without any family wine-making tradition or experience if one really wants to, in a mere handful of years Graillot has become one of the appellation's leading growers.

A change of vocation A job as an international sales representative with a Parisian agricultural products firm left Graillot unsatisfied. Having made up his mind that a change was in order and that he wanted to make wine—and Syrah wine at that—this 40-year-old son of Vienne arrived a mere few weeks before the 1985 harvest, and set about making his first wine with rented vines during leave from his job, with no practical experience. The result was more than promising, and several years later he and his wife had acquired their estate near la Roche de Glun, a few kilometres south of Tain l'Hermitage. Taking the advice of growers such as Marcel Guigal, Gérard Jaboulet and Gérard Chave from whom he used to buy bottles but a few years before, Graillot was rapidly making some of the finest Crozes around.

Excellent soil for red wine The land he chose is at the root of his wines' quality. Lying principally in the Les Chassis locality east of La Roche de Glun, where the soil is composed of several metres of stones, his land is eminently suitable for making quality red wine. The estate's viticultural policy is built around careful cultivation of the vineyard with respect for the soil and its micro-organic life, which means very little use of artificial treatments, soil enriching by organic substances, and no *désherbage*—the grass is left to grow, which obliges the vines to bury their roots deeper, making them less vulnerable to climatic surprises and giving greater *terroir* expression. Graillot aims for moderate yields of perfectly ripe, but not over-ripe, fruit, and his pickers, as might be expected, work by hand, discarding any imperfect fruit as they go along.

The uncrushed grapes are given a long vatting period in concrete and are then reared mainly in Burgundian *pièces*, which have already held several wines. The lack of overt, new-oak flavour sets his wines apart from those of most of his fellow growers.

Crozes-Hermitage La Guiraude The better vintages are the occasion for Graillot to produce his La Guiraude, a selection of the casks which seem to him to have perfect balance and harmony. Such is its quality that the word has got around, and the wine is unfortunately rapidly sold out. Good as the standard *cuvée* is, La Guiraude is significantly richer and more complex, with a thick, juicy morello cherry flavour which gains nuances of tar, herbs and liquorice with bottle age. This really is an exceptional bottle of wine for a modest appellation, and is well worth its price... if one can find stocks! Rib of beef, grilled over a barbecue, enhances its qualities to no end.

- Other red wine: Crozes-Hermitage
- White wine: Crozes-Hermitage
- Owner: Alain Graillot
- Wine-maker: Alain Graillot
- Combined vineyards: 20 hectares
- Production: 106,000 bottles
- Exports: 55%
- Take-away sales: No
- Visits: No

Wine selected:
Crozes-Hermitage La Guiraude

- Grape Variety: Syrah
- Average vine age: 25 years
- Vineyard size: 17 hectares
- Soil type: Alluvial
- Average production: 15,000 bottles

1996

LA GUIRAUDE

CROZES HERMITAGE

APPELLATION CROZES HERMITAGE CONTRÔLÉE

alc. 12.5% by Vol.

Vinifié, élevé et mis en bouteille par

ALAIN GRAILLOT

Les Chênes Verts · Pont de l'Isère · France

PRODUIT DE FRANCE

70cl

L overs of good Crozes-Hermitage would do well to discover the Bernard Chave estate, for it is the source of beautifully made, soft, fruity wines of some complexity. The Chaves are at the forefront of the new generation of Crozes-Hermitage growers who have raised general standards so much.

A new estate comes into being Domaine Bernard Chave was set up in 1970 when Bernard, an independent spirit who was employed on the land, took the step and realized his lifetime dream of starting up his own wine exploitation. As is common in this region so well suited to agriculture in general, vines are not the only crop produced on the estate, for the family also cultivate apricots and peaches. Today Bernard looks after the family fruit business, and his son Yann, summoned from a banking career in Paris to help out, makes the wine.

From small beginnings the estate has gradually been enlarged over the years, and now covers 13.5 hectares in Crozes-Hermitage, of which 12 are planted with Syrah for the red wine, while the remainder, 70% Marsanne and 30% Roussanne, contribute fruit for the white. The family also own 1.5 hectares of Hermitage, enabling them to produce 5,000 bottles of that majestic wine.

Respect for the vineyard environment Vineyard practices amount to what is known as *lutte raisonnée*—respect for the vineyard environment and the soil and its microorganic life—and there are therefore no routine treatments or spraying. All weeding is by ploughing, all soil-enriching organic. Only when there is real danger of fungal attack will the Chaves resort to artificial protective products.

Yields are kept well inside the permitted limits, by severe pruning and systematic green-harvesting. The Chaves pride themselves on picking their fruit only when it is perfectly ripe, particularly so in the case of the white wine, for which they require an ample, *gras* character. The two white varieties, Marsanne and Roussanne, are vinified together in stainless steel at 20-22° and always undergo their malo-lactic fermentations, giving a softer acidity consistent with the type of wine required. They are then aged for a whole year, mainly in vat but also with one tenth in cask. As for the reds, all the Syrah grapes are destalked nowadays, although this was not always the case. Both the Hermitage and the Crozes wines are made in the same way—fermentation in cement vats with regular *pigeage*—with only the length of vatting differing: one week longer for the Hermitage than the Crozes's 2 weeks. Both are matured in *demi-muid* for 12 months before bottling.

Crozes-Hermitage Tête de Cuvée A small vineyard at Pont l'Isère of plants reproduced by *sélection massale* is the source of the Tête de Cuvée. Made for the first time in 1997 exclusively from the free-run wine of their small grapes, it is capable of improving in bottle over 5-6 years. Supple in the mouth, rich and deeply fruity with an intriguing chocolate aspect, it can nevertheless give pleasure from Day One, for its ripe, tannic structure is well enfolded in fleshy matter. This is an excellent Crozes-Hermitage; it merely demands a roast pheasant to set it off to perfection.

- Other red wines:
Crozes-Hermitage Cuvée Traditionnelle, Hermitage
- White wine:
Crozes-Hermitage
- Owner: Bernard Chave
- Wine-maker:
Yann Chave
- Combined vineyards:
14.5 hectares
- Production:
73,000 bottles
- Exports: 70%
- Take-away sales: Yes
- Visits: By appointment

Wine selected:
Crozes-Hermitage Tête de Cuvée

- Grape Variety: Syrah
- Average vine age:
25 years
- Vineyard size:
5 hectares
- Soil type: Sandy silt
- Average production:
12,000 bottles

DOMAINE COMBIER

Fruit lovers in the Pont de l'Isère region have long known the name Combier, for many years the source of fine cherries, apricots, peaches and apples. Now it is the turn of wine-lovers. The word is getting around fast, as people discover the splendid wines of great purity, succulence and character made by Laurent Combier.

Fired with a desire to make wine As has happened at other estates, the arrival of a new generation has signalled an end to the deliveries of grapes to the cooperative. And here, the cooperative's loss is every Crozes-Hermitage-lover's gain! After training in Orange and working in Burgundy, Provence and Châteauneuf-du-Pape, Laurent Combier took over from his parents in 1990, fired with the desire to make wine himself... and not just any old wine! To go about the task, he had a new vatroom and cellars built, designed to make the best use of gravity for movement of fruit and liquid, and equipped it with the necessary stainless steel hardware, with temperature-control facilities.

A pioneer of biological agriculture Combier was fortunate in inheriting a splendid vineyard, not only from a geographical point of view but also from that of the health of the soils and plants. Nine-tenths of the vines lie in the commune of Châssis, on alluvial soil with quartzite stones, which is reckoned the source of the finest red Crozes-Hermitage; the remainder, lying up north around Mercurol in lighter soil, gives excellent white wines. As far back as 1970 Combier's father Maurice recognized the importance to agricultural crops of a healthy, living soil, and embraced the methods of biological agriculture, both for his vines and his other fruit.

Different styles for different occasions Today Domaine Combier has 20 hectares of fruit orchards and 14 hectares of vineyard. Two *cuvées* of red wine are made, the standard Domaine wine and Clos des Grives, and the same is the case for the white wine. The Domaine wines are a conscious attempt to produce typical Crozes-Hermitage in a light, easy-drinking style which is good young, while the Clos des Grives wines are altogether more serious—a selection of the fruit of old vines, from lower yields, the red enjoys longer vatting and rearing in oak casks, while the white is fermented and reared in cask with weekly *bâtonnage*. Any wine which is judged of insufficient quality, which can be anything up to 10% of the production, is sold off in bulk.

Crozes-Hermitage Clos des Grives When making his red wines Laurent Combier prefers to destem his fruit in its entirety and then compensate for that with a longer *cuvaison*, a choice which endows the Clos des Grives with a rich, succulent and fleshy presence on the palate and ripe red-fruit aromas of great intensity. The tannic structure remains discreetly hidden beneath the surface, and when young the wine bears the imprint of its *élevage* in 40% new and 60% recent oak, yet the whole has breeding and harmony from Day One. Most red meats partner the Clos des Grives very well—*tournedos forestière* in particular—as do veal's liver and kidneys.

- Other red wines: Crozes-Hermitage, Saint-Joseph
- White wines: Crozes-Hermitage Clos des Grives, Crozes-Hermitage
- Owner: Combier family
- Wine-maker: Laurent Combier
- Oenologist: Jean-Luc Colombo
- Combined vineyards: 14 hectares
- Production: 80,000 bottles
- Exports: 50%
- Take-away sales: Yes
- Visits: Yes

Wine selected:
Crozes-Hermitage Clos des Grives

- Grape Variety: Syrah
- Average vine age: 45 years
- Vineyard size: 3.5 hectares
- Soil type: Alluvial with quartzite stones
- Average production: 12,000 bottles

CLOS DES GRIVES
CdesG
Appellation Crozes - Hermitage Contrôlée
1997
12,5% vol.
DOMAINE COMBIER
Mis en bouteille au domaine à
Pont de L'Isère 26600 Tain l'Hermitage - F.
Product of France

Château Curson and Domaine Pochon are registered trademarks used by Etienne Pochon, one of the wave of young wine-makers who have taken the Crozes-Hermitage appellation by the proverbial scruff of the neck and given it a good shaking. The wines sold with these labels are absolutely delicious, indeed they now rank among the finest produced in the area.

The emergence of a fine estate When Etienne Pochon brought an end to his contract with the local cooperative in 1987 he had 7 hectares of vines to draw on, enough to produce some 40,000 bottles. By 1999 this figure had doubled. The Pochons live and make their wine in the handsome Château de Curson at Chanos-Curson, which belonged to Diane de Poitiers in the 16th century. The château, built of the Rhône's smooth quartzite stones and calcareous sandstone *mollasse*, has handsome vaulted cellars and a central tower with a spiral stairway giving onto the different levels, and is surrounded by its vineyard.

Two distinct quality levels Viticultural practices are thoroughly organic, in keeping with the times, with much attention devoted to mastering yields and then letting nothing but the finest fruit into the vats. The wine-making also is resolutely modern, and the thinking behind it no less so: two quality levels are produced, one of more consequent and structured wines capable of improvement in bottle, the other of lighter wines bursting with uncomplicated fruit, for drinking relatively early; all the raw material brought in thus finds a suitable outlet. The first level, from the well-exposed and sloping vineyards around the château, is marketed as Château Curson; the second, from young vines or those grown on the plain, as Domaine Pochon.

Secrets of the vatroom For producing his white wine the Pochon vineyards contain roughly 60% Marsanne and 40% Roussanne. The former receives a *macération pelliculaire*, but the latter, notoriously susceptible to oxidation, does not. After pressing there follows 20 hours' settling, then transfer to both new oak barrels and stainless steel and the onset of fermentation. Some 20 days later the 4-month *élevage* starts, with weekly *bâtonnage* of the lees and malolactic fermentation for the Roussanne only. Blending of the two whites takes place in February and the wines are fined and filtered before bottling at the end of May.

The black grapes are systematically destemmed and then macerated for 3 days in stainless steel. Thereafter the fermentation slowly takes off, aided by selected local yeast, and is maintained at 33°C for 7 days with frequent *remontages*, after which comes 20 days' warm maceration. The various vats are blended once the malolactic fermentations are over, and the Château Curson is aged in new and once-used oak, while the Domaine Pochon is lodged in older wood.

Crozes-Hermitage Château Curson Deep purple in colour, the Château Curson has a wonderful, complex bouquet of great purity, in which one can detect nuances of ripe black fruit, violets, liquorice and pepper. Rich, with well-integrated tannin, this wonderful wine needs several years to find its voice, after which it becomes positively talkative in the company of Drôme guinea fowl, partridge cooked with chestnuts or roast saddle of hare.

- Other red wines: Crozes-Hermitage Domaine Pochon, Vin de Pays des Collines Rhodaniennes
- White wines: Crozes-Hermitage Château Curson, Crozes-Hermitage Domaine Pochon
- Owner: Pochon family
- Director: Etienne Pochon
- Wine-maker: Jean-Paul Mounier
- Oenologist: Véronique Perrin
- Combined vineyards: 14 hectares
- Production: 86,000 bottles
- Exports: 60%
- Take-away sales: 2-7 p.m. Fri. and Sat., or by appt.
- Visits: By appointment

Wine selected:
Crozes-Hermitage Château Curson

- Grape Variety: Syrah
- Average vine age: 30 years
- Vineyard size: 3 hectares
- Soil type: Clay and sandy gravel
- Average production: 13,000 bottles

·1997·

Château Curson

CROZES-HERMITAGE
APPELLATION CROZES-HERMITAGE CONTRÔLÉE

Mis en bouteille au Château par

DOMAINES POCHON
Propriétaires à CURSON 26600 Tain l'Hermitage - FRANCE

Produce of France

In common with many other agricultural businesses in the relatively flat area between Tain l'Hermitage and Pont de l'Isère on the left bank of the Rhône, the Cornu family exploitation at Sept Chemins, near Les Châssis, does not rely solely on the vine for revenue, and as much time is spent in fruit orchards as between rows of Syrah or Marsanne. The wine made at this estate though is excellent and may be bought without hesitation.

Adapting to market demand The reputation of Domaine du Pavillon has been acquired in the last few years, for as at many estates in the region, vinification and bottling on site are recent developments, instigated by a young generation of growers who have seen the recent surge in demand for Rhône wine that is affordable and well made, and are keen to supply it and make a name for themselves. The business was originally completely fruit-oriented during the time of its founder, Stéphane Cornu's grandfather, and it was his father Alphonse who planted the vines in the 1970s. For two decades Alphonse Cornu sold his produce to the *négociants* Jaboulet and Delas, until he was persuaded by Stéphane to change to estate-bottling at the end of the 1980s.

Traditional methods and modern rigour Since that crucial change the young Stéphane has been in control of the vats and cellars, using traditional methods to make wine which is thoroughly traditional in character—although that, fortunately, does not include the flaws of yesteryear, the result of rudimentary equipment and an incomplete understanding of the fermentation process!

The family vineyards lie conveniently around the house and winery, and from the 11 hectares Cornu produces two reds and one white. The better red and the white wine are the produce of the original vines planted by Alphonse Cornu (the term "Vieilles Vignes" however would hardly be appropriate yet) on a more sloping part of the vineyard which is looked down on by the *pavillon* in question; the remainder of the vines were planted more recently and are on flatter land, and their produce makes the second red wine, Le Chai Cornu.

Cornu's red wines take their time to develop in bottle, for they are vinified without any destemming, with lengthy maceration and fermentation temperatures which are allowed to rise as they will, which usually means at up to some 36°C. Vinification is in cement vats, and subsequent maturation in cask generally lasts a year, to be followed by bottling without filtration.

Crozes-Hermitage The Domaine du Pavillon Crozes-Hermitage is an excellent, modern representation of healthy Syrah fruit grown in the best Crozes-Hermitage terrain: expressive on the nose with rich, precise morello cherry aromas, it is dense and chewy in the mouth, and packed with concentrated, fleshy fruitiness, supported by a fairly consequent tannic structure and a good degree of acidity. Stuffed lamb *en croûte* partners it very well; and for a winter snack, why not serve it with a bacon and vegetable soup?

- Other red wine: Crozes-Hermitage Le Chai Cornu
- White wine: Crozes-Hermitage
- Owner: Stéphane Cornu
- Wine-maker: Stéphane Cornu
- Oenologist: Michel Laurent
- Combined vineyards: 11 hectares
- Production: 60,000 bottles
- Exports: 90%
- Take-away sales: Yes
- Visits: By appointment

Wine selected:
Crozes-Hermitage

- Grape Variety: Syrah
- Average vine age: 18 years
- Vineyard size: 5 hectares
- Soil type: Alluvial
- Average production: 20,000 bottles

CROZES-HERMITAGE

APPELLATION CROZES-HERMITAGE CONTROLÉE

1997   1997

DOMAINE DU PAVILLON-MERCUROL

Mis en bouteille par
Stéphane Cornu, Producteur Eleveur
à Mercurol 26600 - Drôme (France)
PRODUCT OF FRANCE
Marque déposée   N° Lot 971

Fine Crozes-Hermitage may be had at Cave Desmeure, on the Romans road near Mercurol, where the highly talented Philippe Desmeure goes about his trade. This grower is unstinting in his efforts towards excellence, a fact which shines through in the finished Domaine des Remizières wines. He is representative of the new wave of ambitious young men who have elevated Crozes-Hermitage to levels unheard of a dozen years ago, and deserves to be better known.

Low yields for the finest quality Once he had left school Desmeure learnt his trade over some 15 years of working alongside his father Alphonse, and was therefore not short of experience when the latter took retirement in 1990. Today he has at his disposal a fine estate of 26 hectares, which includes land in Hermitage and Saint-Joseph as well as Crozes-Hermitage, and he makes both red and white versions of all three wines.

Low yields being an essential requisite to concentration, flavour and character in a wine, like his peers Philippe Desmeure addresses the problem during the winter by severe pruning and at the moment of the *véraison*, when the fruit turns colour around late July. That is the propitious moment for eliminating excess vegetation and, particularly for the white varieties, for lopping off excess bunches in order to reduce each vine's crop so that its energy will not be dispersed any more than necessary. However fine judgement is required, for if the grower operates too early the vine will compensate by producing other bunches, while if he does it too late the bunches remaining will not have time to benefit from the new situation.

Fermented in vat and barrel Once the fruit is ripe the harvesters go in, and a selection process to separate the impeccable from the rest takes place in the vineyard. Vinification takes place, after destalking, in stainless steel vats with 3-4 *remontages* per day. The red wines are then run off into barrel and it is there that the malolactic fermentation takes place, as it did in previous times before *vignerons* understood it and wanted to exercise control over it in the vat. The *élevage* subsequently takes place in barrel, lasting one year for the Crozes-Hermitage and some 14 months for the Hermitage, before bottling and sale. The rate of barrel renewal each year is 50% for the former, 80% for the latter.

Crozes-Hermitage Cuvée Christophe Good though the generic red Crozes-Hermitage is, the Cuvée Christophe is a definite step up. Vibrant fruit aromas with a faintly meaty, spicy aspect meet the nose, while the eye is attracted by a limpid, medium-deep violet-red colour. On the palate the attack is fine, the savour invading the mouth's every corner and impregnating it with a delicious draft of blackcurrant, cinnamon and pepper. Tannic structure there is, yet the quality and thoroughness of Desmeure's work is reflected in the softness and elegance of the tannin and the fine length once the wine has been swallowed. This wine also has finesse. Cuvée Christophe is benchmark Crozes-Hermitage, highly suitable for washing down some stuffed breast of veal.

- Other red wines: Crozes-Hermitage, Hermitage, Saint-Joseph, Vin de Pays Cépage Syrah
- White wines: Crozes-Hermitage, Hermitage, Saint-Joseph, Vin de Pays Cépage Viognier
- Owner: Philippe Desmeure
- Wine-maker: Philippe Desmeure
- Combined vineyards: 26 hectares
- Production: 150,000 bottles
- Exports: 25%
- Take-away sales: Mon.-Sat. 9.00-12.00 a.m., 2.00-6.30 p.m.
- Visits: By appointment

Wine selected:
Crozes-Hermitage Cuvée Christophe

- Grape Variety: Syrah
- Average vine age: 30 years
- Vineyard size: 12 hectares
- Soil type: Clay and limestone, granite
- Average production: 10,000 bottles

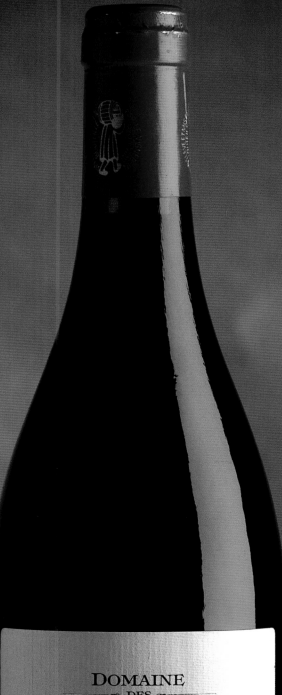

S tretching down the right bank of the Rhône all the way from Condrieu, which appellation it overlaps, to Valence, Saint-Joseph wines come in both the light and fruity variety for quaffing young, and the serious structured variety needing bottle age, and are made to very varying degrees of quality. The best have traditionally come from the original area encompassing the communes Vion, Lemps, Saint-Jean de Muzols, Tournon, Mauves and Glun, and it is in Mauves that one finds the very talented Bernard Gripa.

Extension and reduction of the vineyard area Saint-Joseph's delimited vineyard area has undergone several radical changes over the years. In 1956, when the appellation was created, it covered just 97 hectares of mainly terraced vineyards in the original heartland, and the general level was high, according to those who remember the wines of that period. However in 1969 the area permitted for viticulture was increased to an astonishing 7,000 hectares, encompassing much flat, fertile land incompatible with quality wine. Since the extension many mediocre wines have tarnished Saint-Joseph's name, obliging the authorities to review matters again. In 1992 they therefore reduced the area to 3,004, of which 795 were declared by their owners as producing a crop in 1995. Syrah is the red-wine grape, to which may be blended 10% of either the Marsanne or Roussanne white grapes; these two, together or singly, are responsible for all white Saint-Joseph.

The cradle of the appellation Bernard Gripa is the fourth generation of his family to make wine, having taken over from his father in 1964. At the time other fruit and cereals constituted the bulk of the family production, and even today the grape is not alone on the terraces. Gripa's vineyards are situated in Mauves and Tournon, and he also has one hectare of Saint-Péray, from which he produces a remarkably fresh and elegant example of that wine.

He produces two red and two white Saint-Joseph wines, a standard blend and a *cuvée* named Le Berceau (the cradle), which John Livingstone-Learmonth, in *The Wines of the Rhône*, tells us refers to the Tournon *lieu-dit* Saint-Joseph, the cradle of the appellation, where the fruit is grown. Gripa's red-wine methods are thoroughly traditional: grapes are left on their stalks, and the bunches are tipped uncrushed into the open wooden vats, where they macerate and ferment for some 2-3 weeks with daily treading to extract colour, tannin and fruit, before spending a year in cask prior to bottling. White wines are fermented and aged in barrel, roughly one quarter of which are new.

Saint-Joseph Le Berceau Gripa's red Le Berceau is a very distinguished wine, very deep purple in colour and pungent on the nose, with a deep, spicy, black-fruit flavour, soft and concentrated on the palate and with a structure enabling it to envisage 7-8 years' development. This excellent Saint-Joseph goes very well with a leg of lamb, or stuffed veal's breast.

- Other red wines: Saint-Joseph
- White wines: Saint-Joseph, Saint-Joseph Le Berceau, Saint-Péray, Saint-Péray Les Figuiers
- Owner: Bernard Gripa
- Wine-maker: Bernard Gripa
- Combined vineyards: 10 hectares
- Production: 50,000 bottles
- Exports: 20%
- Take-away sales: 8-12 a.m., 2-7 p.m., Mon. - Sat.
- Visits: By appointment

Wine selected:
**Saint-Joseph
Le Berceau**

- Grape Variety: Syrah
- Average vine age: 50 years
- Vineyard size: 1 hectare
- Soil type: Granite
- Average production: 1,800 bottles

Saint-Joseph | *Mauves*

1996

Saint-Joseph
Le Berceau
APPELLATION SAINT-JOSEPH CONTRÔLÉE
MIS EN BOUTEILLE A LA PROPRIÉTÉ
BERNARD GRIPA
PROPRIÉTAIRE-VITICULTEUR A MAUVES (07) FRANCE
PRODUCE OF FRANCE

DOMAINE JEAN-LOUIS GRIPPAT

Whatever reputation modern Saint-Joseph wines have for being 'serious' rather than fresh, fruity quaffing wines is thanks to the likes of Jean-Louis Grippat, considered by many the finest grower of the appellation. Grippat has been making wine since a young age, and over the years has acquired a very solid expertise of his subject… yet, like all consistently good wine-makers, he is not one for resting on his laurels, for self-satisfaction is a grower's worst enemy!

The trials of the Saint-Joseph grower The Grippat estate has gradually expanded over the years and today covers 9 hectares, situated not only in Saint-Joseph but also on the Hermitage hill. The nucleus though is his holding of 5.3 hectares of Syrah and 1.5 hectares of Marsanne on the Saint-Joseph hill behind Tournon—one of the appellation's finest sites. Here the grower needs to be in good physical condition, for the vines are cultivated on narrow terraces carved out of a precipitous slope of loose granite soil, which is treacherous underfoot and prone to sliding down the slope when it rains. Mechanization is out of the question in many places, and the various vineyard tasks can only be carried out by hand—or, as has recently become the fashion, by helicopter in the case of spraying.

Uncompromisingly rich and structured Grippat trains his vines *en gobelet*, to enhance photosynthesis and aeration, with the supporting stakes traditional in this part of the Rhône valley… although one does see wire used by growers in those plots offering the possibility of mechanization. The crop is naturally picked by hand, and 50-80% of the Syrahs are destalked before being loaded uncrushed into open wooden vats for 18-20 days' vatting. During this period the solid matter is trodden twice daily for maximum extraction of tannin, colour and aroma. The aim, as will be surmised from this treatment, is for uncompromisingly rich and structured wine for development in bottle, yet with reduced risk of stalk tannins adding astringency to the wine. When the vatting period is over the wines change *cuve* for several months to complete their malolactic fermentations, after which they spend up to a year in the traditional *demi-muid*, a large oak cask of varying capacity, usually around 600 litres.

As for the white wines, the Marsannes are pressed and then fermented in stainless steel, then aged in stainless steel and rounded off by several months in cask before bottling, 'malos' completed.

Saint-Joseph Grippat's red Saint-Joseph, a lustrous, dark ruby wine with a classy, slightly smoky black-fruit bouquet, is highly enticing when young… yet that is just the primary fruit talking: it does not really exhibit the depth of its qualities until after a handful of years in bottle, or even more in the best vintages. Patience is the key with this wine! When finally it has reached maturity, it appreciates the company of young wild boar, served with sausage stuffing.

- Other red wines:
Hermitage
- White wines:
Saint-Joseph, Hermitage
- Owner:
Jean-Louis Grippat
- Wine-maker:
Jean-Louis Grippat
- Oenologist:
Michel Laurent
- Combined vineyards:
9 hectares
- Production:
46,000 bottles
- Exports: 30%
- Take-away sales:
By appointment
- Visits: No

Wine selected:
Saint-Joseph

- Grape Variety: Syrah
- Average vine age:
25 years
- Vineyard size:
5.3 hectares
- Soil type: Granite
- Average production:
22,000 bottles

Saint-Joseph

APPELLATION SAINT-JOSEPH CONTRÔLÉE

PRODUIT DE FRANCE

1996

alk. 12,5 % by vol.   750 ml

Mis en bouteille à la propriété

DOMAINE J.L. GRIPPAT SCEA VITICULTEUR A 07300 TOURNON (FRANCE)

In his smart stone cellars in the hamlet of La Ribaudy, high up in the hills above Chavanay, the tall, bearded and bespectacled Philippe Faury crafts Saint-Joseph and Condrieu wines of great distinction, in which *terroir* characteristics predominate, emphasized but not masked by wine-making methods. Faury does not produce much wine, and most is sold on site, making an excursion up the tortuously winding road a delightful necessity.

From polyculture to wine-making When Faury's father settled in La Ribaudy he started cultivating a variety of crops as well as rearing livestock, and it was only in the 1960s that he started increasing his grape production and making wine. He sold it off in bulk at first, and started bottling from 1969 onwards.

Having briefly studied at the *lycée agricole* of Limonest and then gained work experience in an agricultural *négociant* firm, Philippe Faury took over from his father in 1979, and specialized from the start in wine. To make it viable he had to enlarge, for he had only inherited 2.5 hectares of vineyard, and he set about planting abandoned slopes, giving himself in the end 10.5 hectares of south- and south-east-facing land to exploit. At the same time he progressively enlarged his vatroom and cellars.

Wines reflecting their soil and environment Faury is a firm believer in natural wines, which reflect their soil and environment. The high altitude of the vineyards—his Condrieu vines grow at up to 300 metres, the upper limit—has the fortunate effect of reducing to a bare minimum the need for any treatments, and helps him towards this goal. He keeps the vines' yields down by pruning short and then crop-thinning in July or August, and then proceeds to vinify with the minimum of intervention possible: movement of fruit or wine is by gravity when possible, the fermentation is carried out by the grapes' own yeast, there is never recourse to acidification…

Condrieus of finely-controlled opulence The white Saint-Joseph and standard Condrieu are vinified in cask and stainless steel at fairly low temperatures, and undergo their malolactic fermentation. Purity and elegance are the forte of these and Faurie's other Condrieus, none of which shows any of the excessively blowsy opulence which can so easily be a fault of Viognier wines. Besides the standard Condrieu, in 1997 Faury introduced an old-vine *cuvée* named La Berne, intensely rich with finely-controlled opulence, aged in casks of which 60% were new, and a late-harvested *cuvée* Brumaire. This rarity was harvested in 6 tries, the last on 8th December, and demonstrates convincingly how suitable the Viognier is to the production of sweetish wines.

Saint-Joseph Like his white wines, Faury's red Saint-Joseph is a masterpiece of the authentic, harmonious and natural, without the excessive extraction of certain other growers' offerings. Its rich, intense fruit and supporting structure are finely balanced, and lightly perfumed by the wood in which the wine is aged. This Saint-Joseph requires 4-6 years' bottle-age for maximum expression, at which point its qualities are highlighted by the company of roast goose, served with red cabbage.

- Other red wines: Côte-Rôtie, Vin de Pays
- White wines: Saint-Joseph, Condrieu, Condrieu La Berne, Condrieu Brumaire, Vin de Pays
- Owner: Philippe Faury
- Wine-maker: Philippe Faury
- Oenology: Chambre d'Agriculture de la Drôme
- Combined vineyards: 10.5 hectares
- Production: 50,000 bottles
- Exports: 10%
- Take-away sales: 8-12 a.m., 2-6 p.m., by appt.
- Visits: By appointment

Wine selected:
Saint-Joseph

- Grape Variety: Syrah
- Average vine age: 20 years
- Vineyard size: 4 hectares
- Soil type: Granitic
- Average production: 20,000 bottles

1996

Saint Joseph

APPELLATION CONTROLEE

12,5 % vol

Philippe Faury

Viticulteur, La Ribaudy, CHAVANAY, 42410 . France

MIS EN BOUTEILLE À LA PROPRIETE

75 cl

DOMAINE PIERRE COURSODON

One of the best-known names in Saint-Joseph is Coursodon. Four generations of this Mauves family have dedicated themselves to the vine and wine, and the fifth is currently learning the trade. Pierre Coursodon and his son Jérôme today fashion a range of red and white Saint-Josephs of excellent quality.

To obtain fruit of the finest quality... Since Pierre Coursodon took over from his father Gustave in 1982 he has considerably increased the size of the estate, to meet growing demand, clearing and replanting a number of sites which had lain abandoned since Gustave's father's time, and now has at his disposal 12 hectares. The vineyards are on the slopes above Mauves and Saint-Jean de Muzols, and the steepness and openness to the elements make cultivation of the ten-odd parcels hard work indeed, for all operations must be carried out by hand.

The vines, red and white, are impressively old—the two prestige red wines, l'Olivaie and le Paradis Saint-Pierre, are the product of octogenarian plants—and are planted densely. Old age reduces yields, and density of plantation, while also acting as a brake on production, obliges the plants to bury their roots deeply to obtain the mineral salts, oligo-elements and water they need. These two factors go some way to explaining the wines' quality.

A 'green harvest' is carried out in the red-wine vineyards, again to reduce yields, and when it arrives at the reception area the crop is picked through on a sorting table to ensure that nothing but fruit of the finest quality and condition finds its way into the vats. Thereafter its treatment will differ greatly, depending on its colour...

Reds and whites of equal distinction The black grapes are mostly destemmed, then macerated and fermented in open wooden vats for some 18 days with several *pigeages* per day, in order to extract as much colour, aroma and tannin as possible; the Coursodons have always gone for sturdy wines of structure, with ageing potential. The resulting wines are aged for 12-15 months in large barrels and tuns, then bottled without filtration. These, particularly Le Paradis Saint-Pierre and l'Olivaie, are magnificent, full-bodied and flavoursome characters which benefit from 6-8 years in the cellar.

Unlike some, Pierre Coursodon's whites are at least as accomplished as his reds. The juice of his Marsanne grapes is gently extracted by pneumatic pressing, and left to settle overnight. The standard white is then fermented in vat, but fruit destined to make the white Le Paradis Saint-Pierre is fermented in barrel at 18°C, and also undergoes its malolactic fermentation there. It then spends a year enriching itself on its lees with weekly *bâtonnage*, before being bottled.

Saint-Joseph Le Paradis Saint-Pierre Barrel fermentation gives Le Paradis Saint-Pierre fatness and depth which make it that much more serious than the basic Saint-Joseph white, excellent though that is, and destined to a different vocation. With its pure and intense floral aromas and underlining oaky thickness, this is a wine to bring joy to the gourmet's heart, particularly when associated with such delicacies as morels in puff-pastry.

- Other white wines:
Saint-Joseph
- Red wines:
Saint-Joseph Le Paradis
Saint-Pierre, Saint-Joseph
l'Olivaie, Saint-Joseph
La Sensonne, Saint-Joseph
- Owner:
Pierre Coursodon
- Manager:
Pierre Coursodon
- Wine-makers:
Pierre & Jérôme
Coursodon
- Combined vineyards:
12 hectares
- Production:
60,000 bottles
- Exports: 25%
- Take-away sales: Yes
- Visits: By appointment

Wine selected:
**Saint-Joseph
Le Paradis Saint-Pierre**

- Grape Variety:
Marsanne
- Average vine age:
40 years
- Vineyard size:
0.8 hectares
- Soil type:
Clay and limestone
- Average production:
3,000 bottles

Domaine **Coursodon**
1997

PRODUCT OF FRANCE

Le Paradis Saint - Pierre
MARQUE DÉPOSÉE

Saint - Joseph

APPELLATION SAINT - JOSEPH CONTRÔLÉE

MIS EN BOUTEILLE A LA PROPRIÉTÉ

13% vol   PIERRE COURSODON   750 ml
VIGNERON - 07300 MAUVES (ARDÈCHE)

A decade of experiment, analysis and refinement has steadily brought the wines of Pierre Gaillard to their current high standard, making this a very reliable address for the lover of Saint-Joseph, Condrieu and Côte-Rôtie. Yet his vines are still young, and Gaillard is not one for sitting on his laurels; one can confidently expect great things from him in the future...

An entrepreneur studies and starts up Like a number of start-ups of his generation in the northern Rhône Valley Pierre Gaillard did not become a *vigneron* on inheriting a family business but chose to set up as such, and did the necessary studies at Beaune and Montpellier. He then spent a number of years with Vidal-Fleury and subsequently Guigal, initially as *chef de culture*—it was he who planted the La Turque vineyard in 1982—and then working on the wine-making itself. During that period he started buying and planting land, and by 1986 was ready to launch his own exploitation.

Excellence in both colours All his parcels are well-sited, the Saint-Joseph vineyards sloping gently towards the east, while the Côte-Rôtie and latterly-acquired Condrieu face south-south-east on more precipitous slopes.

The meticulous Gaillard has demonstrated a sure touch from the start with his white wines. There are three: a Condrieu, a Saint-Joseph made entirely with Roussanne and a Côtes-du-Rhône Viognier. Severe pruning for low yields followed by patience at harvest-time give Gaillard rich, ripe fruit which he vinifies in barrel at a fairly low 18°C. Once the alcoholic and malolactic fermentations are over the wines are aged in barrel, with weekly *bâtonnage* to keep the lees in suspension and increase the richness and aromatic intensity. The oak barrels are renewed regularly at the rate of 10% per year for the white wines.

Gaillard's reds have taken a little while to achieve their current excellence, for their maker was convinced for a long time that destemming the grapes was an error which detracted from a wine's typicity. Recent years have seen a change of policy, however, much to the wines' benefit. The reds naturally are also treated to oak-ageing, with a more important renewal rate of 20% per year.

Saint-Joseph Clos de la Cuminaille Proving that the slopes above Chavanay, in the northern (extended) sector of Saint-Joseph, can make wine to rival that of the hallowed heartland around Mauves, Tournon and Saint-Jean-de-Muzols, Pierre Gaillard makes a deeply-coloured and superbly complex wine from his 6 hectares of Syrah in the Clos de la Cuminaille.

His method is to give these grapes 5 days' cold maceration, then ferment them rapidly over 5 days at a high 34-35°C with triple *pigeage* daily, and round off the extraction with 10 days' maceration at 30°C. The result is most impressive, a classy wine of great concentration and finely-judged balance, redolent of Syrah's red fruit and spiciness with a touch of vanilla in the background. This has far greater potential for improvement over the years than most red Saint-Joseph, and partners red meats such as beef *à la ficelle* very well.

Saint-Joseph | Malleval

• Other red wines:
Côte-Rôtie, Vin de Pays des Collines Rhodaniennes
• White wines:
Condrieu, Saint-Joseph, Côtes-du-Rhône
• Owner: Pierre Gaillard
• Wine-maker:
Pierre Gaillard
• Oenologist:
Jean-Luc Colombo
• Combined vineyards:
16 hectares
• Production:
93,000 bottles
• Exports: 40%
• Take-away sales:
By appointment
• Visits: By appointment

Wine selected:
**Saint-Joseph
Clos de la Cuminaille**

• Grape Variety: Syrah
• Average vine age:
18 years
• Vineyard size:
6 hectares
• Soil type: Granite
• Average production:
30,000 bottles

DOMAINE ALAIN VOGE

The best wines of Cornas are avidly sought out by connoisseurs, yet on the whole the appellation is little in demand, no doubt because it still suffers from its age-old reputation for producing massive, tannic, rustic and alcoholic brutes. This image is still merited rather too often, yet the better producers do manage to produce wines which, while always equipped for long lives, can nevertheless count fruitiness, charm and balance among their various qualities. There is one, Alain Voge, whose wines are even described as elegant. He has long been among the village's finest growers.

A young man arrives in the village Voge owns 8 hectares of Cornas, a holding which is positively vast in an appellation where the average is less than three. This ex-rugby player arrived in the village in 1958 at the age of 18, and started bottling his production almost from the start. As time went by he bought up additional plots every so often, with the result that his vines are today scattered over a dozen sites, all in prime locations.

A good many of the vines are very old, enabling him to make three different *cuvées* of Cornas: besides the generic wine there is a Vieilles Vignes *cuvée*, produced from 4 hectares of vines aged from 20-80 years, and in the finest vintages a wine named Vieilles Fontaines, a selection of the best grapes from the finest plots.

Experimentation, observation and analysis Voge's wines have been compared by the American writer Robert Parker with the finest Hermitages. This is tribute indeed, for despite the fact that both appellations are made exclusively with the Syrah grape and on similar granite slopes, the extreme heat in Cornas's sheltered, steep vineyards often precludes finesse in the finished product—indeed Cornas in Celtic means 'burnt land'.

Voge sets out to make wines of intense, fresh fruitiness and relative delicacy, and for him they are unbalanced if their alcohol level exceeds 12.5°. Old vines are 50% destemmed, younger ones not at all, and he then ferments the fruit in a mix of stainless steel and cement vats with either *pigeage* or *remontages*, or both; vatting time lasts 15-17 days. The wines are then lodged in oak barrels which have already seen 3-5 vintages and aged for 20-24 months in the case of the Vieilles Vignes or 28-30 months in the case of the Vieilles Fontaines, before being bottled in one fell swoop. This method of proceeding is the result of many years of practice, observation and analysis, yet it is in no way systematic for, like all great wine-makers, Voge is always tinkering and experimenting with the aim of refining even further his product.

Cornas Les Vieilles Fontaines Thanks to the extreme severity with which he selects the raw material for his Vieilles Fontaines, it has a gorgeously fleshy, intense, sensual character, and gives pleasure young, although of course longevity is one of its natural attributes. Drink it with any roast meats, advises Voge, indeed serve a mature bottle with a roast rib of Charolais beef, prepared with slivers of foie gras and fresh truffle and finished with Cornas gravy, as served chez Michel Chabran at Pont-de-l'Isère.

- Other red wines: Cornas, Cornas Vieilles Vignes
- White wines: Saint-Péray sec Mélodie William, Saint-Péray sec Cuvée Boisée, sparkling Saint-Péray
- Owner: Alain Voge
- Wine-makers: Alain Voge & Rémy Desbers
- Oenologist: Jean-François Hebrard
- Combined vineyards: 12 hectares
- Production: 64,000 bottles
- Exports: 30%
- Take-away sales: Yes
- Visits: 8-12 a.m., 2-6 p.m.

Wine selected:
Cornas Les Vieilles Fontaines

- Grape Variety: Syrah
- Average vine age: 35 years
- Vineyard size: 1 hectare
- Soil type: Granite
- Average production: 3,200 bottles maximum

1995

PRODUIT   DE FRANCE

"Les Vieilles Fontaines"
Cuvée
CORNAS
APPELLATION CORNAS CONTROLÉE

12,5% vol.   750 ml

MIS EN BOUTEILLE A LA PROPRIÉTÉ

ALAIN VOGE, Viticulteur à CORNAS (ARDÈCHE) FRANCE

CREATION IMP. REYNAUD - VALENCE

DOMAINE AUGUSTE CLAPE

The village of Cornas owes a lot to its premier *vigneron* and long-time mayor, Auguste Clape, for it has been he who has brought the village name to the attention of faraway critics and consumers, by the superlative quality and laudable regularity of his wines. Thanks to the Clape effect other growers now generally have no problem selling their annual production, and even if Cornas does not enjoy the prestige of Côte-Rôtie and Hermitage, their landholdings have nevertheless taken on some value in recent years.

Against which others are judged Clape is frequently compared with his Mauves counterpart Gérard Chave and Marcel Guigal of Ampuis, for he seems to have an innate feel for blending the produce of his various parcels of vines to produce a harmonious whole. This feel, bolstered by a half-century's experience, makes a single Cornas against which all others are judged—and generally found wanting.

Densely planted on slope and terrace The Clape vineyards are very well sited, mostly on steep slopes and terraces above the village. At 7,500-10,000 plants per hectare they are planted extremely densely, obliging each vine to bury its roots deeply in the search for nutrients and water, and they contain many an old vine, which give far lower yields than when young. These two factors explain the quality of Clape's raw material. On this estate the owner and his son Pierre would never dream of harvesting at anything less than perfect ripeness, and once cut they give the fruit a rigorous quality control.

A champion of traditional methods The grapes are left on their stalks for vinification, and fermentation is conducted by the fruit's natural yeast. Fermentation and then maceration take place over some 12 days in concrete vats with two *pigeages* per day, and the wines are then transferred to *foudre* for their malolactic fermentation and subsequent ageing. New wood is definitely not part of the Clapes' way of doing things.

The wines of the different parcels are not blended until just before bottling, which enables a finer appreciation of their personality. After a light fining the bottling process is carried out without filtering the wines, in several sessions over several months.

Cornas Showing a typical, dense purple-black Cornas colour in its youth, and giving off (with some reticence) classy aromas of blackcurrant, pepper and violets, the Clape Cornas takes no prisoners: extremely rich, sweet and full-bodied, impressively structured and given edge by the right degree of acidity, it is a complete wine of great breed. It needs time to develop its bouquet and harmony: at 20 years of age the legendary 1978 was sumptuously soft, with a splendid, generous and complex bouquet of roasted meat, leather and herb aromas, with young blackcurrant essence still present in the background. A gloriously long finish underlined the sheer quality of the wine. The Clapes recommend serving young vintages with rib of beef, mature ones with hare *à la royale*.

- Other red wine: Côtes-du-Rhône
- White wine: Saint-Péray
- Owners: Auguste & Pierre Clape
- Wine-makers: Auguste & Pierre Clape
- Combined vineyards: 6.5 hectares
- Production: 26,000 bottles
- Exports: 70%
- Take-away sales: No
- Visits: By appointment

Wine selected:
Cornas

- Grape Variety: Syrah
- Average vine age: 15 and 60+ years
- Vineyard size: 4.5 hectares
- Soil type: Granite
- Average production: 15,000 bottles

DOMAINE CLAPE

1996

PRODUIT
DE FRANCE
VIN

PRODUCT
OF FRANCE
WINE

Cornas

APPELLATION CORNAS CONTROLÉE

A.C. 13% BY VOL.   750 ML

RHÔNE WINE

MIS EN BOUTEILLE A LA PROPRIÉTÉ

A. CLAPE, S.C.E.A Propriétaire-Viticulteur à CORNAS (Ardèche)

As the generation of Guy de Barjac, Noël Verset, Marcel Juge and others, having delighted and stunned the palates and senses of Rhône-lovers with many a fine bottle, takes well-earned retirement, it is reassuring to note the emergence of younger growers who are ready and willing to take over and defend Cornas's colours against other regions near and far. One young man doing just that, and showing a definite feel for his calling, is Jacques Leménicier.

From employee to proprietor The long-haired and bearded Leménicier started from scratch, and has built up his exploitation little by little. He started work in the employment of Alain Voge after leaving school at the age of 16. Nine years later, in 1989, he did a year's course at the Beaune *lycée viticole*, and rented his first vines that same year. Work on the Voge estate subsequently went hand in hand with work on his own, to which other rented parcels were little by little added. In 1994 Leménicier finally became a *propriétaire* when he bought a little over 2 hectares of the Domaine de Saint-Pierre, the rest of which was acquired by Paul Jaboulet Aîné. Since then he has been consolidating, gradually paying off his purchase and putting what he has got to the best use. At roughly 500,000 francs per hectare of Cornas vineyard, there are a good number of bottles to be sold!

Rich fleshiness and an imposing tannic structure The main priorities in the vineyard are keeping yields down and preserving the vines' health by respecting their soil's micro-organic life and fauna. By pruning properly while the vines are dormant and debudding in the spring, Leménicier keeps his yields to approximately 30 hectolitres per hectare, and has no need to green-harvest in July. Rarely does he manure the vines, on the principle that the poorer the topsoil the more deeply the vines will bury their roots, giving them greater protection against any climatic difficulties and making their eventual wine that much more complex—a choice of quality over quantity. He waits until the last possible moment before harvesting, in order to obtain a good, rich fleshiness to balance the imposing tannic structure that his wines will have.

Vinification lasts 15-18 days. The fruit of the younger vines is destemmed and fermented with *remontages* morning and evening, while that of the older plants is left on its stems and trodden by foot morning and evening. The two are then blended and matured for 14-18 months in old casks in a hangar down by the railway line, which serves as Leménicier's cellar. The wine is then bottled without filtration.

Cornas Dressed in the classic Cornas purple-black colour, indicative of youth, phenolic ripeness and proper extraction, this wine has a beautifully rich blackcurrant-and-spice flavour, and the supple quality which comes from properly ripe grapes. Its tannic structure is well and truly in place, yet it is ripe and has finesse—an essential difference between good, modern Cornas and the old-style, mouth-lacerating variety. Finally a long finish indicates the promising future with which Leménicier wines are born. Mutton ragout will make a suitable escort for this noble wine.

• White wine: Saint-Péray
• Owner:
Jacques Leménicier
• Wine-maker:
Jacques Leménicier
• Combined vineyards:
3.05 hectares
• Production:
14,000 bottles
• Exports: 50%
• Take-away sales:
By appointment
• Visits: By appointment

Wine selected:
Cornas

• Grape Variety: Syrah
• Average vine age:
90 and 16 years
• Vineyard size:
2.55 hectares
• Soil type: Granite
• Average production:
10,000 bottles

Cornas | Cornas

1996

PRODUIT DE FRANCE

Cornas

APPELLATION D'ORIGINE CONTRÔLÉE

12,5% vol.   *Mis en bouteille à la propriété*   75 cl

Sylviane et Jacques Lemenicier

Viticulteur - Eleveur à Cornas 07130 - France

Tél./ Fax 04.75.40.42.54

DOMAINE JEAN-LUC COLOMBO

O ne of the most influential figures in Rhône wine-making in the last 15 years has been the Bordeaux-trained *œnologue* Jean-Luc Colombo, who advises many a grower on his wine-making and has built up his own estate at Cornas. Colombo's wines demonstrate what he preaches; they are impeccably vinified, richly fruity and heavily oaked wines without rough edges.

An outsider with a message Having tasted widely in all the Rhône appellations and been convinced that many growers were in a wine-making rut Colombo set up his Centre Oenologique in the mid-1980s. The mission he gave himself was to tighten up viticultural practices and change sloppy wine-making habits, the frequent cause of premature oxidation, dried-out fruit, farmyard smells and so on, which often masqueraded as tradition. As an outsider with a relatively undeveloped sense of diplomacy his criticisms grated on many ears, particularly those of older growers whose ancestral methods found themselves in his sights, yet by dint of conviction and sincerity he has built up an impressive roster of clients, including some very prestigious names.

Steps towards purity and richness Good wine can only be made with perfectly ripe grapes from healthy vines, and Colombo therefore advises an organic regime in the vineyard wherever possible. Yield limitation is essential, as is quality control of the grapes at harvest time.

The cellar practices he advocates are hardly innovatory, they are to be observed in Bordeaux châteaux and the *cuveries* of the Burgundian clients of another controversial *œnologue*, Guy Accad. Cellar hygiene is all-important, for dirty conditions are a potential source of rusticity, and destemming is obligatory in order to avoid unripe, green flavours; tannin is extracted not from the stalks but by lengthy maceration, along with colour, aroma and acidity. Malolactic fermentation in barrel is advised for finer harmony between fruit and wood, and when the wine is made *élevage* takes place in new or nearly-new oak, followed by bottling in one single go with neither fining nor filtration.

Colombo's counsels have made for noticeable improvements on many estates, yet he has not let his involvement stop there. He has created Rhône Vignobles, a loose association of some of his clients, the aim of which is to pool their experiences, exchange ideas and generally work as a think-tank on ways of improving the fortunes of the Rhône Valley wines.

Cornas Les Ruchets Use of a Bordeaux bottle and modernist packaging has done nothing to endear Colombo to his fellow growers, yet this also is indicative of a desire to break out of tradition's mould. But appearances aside, it is what is in the bottle which counts: Les Ruchets, an ideally-sited parcel lying high above the village, gives a deeply coloured wine with a fabulous, intense black-fruit fragrance, lushness on the palate and a structure enveloped in ample flesh. A strong toasted flavour and hints of liquorice and spice add to the complexity of the whole, which has a fine long finish. Les Ruchets, paradoxically powerful and delicate, is a magnificently complete wine, which partners jugged hare very well.

- Other red wines:
Cornas La Louvée,
Cornas Terres Brulées,
Côtes-du-Rhône Les Forots
- Owner:
Jean-Luc Colombo
- Wine-maker:
Jean-Luc Colombo
- Oenologist:
Jean-Luc Colombo
- Combined vineyards:
8 hectares
- Production:
40,000 bottles
- Exports: 70%
- Take-away sales: Yes
- Visits: By appointment

Wine selected:
Cornas Les Ruchets

- Grape Variety: Syrah
- Average vine age:
70 years
- Vineyard size: 1 hectare
- Soil type: Granite
- Average production:
3,000 bottles

1996
LES RUCHE
CORNAS
APPELLATION CORNAS CONTRÔLÉE

RÉCOLTÉ ET MIS EN BOUTEILLE
JEAN-LUC COLOMBO
PROPRIÉTAIRE A CORNAS

12.5% VOL.   RHONE TABLE WINE · ALC.12.5% BY VOL · PRODUCT OF FRANCE 750ML

DOMAINE ROBERT MICHEL

The young generation of Cornas growers, inspired by Jean-Luc Colombo, may be modernizing the character of Cornas these days, but there is still the odd grower sticking faithfully to traditional ways and making very fine wine. Robert Michel is one such, a quietly dedicated *vigneron* who produces some excellent *cuvées* which need time to soften up and show their qualities.

Four centuries of wine-making tradition The Michel family are one of the oldest in the village, having lived and made wine there for a good 400 years now. Robert Michel, representing the ninth generation, started working alongside his father in 1965, and had full responsibilities thrust on him when the latter passed away in 1982. After having employed Thierry Allemand for a number of years, he has since been helped by his nephew Vincent Paris, yet the latter plans to start up on his own, as Allemand did. Will Michel's son Jimmy follow in his father's footsteps? Whether he has thought about it or not, he still has a good few years of school ahead of him first!

Five hectares and three wines The Michel estate, which has its cellars in the middle of the village and a warehouse nearby on the main road, covers 5 hectares, from which 3 wines are made. The simplest is the Pied de Coteaux, a wine from the rich, flat land at the foot of the hills, which is fruity and lightly-structured and comes round after several years. The Cuvée des Coteaux is altogether more consequent, made from vines which have had to exert themselves somewhat by burying their roots deep into the sandy clay soil to find the necessary nutrition, and requires proportionally more time to improve in bottle. Finally there is La Geynale, made from vines planted in granite soil on south-facing terraces by Michel's grandfather in 1910, a wine of the power and structure which typified Cornas in those days.

Vinified as in days gone by Fermentation and maceration of the grapes, which have been left on their stalks and lightly crushed beforehand, take place in closed concrete vats, and last some 3 weeks. Unlike some of the younger growers, there is no new wood in the Michel cellars; tradition is the house rule, and new wines are reared in vat and then old wood—one year in each in the case of La Geynale—before being bottled unfiltered.

Cornas La Geynale Fortunately its black colour prepares one for what is to come, for Robert Michel's La Geynale is a very broad-shouldered individual, powerful, structured, and expressing itself with a strong terroir accent... and fine manners are by no stretch of the imagination its strong point! Yet once surly youth has given way to tolerant adulthood, its warm heart and generosity come to the fore, and its pungent breath of leather, game, spice and sometimes undergrowth envelop he who dares approach. This is a great Cornas, the genuine article, and is definitely not for the faint-hearted. When adult it sits easily beside a savoury dish of jugged hare, or even that *dauphinois* speciality, thrush cooked with juniper berries.

- Other red wines: Cornas Pied de Coteaux, Cornas Cuvée des Coteaux
- Owner: Robert Michel
- Wine-maker: Robert Michel
- Combined vineyards: 5 hectares
- Production: 18,600 bottles
- Exports: 30%
- Take-away sales: 8-12 a.m., 2-6 p.m.
- Visits: By appointment

Wine selected:
Cornas La Geynale

- Grape Variety: Syrah
- Average vine age: 88 years
- Vineyard size: 1.5 hectares
- Soil type: Granite
- Average production: 5,000 bottles

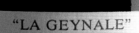

"LA GEYNALE"

Product *of France*

MARQUE DÉPOSÉE

Cornas

APPELLATION CORNAS CONTRÔLÉE

RED RHÔNE WINE

1996

Mis en bouteille à la Propriété

ROBERT MICHEL

VIGNERON A CORNAS (ARDÈCHE) FRANCE

DOMAINE THIERRY ALLEMAND

I n an age when so many school-leavers, lured by the apparently limitless earning possibilities of high-technology businesses such as computing, Internet services, mobile telephones and so on, do not even want to consider a life on the land, it is heartening to see the odd one enthusiastically embracing the noble and traditional *métier* of *vigneron*, and working hard to earn himself a reputation. Thierry Allemand is one such, a young man who appears to have chosen a career for which he has exceptional talents.

Enamoured with the grower's life It is not as if Allemand has wine-making in his blood, for his parents lived and worked in Valence. As a teenager he helped out on Robert Michel's estate, and after leaving school worked there full time, and gradually became thoroughly enamoured with the life.

Naturally enough, before long he was thinking of making his own wine, and started keeping his ears open for any land that might come up for sale. In 1981 he acquired his first plot, which he then spent his weekends planting. Since then he has gradually acquired other land, notably a fine parcel of old vines in the Reynard climat which belonged to Noël Verset, bringing his holding today to 3.4 hectares. However that does not keep him fully occupied, and to supplement his income he still works part-time for the Michels.

A young traditionalist Allemand may be part of the young generation at Cornas, but he holds perfectly traditional views as to how the wine should be made. Low yields are essential for quality, and to ensure this he carries out a crop-thinning *vendange verte* at the moment the fruit turns colour. Then vinifications are carried out in such a manner as to produce wines of structure, density and power... but with perhaps a greater degree of flesh, ripeness and charm than was usual in bygone days. Allemand leaves the fruit on its stalks and treads a small amount to get the fermentation going. The liquid is then allowed to rise gradually to a high 35°C, and is all the time enriched by regular foot treading for maximum extraction of tannin, colour and aroma.

Once the *cuvaison* is over the wines are transferred partly to barrel, partly to stainless steel for ageing, which lasts for 12-18 months. The barrels will already have held wine, for Allemand is not a believer in new oak for ageing Cornas. Finally the wines are racked by gravity, if necessary fined, and bottled without being filtered.

Cornas Reynard Of his two wines, the Reynard is the more profound and complex—it is a simple question of a better site and older vines. The wine has a true young Cornas colour of very dark purple, and a sumptuous Syrah nose of blackcurrant with a touch of tar and cinnamon. Chewy and concentrated on the palate, with mouth-coating tannin and high acidity, it finishes with great length. A good vintage such as 1995 will keep for two decades without any problem. Anyone foolhardy enough to drink this in its youth should prepare a grilled rib of beef, while those who wait will find a stew of wild boar very suitable.

- Other red wine: .
Cornas Chaillot
- Owner:
Thierry Allemand
- Wine-maker:
Thierry Allemand
- Combined vineyards:
3.4 hectares
- Production:
12,500 bottles
- Exports: 45%
- Take-away sales: Yes
- Visits: By appointment

Wine selected:
Cornas Reynard

- Grape Variety: Syrah
- Average vine age:
40 years
- Vineyard size:
1.7 hectares
- Soil type: Granite
- Average production:
6,100 bottles

Cornas | Cornas

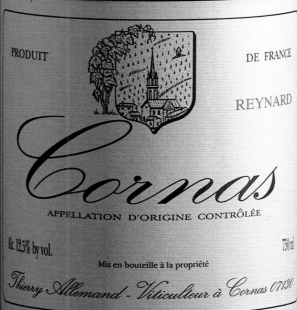

DOMAINE CHABOUD

The sparkling and still white wines of Saint-Péray, the most southerly appellation of the northern Rhône vineyard, are little seen, for this is a wine region which has been inexorably shrinking since its heyday in the late 19th century, and which now covers a mere 58 hectares. Yet there are a handful of growers valiantly fighting on, perpetuating their traditions and their uniqueness, whose produce is well worth discovering. Domaine Chaboud is one.

Ardent defenders of the cause The Chabouds have been in Saint-Péray since before the Revolution, and harvested their first crop of grapes in 1778... and promptly sold it to Champagne producers, a practice apparently common at the time, Remington Norman tells us in *Rhône Renaissance*. Not until around 1830 did growers actually make sparkling wine in Saint-Péray, which initially went by the name "Champagne-Saint-Péray".

In more recent times Jean-François Chaboud, having inherited the estate from his father in 1957, has been one of the most stalwart defenders of Saint-Péray's cause, producing sparkling and still wines of great personality. In 1993 he was joined by his son Stéphan, who had studied in Champagne and is now responsible for the active running and winemaking of this estate, which at 10 hectares is one of the village's largest.

Two idiosyncratic grape varieties Besides their sparkling wine the Chabouds make two still Saint-Pérays, which could be said to be varietals, one being made entirely of Roussanne, the other of Marsanne. This is unusual if not singular, for these two varieties need each other in Saint-Péray's microclimate and are invariably blended, each having its qualities and deficiencies.

Roussanne is a tricky variety to grow and vinify successfully. Indeed there are but a very limited number of 100% Roussanne wines produced up and down the Rhône Valley, for it gives of its best in relatively cool climates, and ripens slowly. It is highly susceptible to oidium and it oxidizes very quickly, both as unfermented juice or during *élevage*, and therefore demands careful inspection and selection before vatting.

On the other hand there are many Marsanne wines, starting with a good number of white Hermitages. Marsanne ripens earlier and can be picked early, for fruitiness, or later, when its richer, sweeter juice gives longer-lasting wines. However its relatively neutral character can easily be lost during vinification, particularly if yields are a little too high, giving boring, characterless wines; a *vigneron* therefore must know exactly what he wants to do with it from the outset.

Saint-Péray The Chabouds' Roussanne wine has a green-tinted light gold colour and an original aromatic personality combining the fruity, the vegetal and the floral: quince, gooseberries, ferns, moss and violets. It is harmoniously constituted with good weight on the palate, richness and just the right level of acidity. What an intriguing wine! This is not the wine which will wean the masses off oak-aged Chardonnay, yet it is definitely a wine to stimulate the oenophile's grey matter. The Chabouds suggest drinking it with a raclette or a fondu, but trout meunière is also perfect.

- Other white wines: Saint-Péray Cépage Marsanne, sparkling Saint-Péray
- Red wines: Cornas, Côtes-du-Rhône
- Owner: Chaboud family
- Wine-maker: Stéphan Chaboud
- Oenologist: Michel Laurent
- Combined vineyards: 10 hectares
- Production: 46,000 bottles
- Exports: 5%
- Take-away sales: 9-12 a.m., 2-6 p.m. (exc. Sunday)
- Visits: Yes

Wine selected:
Saint-Péray

- Grape Variety: Roussanne
- Average vine age: 40 years
- Vineyard size: 2.5 hectares
- Soil type: Clay and limestone
- Average production: 7,000 bottles

CÉPAGE ROUSSANNE
PRODUIT DE FRANCE

SAINT - PÉRAY

APPELLATION SAINT-PÉRAY CONTRÔLÉE

MIS EN BOUTEILLE AU

Domaine CHABOUD

Propriétaire-Récoltant - 07130 SAINT-PÉRAY
France

DOMAINE JEAN LIONNET

A fair proportion of Saint-Péray is made by Cornas growers, which is hardly surprising given the geographical proximity of the two villages, and one can well understand that they should want to produce a little white wine for quenching their thirsts after the gruelling task of blending the latest vintage of immature, tannic Syrah! Jean Lionnet, owner of one of the largest Cornas estates, has 2 hectares in this white-wine village, with which he produces a very fine Saint-Péray *tranquille*.

A look to the future Lionnet has heartily embraced modernism in his Saint-Péray wine-making, which must be the route to take if the growers are to stop the decline of the appellation, which the famous American critic Robert Parker has described as the 'dinosaur of the Rhône Valley'. Having taken over from his father in 1978 and progressively switched to bottling on site instead of selling in bulk, since 1986 Lionnet has been taking the advice of his neighbour, the consultant oenologist Jean-Luc Colombo, who convinced him to forget tradition and adopt thoroughly up-to-date white-wine vinification practices.

Long, slow, cool fermentation Lionnet's 2 hectares are planted with Marsanne and Roussanne in essentially clay and limestone soil. He picks his grapes as late as possible for maximum ripeness and aromatic development, unlike those who produce sparkling wine, for which a slight tartness is desirable. Once the crop has arrived at the modern, well-equipped *cuverie* it is destemmed and then given a 24-hour cold skin maceration in stainless steel, with a light sulphuring to prevent the onset of fermentation. Then the fruit is pressed and the free-run juice, which constitutes some 90% of the total, is run into both stainless steel vats and new oak casks. A little yeast is added and the alcoholic fermentation starts. It is maintained at a very low 14°C, which enables it to be stretched over a month, for long, slow fermentations are the best way of giving a wine flavour complexity. The malolactic fermentation (during which harsh malic acidity is transformed into the softer lactic variety) is blocked in order to retain maximum freshness, and the wine then spends the best part of a year maturing, again in stainless steel and cask, before bottling.

Saint-Péray Straw-gold in colour with green flashes when young, Jean Lionnet's Saint-Péray emerges from the bottle with a very ripe, fresh nose reminiscent of peaches, pears and vanilla. On the palate it is fleshy and succulent, with great purity and elegance. Its oakiness is discernible yet not obtrusive, and the whole is well-balanced, with a long finish. It is light years away from 'traditional' Saint-Péray, just as its maker wished, indeed the authorities have refused him the use of the appellation in the past, not because his wine was faulty but for lack of Saint-Péray *typicité*... Not that that worried him, for this wine sells out rapidly! It is delicious on its own, yet marries very well with a *chaud-froid* of chicken with tarragon, or endives *au jambon*—chicory rolled in ham and baked with béchamel sauce.

- Red wines:
Cornas Domaine
de Rochepertuis, Cornas,
Côtes-du-Rhône
- Owner: Jean Lionnet
- Combined vineyards:
15 hectares
- Production:
53,000 bottles
- Exports: 40%
- Take-away sales:
8-12 a.m., 2-6 p.m.
- Visits: By appointment

Wine selected:
Saint-Péray

- Grape Varieties:
Marsanne 80%,
Roussanne 20%
- Average vine age:
50 years
- Vineyard size:
2 hectares
- Soil type:
Clay and limestone
- Average production:
7,000 bottles

Grand Vin des Côtes du Rhône

— SAINT-PÉRAY —

APPELLATION SAINT-PÉRAY CONTRÔLÉE

1997

MIS EN BOUTEILLE À LA PROPRIÉTÉ

750m

12,5 % vol.

JEAN LIONNET
Propriétaire Viticulteur

Pied La Vigne
à CORNAS
Ardèche - France

There is one Rhône valley estate which is perceived around the world as epitomizing the best that France has to offer. Thanks to the sheer perfection and individuality of its wines, Château de Beaucastel has steadily forged a reputation second to none over the 20th century, and large though it is, its production is nowadays rapidly snapped up by wine-lovers who know what is what.

The Perrins forge Beaucastel's reputation The estate's history starts in 1549, when 'Noble Pierre de Beaucastel' bought a property at Coudoulet. Soon his descendants had built a fine house there, where they were to live for some two centuries. Towards the end of the 19th century Elie Dussaud was master of Beaucastel, and it was he who witnessed the devastation of the vineyard by Phylloxera. He did not replant, and in 1909 sold the estate to Pierre Tramier, who gradually did, before leaving the estate to his son-in-law Pierre Perrin. Pierre, his son Jacques, and since 1978 Jacques's sons François and Jean-Pierre Perrin… each generation of this family has contributed to the construction of Beaucastel's current pre-eminence.

A highly individual estate The wine is individual on two counts: grape mix and vinification method. The vineyard contains all 13 permitted varieties, yet in proportions seen nowhere else. Jacques Perrin was convinced that Mourvèdre should be the dominant grape and built his blends around it, at a time when it was distinctly unfashionable. Beaucastel is today the only red Châteauneuf-du-Pape in which the Grenache is not dominant. The top white wine, made exclusively with Roussanne, equally illustrates this independence of thought. Since Jacques Perrin's time the vines have been cultivated with utmost respect for the soil and the environment, in order to stimulate robust health and thus better-quality fruit, and today the Perrins are proud that bees, birds, cicadas and ladybirds inhabit their vineyards.

Once the black grapes have been checked on arrival at base and then destemmed, they are subjected to a procedure conceived by Pierre Perrin and perfected by his son whereby their skins are steam-heated to 80°C and then cooled to 20°C. This enables the extraction of aroma and colour from inside the skin, and also destroys certain bacteria and enzymes which cause early oxidation—and thus largely renders the use of any SO2 unnecessary during fermentation. The net result is that fermentations are slower and longer, and the resulting wines richer and longer-living. The rest of the wine-making process is traditional, and driven by the Perrin's great perfectionism.

Châteauneuf-du-Pape Hommage à Jacques Perrin To pay homage to the farsightedness and conviction of their father, in the very finest years the Perrin brothers make a largely Mourvèdre-based special *cuvée* which is without doubt one of France's greatest red wines. Despite its thick texture, extraordinary aromatic depth and intensity and its great structure, as with all Perrin wines the accent is on harmony and elegance… which, all elements combined, makes for a very great wine. Lucky owners of this rarity could do worse than choose hare *à la royale* as supporting cast, when the great day eventually comes along!

Châteauneuf-du-Pape | Courthézon

- Other red wines: Châteauneuf-du-Pape, Côtes-du-Rhône Coudoulet de Beaucastel
- White wines: Châteauneuf-du-Pape Roussanne Vieilles Vignes, Châteauneuf-du-Pape, Côtes-du-Rhône Coudoulet de Beaucastel
- Rosé wine: Côtes-du-Rhône Coudoulet de Beaucastel
- Owners: Perrin family
- Combined vineyards: 100 hectares
- Production: 420,000 bottles
- Exports: 80%
- Take-away sales: Subject to availability
- Visits: By appointment

Wine selected:
Châteauneuf-du-Pape Hommage à Jacques Perrin

- Grape Varieties: Mourvèdre 60%, Grenache 20%, Syrah 10%, Counoise 10%
- Average vine age: 55 years
- Vineyard size: 70 hectares
- Soil type: Clay and limestone, quartzite boulders
- Average production: 5,000 bottles

MIS EN BOUTEILLE
DU CHATEAU

1995

GRANDE CUVÉE

Château de Beaucastel

HOMMAGE A JACQUES PERRIN

CHATEAUNEUF-DU-PAPE
APPELLATION CHATEAUNEUF-DU-PAPE CONTROLÉE

Sté FERMIÈRE DES VIGNOBLES PIERRE PERRIN
AU CHATEAU DE BEAUCASTEL COURTHEZON (Vse) FRANCE

PRODUCE OF FRANCE

750 ml
ALC. 13.5% BY VOL

MIS EN BOUTEILLE DU CHATEAU

Seven generations of Coulons have dedicated their lives to wine on the Beaurenard estate, on the south-eastern side of Châteauneuf-du-Pape. "Faites confiance à la tradition" (Place your faith in tradition) is a motto much used at the domaine, yet while the Coulons plainly do this, they also keep abreast of technical advances.

Consistent quality wins an international clientele Domaine de Beaurenard is run by Paul Coulon, his wife Régine and two sons Daniel and Frédéric. In addition to their 30 hectares of Châteauneuf-du-Pape they also have 25 hectares at Rasteau which provide the fruit for a Côtes-du-Rhône and a Côtes-du-Rhône Villages Rasteau. Bottles of the various appellations are despatched as far afield as Japan, Canada and America, as well as the Scandinavian countries and a good many European ones, and the consistency of quality over the years has been born out by regular medals—no less than 225 between 1927 and 1998!

Vineyard and vatroom cares The Coulons are well aware of the importance of the quality of the raw material in wine-making, and their efforts to produce the finest fruit possible are unceasing. They regularly have their soils analysed in order to feed vines with just the right amount of whatever may be lacking, the nutrients being of course organic. In order to keep yields down to a level conducive with quality, debudding is carried out in the Spring and a green harvest takes place as the fruit turns colour if the vines are still producing too much. Parts of the vineyard are kept grassed, as another way of limiting the vines' vigour. Quality control at harvest-time is carried out in the field by the pickers: they each carry two baskets, into one of which goes all the best fruit, into the other anything less good but usable.

In 1988 Paul Coulon took the significant step of investing in a batch of stainless steel temperature-controlled vats, which surely have something to do with the suave, succulent elegance of contemporary vintages. The entire crop is destemmed on arrival at the cellars and then crushed before finding its way into the vats, where it is fermented by its indigenous yeast for greater authenticity. Temperatures in the vats are restrained to 32°C, and the maceration and fermentation period lasts 15-18 days, ensuring that sufficient fruit, colour and fine tannin is extracted for the style of wine required. Wines are then transferred to cask and *foudre* for ageing for 12-18 months, and are finally bottled unfiltered after a fining with fresh egg-whites.

Châteauneuf-du-Pape Two wines, a red and a white, are made at Beaurenard every year, and in the best years an old-vine *cuvée* named Boisrenard is also produced in both colours; the red is rich, fleshy, tannic and Grenache-based, while the white, two thirds Clairette, is a sublime barrel-fermented offering. Exceptional though they are, one should not overlook the domaine's regular red, a masterpiece of elegance, balance, succulent fruit and intense aroma. This is a wine of very good value for money, and a very fine and adaptable table companion, which particularly appreciates red meats and guinea fowl.

- Other red wines: Châteauneuf-du-Pape Boisrenard, Côtes-du-Rhône-Villages Rasteau, Côtes-du-Rhône
- White wines: Châteauneuf-du-Pape Boisrenard, Châteauneuf-du-Pape
- Owner: Paul Coulon & Sons
- Wine-maker: Daniel Coulon
- Oenologist: Noël Rabot
- Combined vineyards: 55 hectares
- Production: 300,000 bottles
- Exports: 50%
- Take-away sales: Yes
- Visits: 8-12 a.m., 1.30-5.30 p.m.

Wine selected:
Châteauneuf-du-Pape

- Grape Varieties: Grenache 68%, Syrah 10%, Mourvèdre 10%, Cinsault and others 12%
- Average vine age: 40 years
- Vineyard size: 23 hectares
- Soil type: Clay and limestone
- Average production: 100,000 bottles

1997   1997

DOMAINE DE BEAURENARD
Châteauneuf-du-Pape
APPELLATION CHATEAUNEUF-DU-PAPE CONTROLEE

14% vol.   MIS EN BOUTEILLE AU DOMAINE   75cl.
S.C.E.A Paul COULON et Fils
PROPRIÉTAIRES-RÉCOLTANTS A 84230 CHATEAUNEUF-DU-PAPE (FRANCE)
PRODUCE OF FRANCE

Bosquet des Papes

Continuing the family tradition of making good, hearty, no-nonsense Châteauneuf-du-Pape, Maurice Boiron is nothing if not consistent in providing very good bottles at a reasonable price. Bosquet des Papes is built for a fairly long life, but by 6-8 years of age it is already well developed, the tannin and rigidity of youth having given way to an assertive, complex bouquet of typical flavours of this region.

An estate of 40 vineyard parcels Five generations of Boirons have now made wine on the Bosquet des Papes estate. Maurice Boiron took over from his father Joseph in 1976, and is today training his own son Nicolas, who will eventually take over when retirement beckons. He inherited 3 hectares from Joseph, and has since bought 6 more, yet the bulk of the estate—some 20-odd hectares—is rented or operated on a crop-sharing basis. Although much of the land is around the village of Châteauneuf-du-Pape, a lot of it is further away, indeed the 27 hectares planted today are composed of no less than 40 parcels, lying principally in the north and the east of the appellation.

Double-checked for quality The harvest generally starts around the 15th September. When the pickers get down to work among the vines, secateurs in hand, they check the fruit quality as they go along and grade it by the traditional two-basket system, whereby the best fruit is kept separate from the unripe, split, rotten or otherwise unusable, which will go to make *rapé*, ordinary table wine. A second examination is carried out by two people on the trailer, following which the fruit is transported to the domaine for vinification.

Effective extraction of tannin, colour and aroma Some 70% of the red-wine grapes are crushed, then the bunches, stalks included, are tipped into the fermentation vats and left to ferment and macerate for 2-3 weeks. The temperature of the liquid in the vats gradually rises, and at the end of the cycle has generally reached 32-34°C, which makes for a very effective extraction of tannin, colour and aroma. Extraction is also maximized by regular *remontages*. Once the alcoholic fermentation is complete, the wine is run out of the vats and the pulp pressed, and this *vin de presse* is then incorporated into the free-run juice, contributing yet more tannin. The malolactic fermentation eventually takes place, after which the wines are blended and run into cask for ageing. They spend 12-24 months in the wood, depending on the quality of the year and in which of the several sessions during the second year they are bottled.

Châteauneuf-du-Pape Cuvée Traditionnelle A young Bosquet des Papes is a fine, intense violet-tinged garnet to look at. The palate is chewy, rich and full of character, very much a traditional, earthy *vin de terroir*, with a flavour of black cherry and *garrigue*. As it matures it becomes even more interesting: at 9 years of age the 1989 vintage was a powerful and beguiling mixture of Port, leather and spice flavours. This wine, not for the faint-hearted, will happily embrace a savoury game pie, for they speak the same dialect.

- Other red wines: Châteauneuf-du-Pape Cuvée Chantemerle, Côtes-du-Rhône
- White wine: Châteauneuf-du-Pape
- Owner: Maurice Boiron
- Wine-makers: Maurice & Nicolas Boiron
- Oenologist: Rock Lauriol
- Combined vineyards: 27 hectares
- Exports: 53%
- Take-away sales: 9.00-12.00 a.m., 1.30-6.30 p.m.
- Visits: Yes. Closed on Sundays and bank holidays

Wine selected:
Châteauneuf-du-Pape Cuvée Traditionnelle

- Grape Varieties: Grenache 75%, Syrah 10%, Mourvèdre 8%, Cinsault, Vaccarèse and Counoise 7%
- Average vine age: 50 years
- Vineyard size: 25 hectares
- Soil type: Clay and limestone, quartzite stones
- Average production: 50,000 bottles

Châteauneuf-du-Pape

Châteauneuf-du-Pape

As its label and name suggest, the excellent Les Cailloux is made from vines growing principally in terrain covered with the much-photographed smooth quartzite stones of Alpine origin. These, as all the growers only too readily insist, have a radiator effect, capturing the intense heat of the day and giving it off at night-time. The grapes therefore have no excuse for not ripening, and the *vignerons* have no excuse for chaptalizing (which in any case is forbidden!)

Two estates are merged Les Cailloux is run by André Brunel. His forbear André, son of Joseph, bought land in what was then known as Châteauneuf-Calcernier as early as the 18th century. Over time other plots of land were added, and finally after the Second World War the Bouachon and Brunel families were united by the marriage of Lucien and Denise, and their two estates became one, making an entity covering 12 hectares.

Since then the estate has expanded even further to 21 hectares, the total surface area being made up of 12 different parcels in all the Châteauneuf *quartiers*. The vast majority of the parcels are oriented southwards, and besides the stones many soil types are represented, including white clay, sand, gravel and red earth.

The emergence of a different style In 1971 André started working alongside his father Lucien, and it was there that his wine-making education was gained, in the vineyard and the vatroom. The wine at that time was very dense and tannic, for Lucien did not destem his fruit and vinified in a thoroughly traditional manner. The 1980s saw some experimentation and the emergence of a different, more modern, style as André, encouraged by the oenological consultant Jean-Luc Colombo, tried destemming, longer vatting and many other refinements, and introduced a little new wood into the cellars for ageing the wines.

Now, drawing on the experience gained from his testing, he evaluates his raw material each year before deciding which path to follow: usually only the Mourvèdre and Syrah are totally destemmed, while the Grenache may be partially destemmed. The Syrah is fermented on its own, then the different components are aged unblended, Grenache in *foudre*, Syrah and the rest in new and used casks. After the wines have been blended, bottling and subsequently sales take place in the Cave Reflets, an association grouping some half-dozen growers founded by the Baron Le Roy de Boiseaumarié.

Châteauneuf-du-Pape Les Cailloux is generally a very deep garnet colour, and offers up a splendidly full, warm bouquet of morello cherry and blackcurrants, gaining liquorice, leather, spice and gamey aspects as it acquires age. It is rich, fleshy and suave on the palate, and its quality is underlined by a long and satisfying finish. It is structured for medium-term development. Duck breast cooked with prunes provides an interesting accompaniment to this very fine Châteauneuf-du-Pape.

- Other red wines: Châteauneuf-du-Pape Cuvée Centenaire
- White wine: Châteauneuf-du-Pape
- Wine-maker: André Brunel
- Combined vineyards: 21 hectares
- Production: 98,000 bottles
- Take-away sales: Cave Reflets
- Visits: No

Wine selected: **Châteauneuf-du-Pape**

- Grape Varieties: Grenache 65%, Mourvèdre 20%, Syrah 10%, Others 5%
- Average vine age: 60 years
- Vineyard size: 17 hectares
- Soil type: Clay, sand, gravel, quartzite stones
- Average production: 75,000 bottles

1996

Châteauneuf-du-Pape

APPELLATION CHÂTEAUNEUF-DU-PAPE CONTROLÉE

Les Cailloux

G.A.E.C. des Vignobles Lucien et André Brunel

Propriétaires à Châteauneuf-du-Pape - 84230 - (Vaucluse) - France

% ALC. BY VOL.   PRODUCT OF FRANCE   750 ML

F ont de Michelle, a Bédarrides estate whose intriguing name—Michelle's fountain—is an allusion to an underground spring in the vineyard (though no one has explained who Michelle was), has made remarkable progress these last years under the impulsion of the two brothers, Jean and Michel Gonnet, who now own and run it. These are very carefully made Châteauneufs, modern in style by their elegance yet wines with all the stuffing one could wish for.

A fine estate is pieced together The estate lies on a site occupied by the Romans. Etienne Gonnet acquired the land at the end of the 19th century, by which time the ravages of the Phylloxera had had their devastating effect, obliging him to grow other crops such as olives and barley as well as the vine.

This polyculture continued until the interwar years, when Jean and Michel Gonnet's grandfather replanted a number of parcels with vines. By 1950 their father Etienne Gonnet, having methodically acquired other plots, could boast one of the rare, large single-block estates in Châteauneuf-du-Pape. In 1970 he had cellars built, which have since been modernized by his sons.

Clay, limestone and quartzite stones This 30-hectare vineyard lies principally on the appellation's south-eastern slope, which has clay and limestone soil covered with the famous *galets roulés*, or Alpine quartzite stones or boulders, and is considered among the area's finest vineyard land. Here the Gonnets cultivate all 13 of Châteauneuf-du-Pape's varieties, to make a red and a white Cuvée Traditionnelle and, if the wines are up to it, a red and a white Cuvée Etienne Gonnet, as well as the standard Côtes-du-Rhônes.

The white Traditionnelle, 50% Grenache blanc, 25% Clairette, 20% Bourboulenc and 5% Roussanne, is vinified in stainless steel after a direct, pneumatic pressing, and is bottled early, 5-6 months after the harvest, having not undergone its malolactic fermentation. It is a delicious example, fragrant and light in style, and superb with a seafood gratin. It is capable of improving over 8-10 years, which give it far greater complexity. The white Cuvée Etienne Gonnet, introduced in 1995, is made of equal proportions of Cuvée Traditionnelle and Roussanne, the latter fermented in barrel, and is naturally weightier and rounder on the palate. As for the red Cuvée Traditionnelle, 70% Grenache and 10% each of Syrah, Mourvèdre and Cinsault, it is 40% destalked and then made classically with 20 days' maceration, with daily *remontages* and *pigeage*. Ageing then takes place in *foudre*.

Châteauneuf-du-Pape Cuvée Etienne Gonnet Inaugurated in 1988 and made only in the better years, the Cuvée Etienne Gonnet is a selection of the best wines rather than the production of a specific part of the vineyard. It is a sumptuously rich and smooth wine made with low yields from very old vines, aged for one year in new and used oak and bottled unfiltered. Confirming its current quality the great 1995 vintage came first in a blind tasting of 40 wines organized by *Vins et Gastronomie* magazine. It will need 12-15 years in the cellar and will be exceptional when mature, and a perfect partner for jugged hare.

Châteauneuf-du-Pape | Bédarrides

• Other red wines:
Châteauneuf-du-Pape
Cuvée Traditionnelle,
Côtes-du-Rhône,
Vin de Table
• White wines:
Châteauneuf-du-Pape
Cuvée Etienne Gonnet,
Châteauneuf-du-Pape
Cuvée Traditionnelle,
Côtes-du-Rhône Cépage
Viognier
• Owners:
Jean & Michel Gonnet
• Wine-makers:
Jean & Michel Gonnet
• Combined vineyards:
30 hectares
• Production:
135,000 bottles
• Exports: 75%
• Take-away sales: Yes
• Visits:
9-12 a.m., 2-6 p.m., by
appointment on Saturdays

Wine selected:
**Châteauneuf-du-Pape
Cuvée Étienne Gonnet**

• Grape Varieties:
Grenache 70%,
Syrah 15%,
Mourvèdre 15%
• Average vine age:
80 and 100 years
(Grenache),
45 years (Mourvèdre),
25 years (Syrah)
• Soil type:
Clay and limestone,
quartzite stones
• Average production:
3,000-15,000 bottles

Château Fortia is well known to those with more than a passing interest in wine as the home of Baron Pierre Le Roy de Boiseaumarié, the prime mover behind the creation of France's *appellation contrôlée* laws. Its vineyard has the potential to make one of the finest Châteauneuf-du-Papes, but sadly in view of the château's important place in the village's history, in recent years the wine has rarely realized this potential. However the corner seems definitely to have been turned since the arrival of the Baron's grandson Bruno Le Roy in 1994. Recent vintages are superb.

A young war hero marries an heiress The estate's history in fact started long before the Baron's arrival. In *Châteauneuf-du-Pape* Michel Dovaz tells us that the *quartier* known as La Grenade in which Fortia lies was under vine at the beginning of the 17th century, and the Fortia vineyard itself might therefore have been planted well before 1763, the date when a small farm surrounded by vines is recorded in the cadastral survey as belonging to the Marquis of Fortia. In 1890 La Fortiasse, as it was known, was acquired by Bernard Le Saint, who restored and enlarged the château built by Paul-Antoine de Fortia. Then in 1919 a young jurist, pilot and war hero named Pierre Le Roy married Le Saint's daughter, heiress to the magnificent estate. Le Roy decided to give up law and devote his life to wine.

A guarantee of authenticity and typicity At the time growers were going through a terrible period: sales were rock bottom, fraudulent passing-off of inferior wine as Châteauneuf-du-Pape was rife, and the after-effects of Phylloxera compounded the growers' problems terribly. Pierre Le Roy devised a revolutionary system which would safeguard authenticity and typicity by means of a series of growing and wine-making restrictions, to which any grower had to comply in order to be able to use his village's name on the label. Le Roy's propositions were adopted by the local growers' syndicate in 1924, and formed the basis of the *appellation contrôlée* system, made law in 1937.

Back on course to former greatness Pierre Le Roy's son Henri succeeded him in 1967, and from the end of the 1970s the wines became thoroughly lightweight and frequently lacking in balance. Then in 1994 Henri's younger son Bruno, qualified in oenology at Montpellier University, took over. With the advice of consulting oenologist Jean-Luc Colombo he has rapidly made great strides, mastering yields through severe pruning and a 'green harvest' if necessary, aiming for a greater degree of ripeness, and by a severe selection of the raw material.

Châteauneuf-du-Pape The 1995 vintage admirably demonstrates the revamped Château Fortia. Dark purple to the eye, this vintage has a rich, pure blackcurrant aroma with a refined spiciness. Its velvet texture and fleshy, ample body point to the care and thought given to its elaboration, and to the ripe, healthy quality of the raw material. All is in balance, and the rich fruit and fine tannic structure seem set to cohabit in harmony over a long period. Fillet of pigeon *au jus de foie gras* matches Fortia 1995 for savour and breed... What class!

- White wine: Châteauneuf-du-Pape
- Owner: Baron Le Roy de Boiseaumarié
- Wine-maker: Bruno Le Roy
- Oenologist: Jean-Luc Colombo
- Combined vineyards: 30 hectares
- Production: 110,000 bottles
- Exports: 70%
- Take-away sales: Yes
- Visits: Yes

Wine selected:
Châteauneuf-du-Pape

- Grape Varieties: Grenache 75%, Syrah 20%, Mourvèdre 5%
- Average vine age: 40 years
- Vineyard size: 25 hectares
- Soil type: Clay and limestone, quartzite stones
- Average production: 70,000 bottles

ESTATE BOTTLED   MISE AU CHATEAU

CHATEAUNEUF-DU-PAPE

1995

PRODUCE OF FRANCE

CHATEAU-FORTIA

PROPRIÉTÉ DU BARON LE ROY DE BOISEAUMARIÉ

S.A.R.L.

CHATEAU FORTIA - 84 CHATEAUNEUF-DU-PAPE

A healthy respect for tradition and a willingness to experiment go arm in arm at Château de la Gardine, where the sons of Gaston Brunel, one of Châteauneuf-du-Pape's most revered figures, craft a range of fine, flavoursome wines. The estate has always been reliable, but since the 1980s the Brunels' ambition and perfectionism have propelled it near the top of the Châteauneuf quality table.

The legacy of Gaston Brunel La Gardine was a small 8-hectare estate when Brunel acquired it in 1943. Fiercely proud of the region and its wines, he set about enlarging it through a large planting programme, giving the estate the form it has today. New wine-making facilities and underground cellars followed, enabling the vinification of the vastly-increased quantities of fruit.

More importantly, he instilled in his sons Patrick and Maxime a love of their inheritance and its traditions, and ambitions for its wine. By 1965 they were seeking the advice of their fellow wine-maker and friend Docteur Dufays, owner of Château Nalys and a renowned geological expert, to advise them on replanting, in order to attain the ideal correlation between the numerous permitted varieties they use and their land, which itself enjoys great geological diversity. That thoroughness is today paying off with great complexity in the wines.

Tradition and a willingness to experiment The quality of their raw material has without doubt played a significant part in the great quality of recent vintages. Lower yields, increasingly organic cultivation and the maintenance of a high average plant age all help to produce excellent grapes on which the Brunels can focus their painstaking attention.

In the vatroom there are no rules, for each vintage's fruit is assessed and vinified as befits it best: most of the fruit is usually destalked, and the various varieties are vatted together, a local tradition dating from bygone days when they grew in intermingled abandon in the vineyards. The stainless steel vats have temperature-control devices and some contain hydraulic *pigeage* equipment, enabling extraction in a shorter time and thereby avoiding excessive dryness and astringency. The Brunels have resurrected the old Châteauneuf tradition of using casks for *élevage*—a century ago the village had 6 cooperages—and sensible use of oak has undeniably given their wine greater refinement than it had in the past.

Châteauneuf-du-Pape Cuvée des Générations Gaston Philippe In years when Nature really rewards them with outstanding fruit, the Brunels release a special *cuvée* in commemoration of their father. Produced from the niggardly yields of their oldest vines, from fruit cosseted and minutely checked for quality, this massive wine is aged entirely in new oak barrels. Violet-black in colour, with a heady perfume of rich black fruit, spice and vanilla, it is so rich and well-balanced that the wood influence is barely detectable after several years in bottle. Ample and smooth, it finishes with great length, a sure sign of its quality and future potential. This magnificent wine, which amply repays long keeping, has the necessary complexity to stand up to a haunch of wild boar, or jugged hare.

Châteauneuf-du-Pape (left margin)

- Other red wines: Châteauneuf-du-Pape Cuvée Tradition, Côtes-du-Rhône
- White wines: Châteauneuf-du-Pape Cuvée Tradition, Châteauneuf-du-Pape Cuvée des Générations Marie Léoncie
- Owner: Gaston Brunel family
- Vineyard Manager: Maxime Brunel
- Wine-makers: Patrick & Philippe Brunel
- Oenologist: Noël Rabot
- Combined vineyards: 106 hectares
- Production: 540,000 bottles
- Exports: 75%
- Take-away sales: 8.30-12.00 a.m., 1-6 p.m.
- Visits: By appointment

Wine selected:
Châteauneuf-du-Pape Cuvée des Générations Gaston-Philippe

- Grape Varieties: Grenache 60%, Syrah 15%, Mourvèdre 12%, all 10 others 13%
- Average vine age: 40 years
- Vineyard size: 0.75-3 hectares
- Soil type: Clay and limestone, quartzite stones
- Average production: 3,000-10,000 bottles

DOMAINE GRAND VENEUR

U p at the northern end of the Châteauneuf-du-Pape appellation and a mere 3 kilometres from Orange, the industrious Alain Jaume produces a range of elegant, fine wines on his Grand Veneur estate from the throng of grape varieties permitted by the appellation rules. This part of the region, a *quartier* known as La Gironde, has a high iron level in its clay and is reckoned less propitious than certain others to the production of quality wine. Jaume's success speaks eloquently of his wine-making talent.

The experience of four generations Jaume has the good fortune to be able to draw on the experience of four generations of *vigneron* forbears, dating back to Mathieu Jaume's time in 1826. Yet Domaine Grand Veneur itself, which came into being in 1979, is Alain Jaume's own creation.

Here, Jaume and his team lavish all the necessary care and attention on the vines, for the vineyard is after all where wine, good or mediocre, is born, and top-quality wine cannot be made with anything less than perfect fruit. Here operations are carried out with great respect for the soil, with no artificial treatments, and with sheep manure and grape compost for soil enrichment. A core activity in the estate's viticultural calendar is pruning, which the team carry out with particular enthusiasm, for this has a direct influence on the vine's productivity, and low yields are essential to good wine. Deciding on the right moment to start the harvest is crucial, and Jaume may be found in his vines every day examining and taking samples, so that the narrow window of perfect ripeness should not be missed.

A trio of elegance and harmony One red Châteauneuf-du-Pape and two whites are produced at Grand Veneur. The red is always impeccably vinified, a wine of elegance and harmony, succulence and concentration. Though not as long-living as some of the more traditional, it is nevertheless a wine which improves over 8-10 years. Grenache makes up 70% of its composition, and all the various varieties are destalked and crushed, then vinified together unless important differences in ripeness dictate otherwise.

The basic white wine is most elegant, an assembly of equal parts of white Grenache, Roussanne and Clairette with the remaining 10% made from other varieties. Like the red, this is fermented in stainless steel, at a cool 18°C, cold-stabilized and bottled 6 months after the harvest. It is fresh, with good balance between roundness and crispness, and attractive honeysuckle and floral aromas; very good *en apéritif* as well as with fish dishes and white meats.

Châteauneuf-du-Pape Cuvée La Fontaine Alain Jaume's most serious wine, however, is his Cuvée La Fontaine, a white wine made entirely from Roussanne, from yields limited at 25 hectolitres per hectare. La Fontaine is fermented and matured in new oak barrels and does not undergo its malolactic fermentation. Like a good Burgundy, this golden yellow nectar is weighty on the palate, concentrated and long, with an essentially floral finish. It is one of the finest white Châteauneufs, thoroughly and proudly untraditional. Serve with trout, cooked with saffron and Nyons olives.

- Other white wines: Châteauneuf-du-Pape, Côtes-du-Rhône Viognier
- Red wines: Châteauneuf-du-Pape, Côtes-du-Rhône-Villages, Côtes-du-Rhône
- Owner: Alain Jaume
- Oenology: Laboratoire Rabot
- Combined vineyards: 38 hectares
- Production: 205,000 bottles
- Exports: 60%
- Take-away sales: 8-12 a.m., 2-7 p.m.
- Visits: By appointment

Wine selected:
Châteauneuf-du-Pape Cuvée La Fontaine

- Grape Variety: Roussanne
- Average vine age: 25 years
- Vineyard size: 0.8 hectares
- Soil type: Clay and limestone
- Average production: 3,000 bottles

Whether he realized it or not, when Aimé Sabon made the decision to stop taking his grapes to the cooperative in 1973 he was laying the foundations of a new star estate in the Châteauneuf-du-Pape firmament. A quarter of a century later, its wines having attained a very desirable reputation, the construction of the edifice might seem long complete… to anyone but Aimé's talented son Christophe. He, however, is not a friend of routine!

Aimé Sabon goes solo The background to this success story is anything but original: a Sabon bought some vineyard land at the turn of the century, when Phylloxera was a recent memory and land for sale was plentiful and inexpensive. Vines were planted, and the land was passed down from father to son. More planting was carried out periodically, notably in 1940, and further land was bought, and all the while the harvests were taken to the local cooperative for vinification. Then came Aimé Sabon's turn in 1967.

From the start Aimé prided himself on the quality of his raw material, and made a point of restricting the yields of his vines. He brought an end to the arrangement with the co-operative and started making and bottling his own wines with the 1973 vintage, which necessitated the construction of wine-making facilities and cellar space. By the time he handed over responsibilities to his son Christophe in 1991 the family had 10 hectares of Châteauneuf-du-Pape vineyard as well as a significant holding of Côtes-du-Rhône and Vin de Pays. Having studied at Beaune, the dapper Christophe has continued to work on the estate's production with great talent, experimenting and refining methods, and using the abundant and excellent raw material to compose new and interesting *cuvées* following his inspiration. Nothing is static at La Janasse!

Great potential complexity The Sabons' 13 hectares of Châteauneuf-du-Pape lie in 5 different sectors, and have varied orientations and soils, providing great potential complexity. After strict quality control the black fruit is usually mostly destemmed (but the vintage is the final arbiter), and spends 3+ weeks' *cuvaison* in concrete vats, followed by some 18 months' *élevage* in *foudre* and both new and used cask. The last operation, bottling, is carried out after a light fining but no filtration.

The majestic white Cuvée Prestige on the other hand, made principally of Roussanne supported by Clairette and white Grenache, is now made entirely in oak casks (two-thirds new) and reared for 18 months with *bâtonnage* of the lees. A masterpiece to enjoy with a Bresse chicken!

Châteauneuf-du-Pape Cuvée Chaupin The *lieu-dit* Chaupin, north-facing and planted with Grenache in 1912, gives a wine which is remarkable not only for its concentration and complexity (a niggardly yield of some 20 hectolitres per hectare and 2 *pigeages* a day see to that) but also for its finesse, harmony and discreet alcohol; these are qualities rare in a Grenache wine, and proof of the talent of the young man at the controls. An eloquent explanation for the increasingly wide demand for his wines. Leg of lamb, seasoned with provençal herbs, has just the finesse of repartee to merit a place at Chaupin's table.

- Other red wines: Châteauneuf-du-Pape Tradition, Châteauneuf-du-Pape Vieilles Vignes, Côtes-du-Rhône-Villages, Côtes-du-Rhône Tradition, Côtes-du-Rhône Les Garrigues, Vin de Pays de la Principauté d'Orange
- White wines: Châteauneuf-du-Pape Prestige, Châteauneuf-du-Pape Tradition, Côtes-du-Rhône
- Owner: Aimé Sabon
- Wine-maker: Christophe Sabon
- Oenologist: Jean-Luc Colombo
- Combined vineyards: 50 hectares
- Production: 266,000 bottles
- Exports: 60%
- Take-away sales: 8-12 a.m., 2-6 p.m.
- Visits: Yes

Wine selected:
Châteauneuf-du-Pape Cuvée Chaupin

- Grape Variety: Grenache
- Average vine age: 80 years
- Vineyard size: 3 hectares
- Soil type: Sandy clay
- Average production: 12,000 bottles

T he Deydier family, makers of Les Clefs d'Or, are well-known and respected in Châteauneuf-du-Pape, having made wine there all through the 20th century. Harmony, finesse and breeding have long been the hallmarks of their production, which may be depended upon to please, whatever the reputation of the vintage.

Coopers and wine-makers Before they made wine the Deydiers were coopers. The change of activity was a natural progression, for wine-making in those days was empirical, and coopers frequently gave growers advice about maturing their wine, racking it and other cellar operations. Modern oenological science was a long way off!

It was Maurice Deydier who first branched out from barrel-making and bought a few vines. He bottled his production from the very early days, and was one of the first to make white Châteauneuf-du-Pape. His son Jean followed in his footsteps and was the one who really put the estate on its feet. Over the years he built up his vineyard holdings, and enjoyed a long and prosperous tenure, before passing away in 1997. Pierre Deydier had already worked with his father Jean for a number of years, and today carries on the good work, with support from his daughter Laurence in the office and his nephew Jean-François Mery in the cellars.

Fine vineyards for the many grape varieties The vineyard is made up of several sloping parcels, very well chosen. The predominantly clay and limestone soils, covered with the region's *galets roulés*, the smooth quartzite stones and boulders of Alpine provenance which litter the region, are planted principally with Grenache Noir, accompanied by Mourvèdre, Syrah and a smattering of Counoise, Muscardin, Vaccarèse and Cinsault for elegance, silkiness and perfume. The family white-wine tradition is maintained with plantings of Grenache Blanc, Clairette and Bourboulenc, which produce some 8,000 bottles annually.

Traditional in production and sales The different varieties of black grape are fermented together in cement vats. They are usually left on their stalks and given a light crushing, and the transformation lasts 15-20 days, conducted at a temperature not exceeding 30°C, which explains to some extent the wine's finesse. The raw liquid is then aged for 12-18 months in *foudre*, the traditional large tun; indeed new oak and small vessels would be inconceivable at this estate!

The Deydiers remain traditional in the range they propose, which comprises just a red and a white Châteauneuf-du-Pape as well as some very fine Côtes-du-Rhône. There is no old-vine *cuvée*, nor second label, and anything sub-standard is sold off in bulk.

Châteauneuf-du-Pape The Les Clefs d'Or red is deep garnet in colour, with a highly seductive nose of morello cherry and blackberry, which takes on hints of undergrowth, game, and sometimes pepper with age. It is richly flavoured yet well-mannered in the mouth, succulent, well-structured, and with good length. Indeed it could even merit the mention 'refined', a rare quality in Châteauneuf-du-Pape. As such Les Clefs d'Or is a perfect accompaniment to chiche kebab, or indeed most barbecued meats.

- Other red wine: Côtes-du-Rhône
- White wine: Châteauneuf-du-Pape
- Owner: Pierre Deydier
- Wine-maker: Pierre Deydier
- Combined vineyards: 34 hectares
- Production: 80,000 bottles
- Exports: 70%
- Take-away sales: Yes
- Visits: Yes

Wine selected:
Châteauneuf-du-Pape

- Grape Varieties: Grenache 70%, Mourvèdre 10%, Syrah 5%, Counoise, Muscardin, Vaccarèse and Cinsault 15%
- Average vine age: 50 years
- Vineyard size: 22 hectares
- Soil type: Clay and limestone, quartzite stones
- Average production: 60,000 bottles

Châteauneuf-du-Pape | Châteauneuf-du-Pape

Connoisseurs of the wines of Châteauneuf-du-Pape have long held the Armeniers' Domaine de Marcoux in high esteem. It might not have the high profile of some of the better-known estates yet the word got around years ago, and today nine-tenths of its production is exported to thirsty, discerning buyers in Brazil, Japan, New Zealand, the United States and many other, nearer destinations.

In the region since the 14th century The Armeniers are one of the oldest families in the region. They lived at Châteauneuf-du-Pape as far back as the 14th century, when the Papacy was installed in Avignon, and their name crops up in numerous documents over the intervening period. The second half of the 20th century saw many a fine vintage of Châteauneuf-du-Pape crafted by Elie Armenier, who ran Marcoux until his death in 1980. Elie was succeeded by his son Philippe, who continued to do things in much the same way as his father until the beginning of the 1990s, when he radically changed his methods.

Adoption of biodynamic methods Having read a book about astrology Armenier decided to visit several famous wine-making proponents of biodynamic methods, and was convinced that adopting these could only be beneficial to his vines and wine. From 1991 he put his new beliefs into action.
Biodynamics are all about homœopathy in the vineyard and respect of planetary movements in all operations, vineyard and cellar. To wean vines off the various synthetic treatments on which they are thoroughly dependant today nothing but organic products are used. Some, spread in the autumn, revive the soil, while others, spread in the spring, take over and reinvigorate the plant. Subsequent cellar operations are carried out whenever possible on preordained days, decided by the movements of the planets and stars.

New-found finesse, harmony and fruitiness The Armeniers are well happy with the results of their new regime, which they reckon has given their wines new-found finesse, harmony and fruitiness, with finer, more supple tannin. Philippe having left the estate in 1995 to recharge his batteries elsewhere, Marcoux is now run by his sisters Sophie and Catherine. The 18-hectare estate is spread over several different terrains, and leans heavily on Grenache. To its indisputable advantage it has many old vines, including 2.3 hectares of centenarians, which must take pleasure in getting back to the organic ways they would have known in their youth!

Châteauneuf-du-Pape Cuvée Vieilles Vignes Whenever the vintage is favourable (which was not the case in 1991 and 1996) the Armeniers isolate part of the produce of the above-mentioned centenarians and some two hectares of 60-year-olds, and produce one of Châteauneuf-du-Pape's greatest wines. This is a powerful wine of massive dimensions, a veritable syrup of Grenache, with a wide flavour range of blackcurrant, liquorice, pepper and toast. It is thick and fleshy on the palate, so much so that its structure is barely perceptible, and has incredible length. This is definitely not a wine to waste on anyone less than passionate about wine! Tournedos Rossini is sufficiently rich and well-bred to keep it company.

• Other red wines:
Châteauneuf-du-Pape,
Côtes-du-Rhône
• White wine:
Châteauneuf-du-Pape
• Owners:
Catherine & Sophie
Armenier
• Vineyard operations :
Catherine Armenier
• Wine-maker:
Sophie Armenier
• Combined vineyards:
18 hectares
• Production:
60,000 bottles
• Exports: 90%
• Take-away sales:
By appointment
• Visits: By appointment

Wine selected:
**Châteauneuf-du-Pape
Cuvée Vieilles Vignes**

• Grape Varieties:
Grenache 80%,
Others 20%
• Average vine age:
60 and 100 years
• Vineyard size:
4.3 hectares
• Soil type:
Clay and limestone
• Average production:
3,500 bottles

DOMAINE DE MONPERTUIS

W hile most Châteauneuf-du-Pape estates now make wines which are more polished and user-friendly than they were in the past—which is generally a very good thing—and others have even gone to the extreme of making lightweight, early-drinking *macération carbonique* offerings, there remain a handful which resolutely continue to produce wine as it was made in days gone by: hard, austere and tannic when young, needing a good few years to develop its bouquet and relax its muscles. These wines demand patience, yet how they reward it when they eventually come round! One such is the very fine Domaine de Monpertuis.

Thirty-two vineyard parcels Monpertuis is run by Paul Jeune, the seventh generation of his family to make wine, and is one of three estates which make up Les Vignobles Paul Jeune, the others being La Croze and La Ramière. The first of these produces Vin de Pays de la Principauté d'Orange, the second Côtes du Rhône and a Vin de Pays du Gard made exclusively with Counoise. The three estates comprise in all 32 different parcels of vine, which no doubt obliges serious reflection as to the picking order at harvest-time, not to mention a good deal of driving over the course of the year.

Long, individual fermentations The two reds and one white Châteauneuf produced at Monpertuis are made with very rigorously selected fruit, from plants the ages of which vary between 45 and 110 years. The whole gamut of the appellation's grape varieties is found on the estate, and these Jeune vinifies individually, each at its specific fermentation temperature—of the whites, for example, Roussanne and Bourboulenc are vinified at 16°C, Clairette at 18°C and Grenache Blanc at 22°C—in order to bring out to the maximum each one's qualities. Vatting lasts, in the case of the reds, for some 3 weeks for the Cuvée Classique and up to 6 weeks for the Cuvée Tradition, and this, allied with the fact that there is only 20% destemming of fruit for the former and none whatsoever for the latter, explain the wines' thickness, structure and initial hardness.

Naturally such powerful new-borns need the calming, refining influence of the *pièce* and the *foudre*, and after several months resting in vat the Classique and the Tradition spend 12 and 24 months respectively in these vessels. Gradually they deposit all matter in suspension, receiving an occasional racking from one vessel to another, before eventual bottling, without filtration in the case of the Tradition.

Châteauneuf-du-Pape Cuvée Tradition Here then is a huge wine, definitely not for lovers of the clean, fruity or simple! The Cuvée Tradition is only made in the finest years, and lives up to its name: uncompromising and resolutely un-modern, it is thick and fleshy on the palate, with the slight sweetness of a high glycerine content, which balances the tannic structure well. Young, one can appreciate its impressive dimensions, yet it needs at least a decade to reveal the extent of its potential. Such is the frustration and the magic of *grand vin*! Needless to say, Paul Jeune's Cuvée Tradition embraces traditional, rustic fare such as *daube dauphinoise* and all manner of game with absolutely no reticence.

- Other red wines: Châteauneuf-du-Pape Cuvée Classique
- White wine: Châteauneuf-du-Pape
- Owner: Paul Jeune
- Wine-maker: Paul Jeune
- Oenologist: Gérard Philis
- Combined vineyards: 33 hectares
- Production: 80,000 bottles
- Exports: 80%
- Take-away sales: Yes
- Visits: By appointment

Wine selected:
Châteauneuf-du-Pape Cuvée Tradition

- Grape Varieties: Grenache 85%, Others (except Syrah) 15%
- Average vine age: 60 and 110 years
- Vineyard size: 6 hectares
- Soil type: Clay and limestone, stones
- Average production: 15,000 bottles

For nigh on a century the Sabon family have been cultivating the vine at Châteauneuf and turning out vintage after vintage of well-crafted, rich, traditionally made wine, to the entire satisfaction of their clients. The generation in charge today proudly continues this relatively low-profile family affair, winning along the way many a medal in local and national competitions.

A thoroughly fragmented vineyard At the origin of the estate there was Romain Jausset, owner of a number of vineyard plots around the town of Châteauneuf-du-Pape. Jausset's only child Marie, who had married Séraphin Sabon in 1904, inherited these on her father's death, and later on left them to her son Joseph. When the moment came for the next generation change, French inheritance laws incited the family to create a *Groupement Agricole d'Exploitation en Commun* in order to preserve the unity of the estate.

The Clos du Mont-Olivet estate is very fragmented, which is certainly not a disadvantage as far as its wine's complexity goes. Plots are owned in all the principal Châteauneuf quarters, but by and large the estate is concentrated in three of them: the youngest vines lie in the Pied-de-Baud quarter in the north, a plateau covered with *galets roulés* over a clay base; the oldest vines are situated on the Montalivet slopes to the east, in clay and limestone soil; and in the south there are vines in Les Gallimardes, which is low-lying stony gravel terrain.

A traditionally-crafted wine In an uncharacteristic show of modernity the Sabons started using a tractor with caterpillar tracks for vineyard tasks as far back as 1957, yet their horse doggedly ploughed on until taking well-earned retirement in 1972. Nowadays, of course, like everyone else they use a four-wheel-drive *enjambeur* which straddles the rows of vines.

Harvesting is carried out by the traditional two-basket method whereby the best fruit is placed in one, the less good in the second, in order to respect the appellation obligation that 5% of the crop be discarded. Back at the domaine the different varieties are crushed on their stalks by Séraphin Sabon's original *fouloir*, then transferred mixed to cement vats for three weeks' vatting, after which there is a change of vat for the 'malo'. Once this is over the wine is lodged in old casks for ageing; new wood is out of the question at Mont-Olivet. Bottling, and ultimately tasting and sales, takes place in nearby premises owned by Reflets, an association of 6 estates including Mont-Olivet, whose members share equipment and notions of quality.

Châteauneuf-du-Pape A fine, very deep garnet ruby always meets the eye as one raises a glass of Clos du Mont-Olivet, yet the taster's attention is rapidly waylaid by its sumptuous bouquet of black olives, bay-leaf, truffles, leather... On the palate it is not as muscular as some, deploying instead a certain elegance and harmony, yet it is unmistakably a wine which requires a lot of time to develop all its innate quality. Its elegance makes Clos du Mont-Olivet eminently well-suited to white meats, seasoned and served with the region's herbs and vegetables, and winged game.

- Other red wine:
Côtes-du-Rhône
- White wines:
Châteauneuf-du-Pape,
Côtes-du-Rhône
- Owners:
Jean-Claude, Pierre &
Bernard Sabon
- Oenology:
Roch Lauriol Laboratory
- Combined vineyards:
25 hectares
- Production:
175,000 bottles
- Exports: 30%
- Take-away sales:
8-12 a.m., 2-6 p.m.
- Visits: Yes

Wine selected:
Châteauneuf-du-Pape

- Grape Varieties:
Grenache 90%,
Others (Syrah, Mourvèdre,
Cinsault, Vaccarèse,
Muscardin) 10%
- Average vine age:
70 years
- Vineyard size:
25 hectares
- Soil type:
Clay and limestone
- Average production:
80,000 bottles

Châteauneuf-du-Pape | Châteauneuf-du-Pape

CHÂTEAU MONT-REDON

I t is probably thanks to the historic Château Mont-Redon more than any other estate that the wines of Châteauneuf-du-Pape are known so well around much of the world. This property, the largest in the region with a total surface area of 160 hectares, was making wine as early as 1334, and its huge production has long been exported, earning it an illustrious reputation.

Geological diversity plays its role   Like all its neighbours, Mont-Redon's vineyards were decimated by Phylloxera in the 1870s, and there were a mere 2 hectares of vines remaining when Henri Plantin acquired the property in 1923. He set about clearing the large tracts of abandoned and overgrown vineyard and planted all 13 authorized varieties, with emphasis on Grenache. Today his descendants, the cousins Didier Fabre and Jean and François Abeille, have a superb 93-hectare vineyard in production at their disposal, sited on the highest slopes of the plateau northwest of Châteauneuf-du-Pape.

Size of course brings geological diversity, which greatly increases the wines' complexity, and this is an essential factor of Mont-Redon's quality. The bulk of the vineyard consists of clay covered by a 2-metre layer of *galets roulés*, in which Grenache, Syrah and Cinsault are in their element, while a richer, sandier part suits Mourvèdre better. Finally there are calcareous soils which are ideal for the white varieties.

Traditional vinification in impeccable conditions   Messieurs Fabre and Abeille produce but two wines, a white and a red, and are against the idea of isolating their best fruit for a 'vieilles vignes' or prestige *cuvée*; far better, they reason, to have better quality in all 350,000 bottles produced of the standard wine.

Like the vineyard, which is run along *lutte raisonnée* lines, the vatroom and cellars are impeccable. Fermentations are traditional, with varieties fermented individually as and when they attain perfect ripeness and are picked. The white wine is fermented at 17-18°C for three weeks in stainless steel and does not undergo its malolactic fermentation. It is reared on its lees for 2-3 months and bottled early in order to preserve its fruit. It is splendid: aromatic and fat yet with enough acidity to give good balance and enable development in bottle.

Châteauneuf-du-Pape   To make the red wine the black grapes are crushed, entirely destemmed and loaded into stainless steel vats with automatic *pigeage*. There they ferment by the action of their own yeast and macerate for 15-21 days, giving up their colour, tannin and aroma. After the numerous lots have been aged for 14-16 months in a mix of new and used barrels, *foudre* and vat, there is a final blending and the wine is bottled and then left to repose in the cellars for 6 months before despatch.

The result is a very dark wine of rich, succulent flavour, which is ample on the palate and structured, yet not excessively powerful. Essentially black fruit and pepper in flavour with a new-oak vanilla backdrop when young, it acquires a more complex and interesting range of flavours after 6-8 years. The wine is harmonious and elegant too, with far more breeding than most, and this aspect of its character makes it a very well suited partner for saddle of hare.

- Other red wines: Côtes-du-Rhône, Lirac
- White wines: Châteauneuf-du-Pape, Côtes-du-Rhône
- Owners: Abeille and Fabre families
- Oenologist: Christian Voeux
- Oenological Consultancy: Laboratoire Rabot
- Combined vineyards: 120 hectares
- Production: 550,000 bottles
- Exports: 60%
- Take-away sales: 7 days per week, 8 a.m.-7 p.m. (Wednesdays 8-12 a.m., 2-6 p.m.)
- Visits: By appointment

Wine selected:
Châteauneuf-du-Pape

- Grape Varieties: Grenache 65%, Syrah 15%, Cinsault 10%, Mourvèdre 5%, Counoise, Muscardin and Vaccarèse 5%
- Average vine age: 45 years
- Vineyard size: 76 hectares
- Soil type: Clay and limestone, quartzite stones
- Average production: 350,000 bottles

CHÂTEAU LA NERTHE

marvellous vineyard location, allied with a tradition of good management and viticultural and wine-making innovation, have resulted in the long pre-eminence of La Nerthe among Châteauneuf-du-Pape's estates. Today it continues to benefit from the investment and the intelligent management necessary to ensure the production of great wine, and its wines are regularly among the most accomplished of the region.

The legacy of enlightened owners The estate existed as far back as 1560, when it was known as Beauvenir and was the property of the Tulle de Villefranche family. By 1750 it covered 50 hectares, made wine, and its owners had already set up a network of agents, indeed its production was selling as far afield as London, Moscow and America. Bottling was introduced on site in the ensuing years, and the writer Jullien, in his *Topographie de Tous les Vignobles Connus* of 1822, called it a "vin de première classe".

A solution to the Phylloxera problem La Nerthe's vineyards were destroyed by the dreaded Phylloxera bug in the 1870s, and the Tulle de Villefranches sold the estate to Commandant Joseph Ducos. While all around him were replacing their decimated vineyards with fruit trees, Ducos, convinced that grafting Rhône vines onto Phylloxera-resistant American rootstock was the answer, set about rebuilding his vineyard by that method. He was initially observed with disbelief, and then curiosity, by fellow growers, but was eventually imitated by them all. He conducted lengthy research into vine varieties, planting 10 on his estate, and the results of his experiments were influential in the drawing-up of Châteauneuf-du-Pape's appellation laws in 1936.
After suffering extensive damage during the war and then a difficult post-war period the property was acquired in 1985 by the Richard family and David & Foillard, and entirely restored. Alain Dugas, who had studied with Dr. Dufays of Domaine de Nalys, was appointed to run it and make the wine.

Expressing La Nerthe's terroir A good number of the last century's traditions still stand today at La Nerthe, for they have long proved their value. Systematic destemming, followed by a light crushing and 15-18 days' vatting, were how the wine was made in 1860, and are more or less how it is made today. The multiplicity of vine varieties is essential to the balanced expression of La Nerthe's *terroir*, and the Grenache has thus never been particularly predominant in the blend. And then its marvellous site, its old vines, very low yields and perfect grape ripeness, these all contribute to La Nerthe's quality.

Châteauneuf-du-Pape Cuvée des Cadettes Dugas produces four wines: a very fine standard red and white Châteauneuf-du-Pape, and in favourable years a magnificent barrel-fermented white Clos de Beauvenir and the red Cuvée des Cadettes. The latter is made in wooden vat and aged in nothing but new oak barrels. Its impressive structure destines it for great longevity, and in the mouth it is very concentrated and ample, with a rich, spicy blackcurrant flavour and the toasted flavour of its new oak. This glorious wine, awarded three stars by the *Guide Hachette des Vins* for its 1995 vintage, calls out for a haunch of venison.

- Other red wine:
Châteauneuf-du-Pape
- White wines:
Châteauneuf-du-Pape
Clos de Beauvenir,
Châteauneuf-du-Pape
- Owners: Richard family
- Director: Alain Dugas
- Wine-maker:
Alain Dugas
- Oenologist: Alain Dugas
- Combined vineyards:
90 hectares
- Production:
350,000 bottles
- Exports: 75%
- Take-away sales:
9-12 a.m., 2.30-5.30 p.m.
- Visits: Groups of 10,
by appointment

Wine selected:
**Châteauneuf-du-Pape
Cuvée des Cadettes**

- Grape Varieties:
Grenache 44%,
Mourvèdre 28%,
Syrah 28%
- Average vine age:
90 years
- Vineyard size:
5 hectares
- Soil type:
Sand and quartzite stones
- Average production:
15,000 bottles

Château La Nerthe

Châteauneuf-du-Pape

APPELLATION CHÂTEAUNEUF-DU-PAPE CONTRÔLÉE

CUVÉE DES CADETTES 1995

Mis en bouteille au Château

13,5% vol.   75 cl

Château La Nerthe S.C.A. · Propriétaire-Récoltant à Châteauneuf-du-Pape · Vaucluse · France

PRODUCT OF FRANCE

Any listing of the finest producers of Châteauneuf-du-Pape invariably includes the Avril family and their Clos des Papes estate, for year in, year out, this father-and-son team make extremely good wine. What is more, their welcome is warm and their wines remain affordable.

Three centuries of wine-makers The Avrils were First Consuls and Treasurers of Châteauneuf-du-Pape from 1756 to 1790. Yet more importantly from the point of view of today's wine-lover, over some 3 centuries they have been wine-makers. They started bottling their produce very early on; a gold medal won in 1882 at the Avignon Fair attests to its quality at the time. The first wines to be sold under the name Clos des Papes appeared in 1896, both white and red selling for 5 francs a bottle, and Paul Avril, grandfather of the present Paul, registered the name as a trademark in 1902. Recognizing the necessity of setting and safeguarding standards for his region's wines, Avril was the driving force behind a committee organized as early as 1911 to draw up basic production rules, which later on were to form the basis of the A.O.C. Since his days three generations have delighted the palates of wine-lovers with many a fine vintage.

The advantages of a fragmented estate Clos des Papes is a highly fragmented estate which counts 18 parcels spread over the length and breadth of the appellation. A logistic disadvantage perhaps, yet since there is climatic variation between the different sectors it has the advantage of staggering the ripening of fruit—the northern part of the appellation can be up to 10 days behind the southern part—enabling the harvesting of different parcels at peak ripeness. What is more, the fact that the grapes are grown in a wide diversity of soils and subsoils also enhances the complexity of the wine. Clos des Papes, as one might suspect, is not simply a brand name but is one of the Avrils' vineyards; lying inside the grounds of the ruined château, it once formed part of the Papal estate.

The inescapable requisites of quality Low yields and strict selectivity are the inescapable requisites for the production of quality wine, in the Avrils' view. To this end they take great steps to reduce the vine's natural productivity by severe pruning, debudding in the spring and green harvesting in July. Then once the harvest has started the fruit is examined and if necessary rejected either as it is cut, as it arrives at the trailer, or on the conveyor belt in the reception area.
The vinification which follows is thoroughly classic, taking place in enamel-lined vats at a relatively high temperature whichever colour. The white wine is bottled without any wood contact, while the red is aged in *foudre* and cask for 12-18 months.

Châteauneuf-du-Pape The red Clos des Papes, so dark it seems black, develops a sumptuous, soft bouquet of morello cherries, cloves and cinnamon after a few years in bottle, with an attractive smoky aspect. It is remarkable for its balance and harmony and the opulence of its flesh, which hides its tannic structure. Grilled red meats suit it down to the ground, indeed a barbecued rib of beef will show off its qualities to perfection.

• White wine:
Châteauneuf-du-Pape
• Owner:
Clos des Papes - Paul Avril
• Manager: Vincent Avril
• Combined vineyards:
32 hectares
• Production:
130,000 bottles
• Exports: 65%
• Take-away sales:
8-12 a.m., 2-6 p.m.
(Fri. 5 p.m.)
• Visits: Yes

Wine selected:
Châteauneuf-du-Pape

• Grape Varieties:
Grenache 70%,
Mourvèdre 20%,
Syrah 8%,
Counoise, Muscardin and
Vaccarèse 2%
• Average vine age:
30 years
• Vineyard size:
26 hectares
• Soil type:
Clay and limestone
• Average production:
110,000 bottles

Châteauneuf-du-Pape | Châteauneuf-du-Pape

DOMAINE DU PÉGAU

One could hardly find a more traditional wine estate than Domaine du Pégau, where the Féraud family produce wines of enormous character, power and structure, no-holds-barred Châteauneuf-du-Pape which pays no lip service to modern fashions and techniques. If one is to buy a few bottles of Pégau a cellar and lots of patience are required, but the reward at the waiting's end makes it thoroughly worthwhile.

Long established in the region The Férauds and their ancestors have lived in the region since 1670, and have always been attached to the land and earned their living from crops. Over the course of the 20th century the family acquired the occasional little plot of vineyard land, yet it was only in 1987, the year when Laurence Féraud joined her father Paul, that the estate Domaine du Pégau formally came into existence. Pégau is a 13th-century Provençal word for an earthenware jug used for serving wine at table, examples of which have been found in diggings on the site of the Papal palace in Avignon.

Maintaining healthy soils and plants The estate, enlarged several times since 1987, is composed of 9 different parcels on well-exposed hillsides facing east-south-east. Their soils are predominantly clay and limestone, covered with *galets roulés*, the smooth quartzite stones of Alpine origin which give out at night the heat they have accumulated during the day, and also prevent evaporation of the water in the soil. All 13 different permitted varieties are planted, the vines having been grafted onto Rupestris du Lot rootstock which resists the strong, cold blasts of the Mistral wind very well, enabling the vine to grow straight.

Viticultural practices are firmly oriented towards maintaining healthy soils and plants and keeping the latters' production to a low level of no more than 25-30 hectolitres per hectare. Pruning is severe, and the only fertilizer used is the ash of the burnt vine-shoots and sheep dung. Ploughing, and not weedkiller, keeps the vineyards weed-free, and no insecticide is used. *Epamprage* (leaf-stripping) is carried out in June to improve grape-ripening, by increasing insolation and reducing the rising of valuable sap into fruitless shoots.

Vinified to last Once picked and examined, the grapes undergo a traditional vinification. The black varieties are left on their stalks and crushed, then fermented and macerated for 15 days with two *remontages* per day for extraction of colour, tannin and aroma, and finally run into *foudres*, press-wine incorporated, for between 18 months' and 5 years' rearing. White grapes have a day's skin maceration and are then vinified in 5-year-old Meursault barrels, with maturation on their lees.

Châteauneuf-du-Pape Cuvée Réservée A young Pégau red wine shows a dense, dark purple colour, and can surprise the taster by its sheer massive, rich and tannic constitution. Sumptuous aromas of black cherry, liquorice, herbs and black olives assail the senses, to be joined by nuances of leather, coffee, cinnamon and pepper as the wine ages. This is a magnificent, complex and memorable Châteauneuf-du-Pape, demanding nothing less than a stew of wild boar or some other similarly full-flavoured dish.

- Other red wine: Châteauneuf-du-Pape Cuvée Laurence
- White wine: Châteauneuf-du-Pape
- Owners: M. and Mme. Paul Féraud, Laurence Féraud
- Wine-maker: Paul Féraud
- Combined vineyards: 18 hectares
- Production: 80,000 bottles
- Exports: 85%
- Take-away sales: Yes
- Visits: 8.30 a.m.-5.30 p.m., weekends by appointment

Wine selected:
Châteauneuf-du-Pape Cuvée Réservée

- Grape Varieties: Grenache 70%, Syrah 15%, Mourvèdre 10%, Counoise and others 5%
- Average vine age: 50 years
- Vineyard size: 17 hectares
- Soil type: Clay and limestone, quartzite stones, sand
- Average production: 65,000 bottles

Châteauneuf-du-Pape | Châteauneuf-du-Pape

1996

CUVÉE RÉSERVÉE

DOMAINE DU PEGAU

Product of France

Châteauneuf du Pape

APPELLATION CHÂTEAUNEUF-DU-PAPE CONTRÔLÉE

13,5 % vol.   Mise en Bouteille à la propriété   750 ml

...au FÉRAUD et Fille, Propriétaires Récoltants à CHATEAUNEUF-DU-PAPE - 84 - France

There are few estates in France or indeed anywhere in the world which make a wine of such sublime, concentrated brilliance as Château Rayas. And there can be none which come near it for legend: so much has been written about this small, hidden, run-down property, its unorthodox methods and its eccentric proprietors, that the visitor, assuming he manages to find the place, may be forgiven a little apprehension...

A very unusual vineyard As a wine estate Château Rayas is young. Its vineyards—some 15 parcels, many surrounded by woods—were planted by Louis Reynaud in 1922, and are mostly north-facing. Intuition on the part of the young man? The vines as a result get both respite from excessive heat and a longer, gentler ripening curve. They are composed of friable clay, limestone, and in some places sandy soils, without any of the smooth quartzite stones; rumour has it that Reynaud removed them all by hand. And in an appellation where 13 varieties are permitted for red wines, Rayas uses but one—Grenache, which generally does not age well.

Father and son nurture a legend Over the decades Rayas's reputation was forged by the eccentric Louis Reynaud, who held sway until his death at a ripe old age in 1978, when he was succeeded by his son Jacques, an equally exotic personage of great culture, intellect, and wine-making talent. The reclusive Jacques had no love of journalists and the warmth of his welcome was unpredictable—the estate is tucked away off the beaten track and visitors are discouraged—yet he made wines which mostly stood up brilliantly under the piercing spotlight of the world's wine critics. A bachelor, he passed away in 1997, since when the estate has been run by his young nephew Emmanuel Reynaud, who shows all the signs of being capable of perpetuating the Rayas standards.

The apotheosis of Grenache Noir Extremely low yields of 15-18 hectolitres per hectare, which would be regarded by many as excessive and unprofitable, have always been at the root of Rayas's quality. The almost over-ripe grapes, often with potential alcohol of 15°, are vinified slowly by thoroughly traditional methods, in cellars which belie the adage that fine wine can only be made in clean surroundings. The wine is then aged in a motley collection of old casks of various sizes, the contents of which are unhesitatingly refused inclusion into the *grand vin* if they are not utterly worthy. Stainless steel, thermoregulation, new oak... none of the trappings of the modern wine estate are to be found at Rayas.

Châteauneuf-du-Pape Sporting its famous label and disdaining the bottle with the Papal emblem, Rayas is proud to be judged on its own intrinsic merits. Great breeding, extraordinary thickness and concentration, surprising refinement, it is the apotheosis of Grenache Noir. It speaks with waves of sumptuous, sweet flavour and a very consequent alcohol level, yet can be relied on for perfect balance and harmony. A *tour de force* by which others are judged, it needs a dozen years to develop its complexity, yet will last twice that in a good year. Truffled capon in a coarse salt crust makes a very successful accompaniment to Château Rayas at table. A toast to the Reynauds of this world!

- Other red wine: Châteauneuf-du-Pape Pignan
- White wine: Châteauneuf-du-Pape
- Owners: Reynaud family
- Wine-maker: Emmanuel Reynaud
- Combined vineyards: 13 hectares
- Production: 38,000 bottles
- Exports: 70%
- Take-away sales: No
- Visits: No

Wine selected:
Châteauneuf-du-Pape

- Grape Variety: Grenache Noir
- Average vine age: 15 and 70 years
- Vineyard size: 8 hectares
- Soil type: Clay, limestone, sand
- Average production: 24,000 bottles

RÉSERVE
1996

CHATEAU RAYAS

14% CHATEAUNEUF-DU-PAPE

APPELLATION CHÂTEAUNEUF-DU-PAPE CONTRÔLÉE

S.C.E.A
CHATEAU RAYAS

750 ml

CHATEAUNEUF-DU-P
VAUCLUSE
FRANCE

The 1990s have witnessed much change at the La Vieille Julienne estate, which has coincided, as so often happens, with the handing over of responsibilities from a father to his son. In a short number of years the young and articulate Jean-Paul Daumen has reviewed a number of the estate's traditions and improved the wine considerably. La Vieille Julienne was always renowned for size and staying-power, but these days richness, complexity and irresistible succulence are its major qualities.

A haven from the dreaded Phylloxera The estate, which came into being in the early 18th century, takes its name from the Julienne family, its original owners. Daumen's family acquired it in 1905. At that time there were relatively few vines, yet somehow what there were mercifully escaped the depredations of the dreaded Phylloxera. Initially the wine was made for the consumption of family and friends, but in the 1920s the step was taken to start selling to the local merchants. Gradually demand from private customers for the wine in bottle grew, and by the 1950s the greater part of the production was being bottled. Today La Vieille Julienne finds its way to wine-lovers all around the world.

Several essential changes Grenache has always been the linch-pin of this wine, indeed the centenarian plants which escaped the Phylloxera are of that variety. Having observed the great quality of certain other Châteauneufs, Daumen knew when he took over in 1990 that there were several essential changes to be introduced. Perhaps the most important was the introduction of destalking, permitting a lengthier vatting period of some 25 days at controlled temperatures of 28-33°C, with the extraction of tannin, colour and aroma enhanced by pumping up and spraying the wine over the cap of solids (*remontage*) 4 times per day. Daumen ferments the different varieties individually, each in the company of an equal part of Grenache; that way he never has to pick a variety or a plot until it is perfectly ripe, and can carry out the stringent controls essential for quality.

After two rackings the wines are blended and then transferred to barrel. There were experiments with various proportions of new oak until 1995, since when a mix of wood of between 1 and 4 years' age has been used, as well as 50-hectolitre tuns. After some 12-18 months' ageing followed by a fining the wine is bottled in one go, without filtration. This quality *élevage* and the single bottling have been greatly instrumental in ridding the wine of its previous rusticity and solidness.

Châteauneuf-du-Pape Cuvée Réservée The finest wine at La Vieille Julienne is made almost entirely with Grenache, from a niggardly yield of 20 hectolitres per hectare. The Cuvée Réservée, which is only made in exceptional years, is a wine of extraordinary depth and seduction, with a large tannic structure clothed in voluminous flesh and a refined flavour of spicy, cooked fruit with a vanilla backdrop. It is actually delicious young, yet is made for a decade's keeping, and will live far longer than that. This masterpiece is made for a stew of wild boar.

- Other red wines: Châteauneuf-du-Pape, Châteauneuf-du-Pape Cuvée Vieilles Vignes, Côtes-du-Rhône, Côtes-du-Rhône Cuvée Vieilles Vignes, Vin de Pays de la Principauté d'Orange
- White wines: Châteauneuf-du-Pape, Côtes-du-Rhône
- Owner: Daumen family
- Manager: Jean-Paul Daumen
- Wine-maker: Jean-Paul Daumen
- Oenologist: Noël Rabot
- Combined vineyards: 32 hectares
- Production: 185,000 bottles
- Exports: 40%
- Take-away sales: Yes
- Visits: By appointment

Wine selected:
Châteauneuf-du-Pape Cuvée Réservée

- Grape Varieties: Grenache 95%, Syrah 5%
- Average vine age: 70 years
- Vineyard size: 1.3 hectares
- Soil type: Clay and limestone
- Average production: Up to 4000 bottles

PRODUCE OF FRANCE

1995

RÉSERVÉ

Châteauneuf-du-Pape

APPELLATION CHATEAUNEUF-DU-PAPE CONTROLÉE

DOMAINE DE LAVIEILLE JULIENNE

750 ML

MIS EN BOUTEILLE DU DOMAINE
SARL DAUMEN PERE ET FILS PROPRIÉTAIRES ORANGE (VSE) FRANCE

The wines of Domaine du Vieux Télégraphe are looked upon by many as yardstick Châteauneuf-du-Pape, indeed it is by them that many foreigners discover the appellation, for 80% of the estate's sizeable production is exported to destinations around the world. The region could hardly have a finer ambassador. Recent years have seen the wine continue to excel, thanks to a lot of devotion and hard work.

A century of prosperity The Brunier family can be proud of what they have achieved. The estate celebrated its centenary in 1998, and with faultless continuity has been passed down four generations: Hippolyte the founder, Jules, Henri, and now Frédéric and Daniel…

Prosperity has permitted expansion, not only of Vieux Télégraphe but also, in 1986, with the purchase of Domaine de la Roquette, another Châteauneuf-du-Pape estate of 28 hectares, and then in 1998 with Domaine Les Pallières, a Gigondas estate of great if somewhat fading reputation.

The dangers of routine Vieux Télégraphe's eminence derives primarily from its vineyard site, a magnificent single block on the La Crau plateau in the appellation's south-eastern section. This vast, south-facing terrace of clay and limestone soil, covered with smooth, heat-reflecting quartzite stones and lying over a stratum of water-retaining impermeable red clay, is ideally suited to the climate's demands, and often serves as a model for viticultural experiments.

It is cultivated with the utmost respect by the Bruniers. Going further than simply being ecological in their practices, the brothers ceaseless reflect on the 'why's and 'how's of all they do, and the effect on the grape-quality of their actions, for they have an acute awareness of the dangers of routine. Traditional treatments against fungal outbreaks are limited and targeted with precision, while the grapeworm is combated by means of 'sexual confusion', which involves diffusing the scent of the female Eudemis butterfly, its mother, in order that the male cannot find her.

Analysis of the grapes' needs Low yields are viewed as essential, and are achieved by debudding in the spring and, if necessary, green harvesting in July. Fruit quality is meticulously controlled during the harvest, and vinification then proceeds in a winery designed to move the raw material and then the wine by gravity, rather than pumping. Vinification is traditional yet, like vineyard operations, it is subject to analysis of the needs of the different grapes every year. It is ended with a protracted *élevage* and regular racking, permitting bottling without filtration.

Châteauneuf-du-Pape In style the modern Vieux Télégraphe red is situated in between the truly long-term wines and those made for consumption young. Contrary to the structured, dense wines made before the mid-1980s, the accent is now on aroma and balance, and concentrated, juicy fruit which makes the wine delicious from youth onwards. Delicious aromas of black fruit, liquorice, Provençal herbs and *garrigue* perfume this generous wine, making it a fine partner for grilled red meats seasoned with herbs.

- White wine: Châteauneuf-du-Pape
- Owner: Brunier family
- Managers: Frédéric & Daniel Brunier
- Wine-maker: Frédéric Brunier
- Combined vineyards: 70 hectares
- Production: 306,000 bottles
- Exports: 80%
- Take-away sales: 8-12 a.m., 2-6 p.m.
- Visits: By appointment

Wine selected: **Châteauneuf-du-Pape**

- Grape Varieties: Grenache Noir 60%, Mourvèdre 15%, Syrah 15%, Cinsault 5%, Others 5%
- Average vine age: 50 years
- Vineyard size: 63 hectares
- Soil type: Clay and limestone, quartzite stones
- Average production: 200,000 bottles

1996

Châteauneuf-du-Pape

"LA CRAU"

Domaine du

Vieux Télégraphe

APPELLATION CHATEAUNEUF-DU-PAPE CONTROLÉE

MIS EN BOUTEILLE AU DOMAINE

H. BRUNIER ET FILS, PROPRIÉTAIRES-RÉCOLTANTS 84370 BÉDARRIDES FRANCE

PRODUCE OF FRANCE

The Faraud family is well known in Gigondas, and one can hardly miss the faded mural sign on the left-hand side announcing the presence of the cellars as one enters the village. The name is also well known in far-away countries, for four-fifths of the yearly production are exported. Domaine du Cayron is one of the richest and most powerful Gigondas, a yardstick wine of great concentration and character.

Time-honoured family methods The estate takes its name from the *col*, part of the Dentelles de Montmirail, which lies above the village and at the base of which the Farauds own land. Four generations have built up the estate. Michel Faraud learnt his trade at his father Georges's side and took over from him in 1976, since which time he has made many a vintage by the time-honoured family methods. There is but one wine, for this grower is not interested in prestige or old-vine *cuvées*—he is not about to bend to the requests of his clients, as some do, and start changing his methods, ageing in new oak, filtering and what have you!

An unusual blend The Cayron vineyards, which lie essentially on clay and limestone soils, are scattered all over the appellation, those at the foot of the Col du Cayron being the finest. In this particular part of the Vaucluse the Cinsault performs remarkably well, contributing freshness and fruit and not losing acidity despite the high temperatures, and 15% of the Cayron vineyard is therefore planted with this variety. Unusually there is but a token presence of Mourvèdre, for it is not one of Faraud's preferred varieties, and Grenache and Syrah make up the rest of the blend.

Slow, traditional wine-making Vinification then takes place in cellars in which the visitor can imagine himself back in the 19th century. The fruit is fermented with no prior destemming in sunken concrete vats. These, being naturally cool, present the advantage of natural heat regulation; the disadvantage is that *décuvage*, the post-fermentation operation of removing the solid matter from the vat in order to press it, involves getting down into the vat and forking it out through the hole above—a thoroughly *pénible* chore! The *marc* is pressed by means of an ancient hydraulic press, the press wine is then added to the free-run, and the Farauds' venerable *foudres* then come into service for ageing the wine. Over several years it gradually falls bright, and several rackings separate it from its deposit. Then bottling takes place, 20 hectolitres at a time, when stock is needed.

Gigondas Year after year Michel Faraud manages to make a very rich, savoury Gigondas, which develops a remarkably intense bouquet after some 8 years. Never complicated by extraneous influences such as new wood, it is beautifully and densely fruity, wonderfully silky on the tongue and with a structure of fine tannin which is anything but aggressive. The wine's extremely long finish only confirms what the taster divines from the start: this is a great Gigondas, made for the long-term. Beef *paupiettes* or a haunch of wild boar are the sort of meats it requires.

- Owner:
EARL Michel Faraud
- Wine-maker:
Michel Faraud
- Oenologist:
Gérard Philis
- Vineyard size:
15 hectares
- Grape Varieties:
Grenache 69%,
Syrah 15%,
Cinsault 15%,
Mourvèdre 1%
- Average vine age:
45 years
- Soil type:
Clay and limestone
- Production:
60,000 bottles
- Exports: 80%
- Take-away sales:
9.00-12.15 a.m.,
2.00-6.30 p.m.
- Visits: By appointment

Gigondas | Gigondas

I f the wines of Gigondas have made great strides forward in the last few decades it is thanks to growers like Jean-Pierre Cartier, the free-thinking innovator who is responsible for the destiny of the excellent Domaine Les Goubert. There is nothing frivolous made on this estate, for Cartier is unashamedly pro-*vin de garde* when it comes to red wine, and also makes deliciously full-flavoured whites.

A wealth of different plots are united Cartier was born into a family of *vignerons* which goes back many a generation—Goubert was the name of his mother's family—and by the time he was 14 he was already helping out in the vineyard, listening and observing. By 1973, the year when his father left him 3 hectares, he had thoroughly solid notions not only of how to make wine but of the quality level he wanted to attain. From the outset he started bottling his produce and looking around for land in order to increase his production and be able to make a better living.

Nowadays Jean-Pierre and Mireille Cartier own a splendid 23-hectare estate, made up of over 40 parcels of vine on terraces or slopes in the communes of Beaumes-de-Venise, Lafare, Sablet and Séguret as well as Gigondas. This wealth of different plots comprises a lot of geological diversity, which, emphasised by Cartier's traditional methods of cultivation using neither chemical fertilizers nor insecticides, in turn brings great complexity to the finished wines.

Wine-making 'à l'ancienne' Vinifications at Les Goubert could hardly be more traditional. The fruit for the red wines is mostly left on its stems and lightly crushed, and then loaded into concrete vats for *cuvaison*, which lasts for 3-4 weeks or more. Temperatures are allowed to rise to some 32°C for better extraction, but if they look like rising further, since he has no cooling equipment Cartier controls them the way it was no doubt done by his forbears, by transferring the liquid to another vat overnight and then reuniting it with its *marc* the following day. After ageing, the length of which depends on the wine and the vintage quality, there is *égalisation* of the different recipients and finally bottling, which is all done in one go. The whites wines are made at 18-20°C in either a mix of stainless steel and barrel or simply, in the case of the Viognier wine, 10 months' barrel.

Gigondas Cuvée Florence In celebration of the birth of his daughter, in 1985 Cartier introduced a prestige wine of Grenache and Syrah, made from very low yields. Going against local practice he gave it a long ageing in mainly new oak barrels. The result was a superbly successful wine, opulent and fleshy, of fascinating complexity in the mouth. Fortunately Florence's birth has since been celebrated with great regularity, and with particular distinction in 1995: 50% new oak, 24 months' ageing, and bottling with neither fining nor filtration, this splendour breathes vanilla, violets, black fruit and spice, in a supremely harmonious whole which finishes very, very long. It is well structured and will no doubt live at least 20 years. It deserves a flavoursome red meat or game at table, followed by some mature Gouda.

• Other red wines: Gigondas, Côtes-du-Rhône-Villages Beaumes-de-Venise, Côtes-du-Rhône-Villages Sablet, Côtes-du-Rhône
• White wines: Côtes-du-Rhône-Villages Sablet, Côtes-du-Rhône Viognier
• Owners: Jean-Pierre & Mireille Cartier
• Wine-maker: Jean-Pierre Cartier
• Combined vineyards: 23 hectares
• Production: 120,000 bottles
• Exports: 70%
• Take-away sales: 9-12 a.m., 2-6 p.m. By appointment over the weekend.
• Visits: By appointment

Wine selected:
Gigondas Cuvée Florence

• Grape Varieties: Grenache, Syrah
• Average vine age: 30 years
• Vineyard size: 9.91 hectares
• Soil type: Clay and limestone
• Average production: 12,695 bottles

Gigondas | Gigondas

Domaine Les Goubert

Cuvée Florence

Gigondas
APPELLATION GIGONDAS CONTRÔLÉE

Cette cuvée, millésime 1995, représente 12695 bouteilles, celle-ci porte le

RED RHONE WINE   N° 12502

S.C.E.A. JEAN PIERRE CARTIER PROPRIÉTAIRE RÉCOLTANT à GIGONDAS FRANCE

ALC. 13.5% BY VOL.   MIS EN BOUTEILLE AU DOMAINE   750 ml

PRODUCE OF FRANCE   LCF95

DOMAINE RASPAIL-AY

Gigondas | Gigondas

T he admirable Raspail-Ay estate produces a single red wine, a Gigondas of exceptional depth and dimension, which is regularly amongst the very finest produced in the village. Here is a very good example of the *vigneron* letting Nature get on with producing the finest fruit possible, and then giving the wine the time to make itself, unhurriedly, with the least intervention possible from him.

In the image of its maker   The *vigneron* in question is Dominique Ay, a man with a physique which mirrors that of his wine: full-bodied, powerful… and doubtless just as generous and warm. Ay is a direct descendant of Eugène Raspail, who founded the estate half a dozen generations ago. It was originally far bigger than it is today, but somewhere along the line it was quartered in order to accommodate four heirs equally, as French law requires. Raspail-Ay should not be confused with Château Raspail, twice its size, which was also part of the original estate but today does not produce wines of the same ambition and distinction. Dominique Raspail has been at the helm since taking over from his father François in 1982.

Healthy vines for perfect grapes   The estate's vineyards almost all lie around the elegant château, and have complementary soil characteristics, most consisting of clay and limestone, some of stony alluvial soil. They slope gently, and their situation at the foot of the Dentelles de Montmirail affords a degree of protection from excessive sunlight, mist, humidity and hailstorms. Aware of the importance of top-quality raw material, and thus by necessity healthy vines, Dominique Ay uses as little fertilizer as he can get away with, and only uses treatments against the vine's occasional ailments when absolutely necessary.
He is lucky in having enough cellar space to enable him to process the different arrivals of fruit unhurriedly, where many in the region are obliged to force their vinifications somewhat in order to free vats for the next arrivals of fruit. After the pickers have moved down the rows selecting the best bunches, the harvest is destalked and crushed and then loaded into closed cement vats, in which it ferments and macerates for 3 weeks. When all bacterial activity is over the wines are transferred to *foudre* for 16-18 months for ageing, after which bottling starts; this takes place in several stages as stock is required, there generally being 3 bottlings over a year. The wine is neither fined nor filtered before bottling.

Gigondas   Thanks to its unhurried vinification and ageing, and thanks to its not being tampered with before bottling, Dominique Ay's Gigondas is absolutely representative of the best that the village can produce: full-bodied, well-structured, rich and potent, with a fine blend of spicy fruitiness ever so lightly seasoned with the surrounding *garrigue*, it is a wine which has remarkable staying power in top vintages, and even in difficult ones improves over 8-10 years. A dish to bring out its qualities to the full? *Daube provençale*, recommends Monsieur Ay.

- Rosé wine: Gigondas
- Owner: Dominique Ay
- Wine-maker: Dominique Ay
- Oenologist: Gérard Philis
- Combined vineyards: 18 hectares
- Production: 75,000 bottles
- Exports: 50%
- Take-away sales: 9.00-12.30 a.m., 2.30-6.00 p.m.
- Visits: No

Wine selected:
Gigondas

- Grape Varieties: Grenache 70%, Syrah 15%, Clairette 9%, Mourvèdre 6%
- Average vine age: 40 years
- Vineyard size: 18 hectares
- Soil type: Clay and limestone, stones
- Average production: 60,000 bottles

Domaine Raspail-Ay

Récolté, élevé et mis en bouteille dans la cave du propriétaire par

E.A.R.L. **Dominique AY** - à GIGONDAS (Vaucluse) - France

Alc. 14% vol.   750 ml

PRODUIT DE FRANCE

L ouis Barruol is the heir to a 14-generation family tradition at the historic Château de Saint-Cosme, several hundred metres north of the village of Gigondas. Yet while the family are well known in the area the wine is little known on the international stage, for bottling on the estate has only recently recommenced. So pure and authentic are Barruol's wines, however, that Saint-Cosme is destined to become one of the great names of the southern Rhône.

A historic vineyard slope Saint-Cosme is the most ancient estate in the region. Lying on the site of a Gallo-Roman villa which very probably already had its own vineyard, the estate's existence in 1416 is attested by a document mentioning the granting by Jean de Châlon, Prince of Orange, of "land for the planting of vines on the Saint-Cosme slope". The Barruols' ancestors acquired it in 1490, and at the end of the 16th century built a splendid residence over existing cellars.

The slope covers 15 hectares and is looked down on by the 10th-century chapel dedicated to Saint Cosme, who shares with Saint Damien the responsibility of patron saint of the parish. The site is perfect for viticulture, and the Grenache, Syrah, Mourvèdre and Cinsault vines are immaculately tended. Louis Barruol tries to maintain a high vine age of at least 60 years, for this, he tells one, is the key to quality, particularly when it comes to Grenache. Pruning is severe in order to maintain low yields (as low as 25 hectolitres per hectare) and harvesting is never started until the grapes become overripe.

Purity of fruit, expression of terroir Barruol makes his wine without recourse to SO2 whenever possible in order to preserve the fruit's purity, and with minimum manipulation. Fermentation is conducted in concrete vats by the grapes' natural yeast, and maceration lasts some 40 days, with two sessions of foot-treading per day. Then the wine is transferred half to tank and half to cask (of which 50% are replaced annually) for a year's *élevage*, during which it is not racked, again to preserve the fruit's purity. At the end of the year it is bottled with neither fining nor filtration. The bottles then await purchasers in the estate's medieval cellars, which contain what are possibly the oldest fermentation vats in France, cut into the sandstone walls.

Gigondas Cuvée Valbelle Whenever the end of the growing season permits harvesting at sufficient *surmaturité* Barruol makes a second Gigondas, which is a selection of the wines of the oldest vines. Valbelle is matured exclusively in casks, half of which are new, the remainder having already served several times. Again there is neither SO2 nor racking. It is a dense wine, velvet of texture and extraordinarily rich, with a magnificent, smoky bouquet of pepper and ripe black fruit, and nuances of tobacco, leather or game, depending on the vintage and age of the bottle. A magnificent triumph of old vines and non-interventionism! Stuffed shoulder of lamb with a mature Valbelle (or indeed the excellent Cuvée Classique) will send even the most blasé gourmet into raptures!

- Other red wine: Gigondas Cuvée Classique
- Owner: Louis Barruol
- Wine-maker: Louis Barruol
- Combined vineyards: 15 hectares
- Production: 60,000 bottles
- Exports: 60%
- Take-away sales: Yes
- Visits: No

Wine selected:
Gigondas Cuvée Valbelle

- Grape Varieties: Grenache 70%, Syrah 30%
- Average vine age: 80 years
- Vineyard size: 4 hectares
- Soil type: Clay and limestone
- Average production: 12,000 bottles

CHATEAU
DE
SAINT COSME

1996   1996

"Valbelle"

GIGONDAS

Appellation Gigondas Contrôlée

13,5% vol.   75cl

Mis en Bouteille au Château

EARL BARRUOL Propriétaire Récoltant à Gigondas 84190 France

Product of France

DOMAINE SAINT-GAYAN

One of the oldest Gigondas estates is that of Saint-Gayan, which lies at the northern limit of the village's appellation, not far from Sablet. It is the property of Roger Meffre and his family, whose ancestors have been making wine there for nigh on 400 years. Today Saint-Gayan is one of the greatest names in Gigondas.

At home in an arid environment After half a century presiding over the destinies of Saint-Gayan Roger Meffre retired in 1993, handing over responsibility for the running of the estate to his son Jean-Pierre and daughter-in-law Martine. The family possesses 16 hectares of Gigondas and a further 24 of Rasteau, Châteauneuf-du-Pape, Côtes-du-Rhône and Vin de Pays, which provide them all told with some 1500 hectolitres per year.

The Gigondas vineyards lie on the gently-sloping plain around the house, where the soil is very poor and composed essentially of clay and limestone littered with stones from the Dentelles de Montmirail, with an important presence of compacted sand known as *safres* in places. The Grenache, Syrah and Mourvèdre vines which hug the ground and struggle to prosper in this arid terrain, frequently blasted by the Mistral wind, are of a very respectable average age of 50 years, and there are also scattered bands of centenarian vines to be found.

A permanent and visible presence during harvest The Meffres' Gigondas is one of the richest and sturdiest of the village. Not only is this high vine age a contributory factor to the wine's character, but moderate yields, attained by severe pruning, debudding and then green-harvesting where necessary, also play an essential role. Selection is of course necessary, obliging the Meffres like any serious vineyard owners to be permanently and visibly present during the harvest, failing which the tired pickers, backs aching, soon lose interest in discarding unripe or rotten grapes and cut anything and everything.

Vinified for maximum extraction The Gigondas is fermented in stainless steel and cement vats and macerated for a prolonged period of at least 3 weeks at a relatively high temperature for maximum extraction of its colour, tannin and aroma components. After *décuvage* the skins and pulp are pneumatically pressed and the press wine is added to the free-run wine. At that point the wines of the three varieties, which until then have been kept separate, are blended and spend the following two years in tank, followed by one year in *foudre*, before being bottled unfiltered in monthly sessions over the best part of the following year.

Gigondas The Meffres' very conservative cellar practices result in a dense garnet wine with a powerful and heady bouquet of red fruit and pepper with a touch of *garrigue*, which requires a good few years to open up completely. In the mouth its density, concentration, power and structure are utterly impressive, and its finish is no less so. As the years roll by (for Saint-Gayan is one of the longest-living Gigondas) aromas of truffle, earth and leather often emerge, making for a most enjoyable tasting. The complex and generous Saint-Gayan calls for a hearty game dish such as jugged hare, or duck with olives.

- Other red wines: Châteauneuf-du-Pape, Côtes-du-Rhône-Villages Rasteau, Côtes-du-Rhône, Vin de Pays de la Principauté d'Orange
- White wine: Côtes-du-Rhône
- Owner: G.F.A. de L'Oratory - Roger Meffre family
- Wine-maker: Jean-Pierre Meffre
- Oenologist: Gérard Philis
- Combined vineyards: 40 hectares
- Production: 200,000 bottles
- Exports: 50%
- Take-away sales: 9.00-11.45 a.m., 2.00-6.30 p.m.
- Visits: No

Wine selected: **Gigondas**

- Grape Varieties: Grenache 80%, Syrah 15%, Mourvèdre 5%
- Average vine age: 50 years
- Vineyard size: 16 hectares
- Soil type: Clay and limestone
- Average production: 60,000 bottles

Until the mid-1980s few had heard of Santa Duc, an estate producing what was no doubt good wine but selling it all off in bulk, like many others, to the *négoce*. Then with a change of generation came a change of ambition, and very quickly the name got around and the wine started to be talked about and favourably reviewed. It is no surprise to note that today Santa Duc is one of the most highly rated Gigondas producers.

Respect for the vineyard environment   Santa Duc has now been in the Gras family for four generations. When the young Yves Gras took over from his father Edmond in 1985 he had definite ideas about his role as grower and about the type of wine he wished to make. The vineyard was where his time should be spent, he felt, since no good wine is made with anything less than top-quality fruit, and like many of his generation he was convinced that his vines would produce the finest fruit only if cultivated in as natural and ecological way as possible. Respect for the vineyard environment therefore dictates all Santa Duc's viticultural operations, and today neither insecticides nor chemical fertilizers are used, and treatments are only carried out if the crop would be at risk were they not, and then very sparingly; in short, *lutte raisonnée*, which proscribes the unthinking, routine use of chemical products.

Top quality fruit only comes from low yields, so Yves goes out among the vines in July and enthusiastically lops off excess bunches. At harvest time he always waits until his crop is almost overripe before picking, for Grenache wines particularly need respectable alcohol levels, and fusses worriedly among his *vendangeurs* making sure that they are being sufficiently selective in the fruit they collect in their baskets.

The making of an authentic Gigondas   While Grenache naturally holds pride of place in his vineyard, Yves Gras cultivates a significant proportion of Mourvèdre, of which he is very fond, and some Syrah, for he is out to make 'authentic' Gigondas, of the firm, tannic and muscular sort, and these varieties contribute colour, tannin and bouquet to complement the Grenache's flesh and alcohol.

The family vineyards are very scattered, which makes for more complexity in the wines. Some are on the higher slopes, composed of poor sandy limestone, while the bulk are on flatter red clay below the village known as Les Hautes Garrigues. The former contribute finesse, elegance and *terroir* character, growers tell one, while the latter give body, warmth and bouquet.

Gigondas Prestige des Hautes Garrigues   Since 1989, in the finest years Yves Gras has produced a *cuvée* exclusively made from the Hautes Garrigues, which is a formidably rich, powerful and structured wine of around 15°, made for long ageing. This is made with selected Grenache and Mourvèdre, picked very late and vatted uncrushed without destemming, and then aged in new and one-year barrels for some 18 months before bottling. Thick in extract it may be, but it is nevertheless as fresh as one could wish. Prestige des Hautes Garrigues is a great Gigondas, which may be served with jugged hare with truffles.

• Other red wines:
Gigondas Tradition,
Côtes-du-Rhône,
Vin de Pays de la
Principauté d'Orange
• Owners:
Edmond & Yves Gras
• Wine-maker: Yves Gras
• Combined vineyards:
22 hectares
• Production:
130,000 bottles
• Exports: 80%
• Take-away sales:
Stock permitting
• Visits: By appointment

Wine selected:
**Gigondas Prestige
des Hautes Garrigues**

• Grape Varieties:
Grenache 80%,
Mourvèdre 20%
• Average vine age:
50 years
• Vineyard size:
3.5 hectares
• Soil type:
Clay and limestone
• Average production:
12,000 bottles

Prestige des Hautes Garrigues

GIGONDAS

Appellation Gigondas Contrôlée

Domaine Santa Duc

1996   1996

ALC 15% BY VOL   CONTENTS 750 ML

Mis en bouteille au Domaine

E.a.r.l. Gras Edmond et Fils Vignerons à 84190 Gigondas (Vaucluse) France

RED RHONE WINE - PRODUCE OF FRANCE

Château du Trignon

The Roux family at Château du Trignon have long been known both for the quality of their wines and for their innovative spirit, which has led them to much experimentation in vinification methods over the years. Success has enabled them to build a fine portfolio of holdings in a number of appellations, which is topped by their very good Gigondas.

Vineyard expansion and vinification experiments It was in 1895 that Etienne Roux and his son Joseph bought the 15-hectare Château du Trignon. Until the end of the 1950s it was polycultural, growing olives and various soft fruit as well as vines. In 1956 Joseph's son Charles and grandson André expanded their wine-making activities when they acquired land in the Rasteau, Sablet and Côtes-du-Rhône appellations, bringing their total vineyard holdings to 50 hectares. Shortly afterwards a new and very modern winery was built, and as early as 1960 the father-and-son team, working with Dr. Dufays of the Châteauneuf-du-Pape estate Domaine de Nalys, had perfected and were using the semi-carbonic maceration method, which produces richly fruity wines without the tannic structure acquired by the traditional method.

In 1991 Charles's grandson Pascal took over responsibility for the business. The Gigondas vineyards were increased by the addition of 15 hectares of prime land on the slopes of the Dentelles de Montmirail and, to complete the portfolio of southern-Rhône wines the Châteauneuf-du-Pape estate Domaine des Sénéchaux was acquired in 1993.

Improvements in the raw material The vatroom and vinification process have not monopolized the attentions of Pascal Roux to the exclusion of all else, for he has made large strides in the vineyard, improving the quality of his raw material thanks to a generally more organic viticultural regime. Weeds are kept at bay not with weedkiller but by hoeing, and the soil is enriched by organic manure. Yields are kept to levels compatible with quality by severe pruning, and the fruit is examined and rejected if necessary as the pickers go down the rows of vines.

In the vatroom all the red wines save the Gigondas are made by carbonic maceration with 12-16 days' vatting, which gives wines of beautiful purity and fruit for drinking within some 5 years of the vintage; the white wines are pressed pneumatically, left to settle at 15°C and fermented at 20-21°C.

Gigondas The two distinct types of terrain from which its grapes come give the Gigondas a fine, ample and generous nature, with great aromatic complexity. After some 6 years the superb bouquet of ripe red fruit, pepper, liquorice and hints of roast coffee presents an irresistible invitation to linger awhile over the glass before tipping back the dark liquid and savouring its succulence. Unlike its stablemates this wine is the result of a traditional vinification of partly-destemmed fruit over 18-25 days, with *élevage* in concrete and wooden casks of various sizes for 15 months. Lamb chops *à la provençale*, or even couscous, provide warmth and colour that the wine recognizes and appreciates.

- Other red wines: Côtes-du-Rhône-Villages Rasteau, Côtes-du-Rhône-Villages Sablet, Côtes-du-Rhône Cuvée du Bois des Dames, Côtes-du-Rhône
- White wines: Côtes-du-Rhône-Villages Sablet, Côtes-du-Rhône Viognier, Côtes-du-Rhône
- Owner: Pascal Roux
- Wine-maker: Bruno Gaspard
- Oenology: Laboratoire Rabot
- Combined vineyards: 62 hectares
- Production: 305,000 bottles
- Exports: 70%
- Take-away sales: 9-12 a.m., 2-7 p.m. Mon.-Sat.
- Visits: Yes

Wine selected:
Gigondas

- Grape Varieties: Grenache 65%, Syrah 20%, Mourvèdre/Cinsault 15%
- Average vine age: 40 years
- Vineyard size: 25 hectares
- Soil type: Sandy limestone, alluvial with stones
- Average production: 90,000 bottles

GRAND VIN DES CÔTES DU RHÔNE

CHÂTEAU DU TRIGNON
1997
GIGONDAS
APPELLATION GIGONDAS CONTRÔLÉE

MIS EN BOUTEILLE AU CHÂTEAU

S.C.E.A CHÂTEAU DU TRIGNON A GIGONDAS - 84190 - FRANCE

750 ML   ALC. 14% BY VOL

DOMAINE LA FOURMONE

The pretty village of Vacqueyras, which lies between Gigondas and Beaumes-de-Venise in some of France's most picturesque vineyard country, was upgraded from Côtes-du-Rhône Villages to its own *appellation contrôlée* in 1990. This had been on the cards for some time, thanks to the excellence of the wines of estates such as Domaine La Fourmone.

A well-known local personality La Fourmone is owned by Roger Combe and his family, whose ancestors have been in the region since 1634. Combe is a well-known local personality who speaks the Provençal language fluently and writes verse in it, and is fiercely proud of his origins. He produces not only a range of three red and one white Vacqueyras but also, under the L'Oustau Fouquet label, two Gigondas wines. His wine-making is thoroughly traditional. Grenache forms the backbone of the wines, which are completed with Syrah and, in the case of the more serious *cuvées*, Mourvèdre. Vines are tended by *lutte raisonnée*, a philosophy which is as ecological as possible yet which does not rule out the recourse to chemical treatments; these may be sparingly used if sufficient reflection has not come up with any other way of getting round a problem. The red-wine crop is left on its stalks and lightly crushed, and then spends approximately 10 days fermenting and macerating in cement vats before being run off for ageing, again in cement but with a subsequent passage in *foudre* in the case of the top *cuvées*. The solids are pressed *à l'ancienne* in a vertical press, enabling the addition of press wine if the short vatting period has not conferred on the wines sufficient structure. Finally bottling is carried out in anything up to 6 sessions over roughly a year.

A Vacqueyras for every occasion The three red Vacqueyras wines that Combe makes—or more exactly that his daughter Marie-Thérèse makes, for officially he has retired—have different vocations. The most serious is the *cuvée* called Les Ceps d'Or, which is only made in the finest years, from venerable Grenache vines, many of which are centenarian. This is a splendidly rich, deep and intensely-flavoured bottle, which attains perfection after a dozen years. The bulk of the house production goes to make the *cuvée* Sélection Maître de Chais, which while not possessing as much depth as the Ceps d'Or is all the same a fine, mouth-filling wine needing a half-dozen years in bottle. The lightest of the three is the Trésor du Poète.

Vacqueyras Trésor du Poète A combination of sandy limestone soil, favouring elegance and relative lightness, and a varietal blend excluding Mourvèdre and the structure and firmness that it brings to a blend, give birth to the exquisite 'Poet's Treasure', the lightest and most insouciant of the Combes' range. Fresh and spicily perfumed with a definite suggestion of raspberries, this is the perfect lunchtime Rhône wine, asking nothing but unhurried enjoyment from those who uncork it—and certainly not excessive analysis!—over simple fare such as roast poultry with garlic or grilled lamb cutlets.

- Other red wines: Vacqueyras Sélection Maître de Chais, Vacqueyras Les Ceps d'Or, Gigondas L'Oustau Fouquet Tradition, Gigondas Cuvée Cigaloun, Côtes-du-Rhône
- White wine: Vacqueyras Cuvée Fleurantine
- Owner: Roger Combe & Filles
- Wine-maker: Marie-Thérèse Combe
- Oenologist: M. Constantin
- Combined vineyards: 37 hectares
- Production: 225,000 bottles
- Exports: 10%
- Take-away sales: 9-12 a.m., 2-6 p.m.
- Visits: No

Wine selected:
Vacqueyras Trésor du Poète

- Grape Varieties: Grenache 85%, Syrah 15%
- Average vine age: 30 years
- Vineyard size: 8 hectares
- Soil type: Sand and limestone
- Average production: 30,000 bottles

TRÉSOR du POÈTE

DOMAINE la FOURMONE
VACQUEYRAS
APPELLATION VACQUEYRAS CONTRÔLÉE
RÉCOLTÉ ET MIS EN BOUTEILLES AU DOMAINE PAR
ROGER COMBE ET FILLES
E.A.R.L - VIGNERONS À 84190 VACQUEYRAS - VAUCLUSE - FRANCE - ℗ 04 90
PRODUCE OF FRANCE

DOMAINE LA GARRIGUE

On their huge Domaine La Garrigue the Bernard family make a small range of wines of uncompromising character, which demonstrate succinctly what 'traditional' wine-making is all about in the Vaucluse. The wines require time to come together in bottle, soften up and develop their bouquet, failing which their rigidity and structure can surprise the unsuspecting taster.

A continuing family concern Like numerous estates in the area this one is a family concern which has been passed down over several generations, and has been gradually built up to its present size over the years. Today La Garrigue is run by Maxime and Pierre, sons of the late Albert Bernard, along with their sisters, who look after the administrative side of things—a responsibility the importance of which can not be understated, so unceasing is the deluge of forms of all sorts to which the authorities submit France's harassed *vignerons*! Continuity in the future seems to be assured, for Maxime's son and daughter are learning the ropes on the estate and at wine school.

Aromatic intensity and terroir characteristics The Bernards are firm believers in the virtues of old vines, and maintain an average age of 40 years for their Grenache, Syrah, Cinsault and Mourvèdre. The plants are less productive, but the juice of their fruit is richer, and their roots are buried more deeply, enabling them to express a *terroir's* characteristics with greater definition. The bulk of the vineyard is formed by 3 blocks of 15 hectares around the house, with the remainder being fairly scattered; it lies partly on a stony plateau, partly on a clay plateau, and, unsurprisingly, the *garrigue* is all around!

Vinification could hardly be more traditional. The grapes, picked by hand and sorted in the vineyard, are left on their stalks and lightly crushed, and undergo extended fermentation and maceration in enamel-lined concrete vats. Ageing lasts at least 18 months, and at most a lot longer, for the wines are stored in concrete tanks until needed, which can mean a wait of 4 years or more. Then, when at last they are bottled, it is with neither fining nor filtration.

Vacqueyras Cuvée de l'Hostellerie The style of wine aimed for by the Bernards is perfectly illustrated by their Vacqueyras Cuvée de l'Hostellerie, so named because Pierre Bernard is proprietor of the Les Florets restaurant near Gigondas. A very dark, dense purple in colour, powerfully peppery and spiced on the nose, the Cuvée de l'Hostellerie assails the palate with its massive framework and lithe, muscular flesh. This is quintessential, traditional Vacqueyras, which can be safely forgotten in a corner of the cellar for a dozen years. It is the ideal wine for a cold winter's night, for serving with red meats and rich sauces such as *daube dauphinoise*.

- Other red wines: Vacqueyras, Gigondas
- White wine: Vacqueyras
- Rosé wine: Vacqueyras
- Owner: EARL A. Bernard & Fils
- Wine-maker: Pierre Bernard
- Oenologist: Christophe Coupez
- Combined vineyards: 65 hectares
- Production: 400,000 bottles
- Exports: 60%
- Take-away sales: 8.00-12.00 a.m., 2.00-7.30 p.m. By appt. on Sun.
- Visits: Yes

Wine selected:
Vacqueyras Cuvée de l'Hostellerie

- Grape Varieties: Grenache 75%, Syrah 25%
- Average vine age: 40 years
- Vineyard size: 3 hectares
- Soil type: Clay and stone
- Average production: 15,000 bottles

DOMAINE "LA GARRIGUE"

Cuvée de l'Hostellerie

VACQUEYRAS

APPELLATION VACQUEYRAS CONTROLEE

C. A. BERNARD & FILS PROPRIÉTAIRES-EXPLOITANTS - VACQUEYRAS
MIS EN BOUTEILLE A LA PROPRIÉTÉ

PRODUIT DE FRANCE

T he Vaucluse village of Vacqueyras, which was granted its own appellation in 1990, does not have the reputation of nearby Gigondas, whose wines are generally rather finer and less rustic. Yet of the several estates which stand out, one in particular is worthy of close attention: Château des Tours, lying between Sarrians and Jonquières, is making progressively finer wine as its young owner accumulates experience, and its output may already be described as exceptional.

The winery is built The young man in question is Emmanuel Reynaud, and when one knows that he is of the Reynaud dynasty of Château Rayas fame, all is explained. This is a family whose patriarch Louis long ago realized what was necessary to produce the best wine in the region, and passed down the message to his sons Jacques, who succeeded him at Rayas, and Bernard, Emmanuel's father.

Louis Reynaud acquired the Château des Tours estate (so named because of its small but very handsome twin-towered castle) just after the Second World War, as he did his other estate, Château de Fonsalette. He left it to Bernard, and for many years it produced a variety of crops which covered some 20 hectares of the 38 which comprise the estate; the grapes which were produced on the remaining land were taken to the cooperative. It was under the impulsion of the young Emmanuel, who had started working in 1980 beside his father, that a *cuverie* and cellars were built in 1989 and that the grape crop took on a different importance in the scheme of things.

Traditional methods and self-imposed discipline Having worked for a while with his late uncle Jacques, Emmanuel had seen just how things are done at Rayas, and duly started applying equally strict discipline to viticultural practices on the Vacqueyras estate. The vineyard, like Rayas, is planted almost entirely with Grenache, and is run along thoroughly traditional lines. Very strict limitation of yields is at the heart of viticultural policy—20 hectolitres per hectare is the average production figure—and fruit is always harvested very late, just slightly overripe, again as at Rayas. Only so is it possible for such rich, concentrated and aromatic wine to be produced.

All the bunches are left on their stalks for *cuvaison*, which takes place in stainless steel, and regular *remontages* help extract a maximum of colour, aroma and tannin from the cap of skins and stalks. Maturation takes place in concrete vats, with a few months' finishing in old wood, and the wines are then bottled with a light filtration.

Vacqueyras Reynaud's progress during the 1990s has been very apparent, which bodes well for Rayas and Fonsalette as well as Tours, for since his heirless uncle Jacques's death he has found himself in charge of all three. Château des Tours, dense, rich and magnificently aromatic, is destined to become highly *recherché*. It is capable of improving over 10-12 years, or even longer in the best vintages, and accompanies all the regional specialities; mutton *daube* or beef *paupiettes* do very well.

- Other red wines: Côtes-du-Rhône, Vin de Pays de Vaucluse (sold under the Domaine des Tours label)
- White wine: Vacqueyras
- Owner: Reynaud family
- Wine-maker: Emmanuel Reynaud
- Combined vineyards: 39 hectares
- Production: 186,000 bottles
- Exports: 80%
- Take-away sales: By appointment
- Visits: By appointment

Wine selected:
Vacqueyras

- Grape Varieties: Grenache 98%, Syrah 2%
- Average vine age: 30-70 years
- Vineyard size: 6 hectares
- Soil type: Clay and limestone
- Average production: 16,000 bottles

Vacqueyras | Sarrians

DOMAINE DE LA MORDORÉE

Until the 1980s the wines of Lirac had enjoyed little more than local popularity, as a result of the collective lethargy of the region's growers. In recent years however they have acquired wider renown thanks to the efforts of several estates, in particular Domaine de la Mordorée. La Mordorée has shown that the region is thoroughly capable of producing rich and flavoursome wines with some ageing potential, and its convincing performance has been duly noted and appreciated by the world's critics and Rhône-wine lovers.

A viable estate is created The estate's origins go back to 1974, when Francis Delorme's wife inherited some vines. Delorme, a businessman with his own firm, started learning about and making wine as a sideline. By 1986 he was ready to retire, and sold up. With the proceeds he decided to buy more vineyards in order to create a wine estate of a sufficiently large size to afford his two sons a decent living.
As well as buying more land, the existing buildings were extended and more modern equipment was acquired. Delorme's eldest son Christophe duly joined his father once he had left school, and there followed a fruitful period of discussion, experimentation and learning. Experimentation in the vineyard involved the cultivation of one parcel by biodynamics, eventually abandoned as insufficiently effective, the introduction of 'sexual confusion' of the Eudemis butterfly to prevent the hatching of the grapeworm, the grassing of the vineyards to favour deeper root systems... Respect for the soil and its micro-organisms and fauna is regarded by the Delormes as essential to healthy vines and thus juicy grapes.

For drinking young or laying down Yields are kept extremely low, and the fruit is only picked when perfectly ripe. The Delormes have a strong dislike of bitterness and astringency in wine, so all grapes are destalked before vinification, which takes place in stainless steel. They set out to make wines which may be enjoyed from the first year, yet which have decent ageing potential. The different varieties are always fermented together for maximum aroma preservation, at around 30-32°C, with regular *remontages*. Once the period of fermentation and maceration has lasted long enough the better red wines are run off into barrel, in which they enjoy a judiciously-judged *élevage* before being bottled, generally without filtration.

Lirac Cuvée La Reine des Bois Refering to the *mordorée*, or woodcock, the red 'Queen of the Woods' is a wine destined for laying down, and as such is only made in years when the Mourvèdre, contributing structure and colour, is of sufficient quality. Dark, concentrated and so fleshy that its soft tannin is barely perceptible, this is probably the finest red Lirac available today, and all the proof one could ask of the talent of Francis and Christophe Delorme. They have chosen the right direction and are pursuing it with single-minded determination. Stuffed veal's breast makes a persuasive suitor for La Reine des Bois.

- Other red wines: Lirac, Châteauneuf-du-Pape, Côtes-du-Rhône
- White wines: Lirac Cuvée La Reine des Bois, Lirac, Côtes-du-Rhône
- Rosé wine: Tavel
- Owners: Delorme family
- Oenologist: Noël Rabot
- Combined vineyards: 45 hectares
- Production: 240,000 bottles
- Exports: 80%
- Take-away sales: 8.00-12.00 a.m., 1.30-5.30 p.m.
- Visits: By appointment

Wine selected:
Lirac Cuvée La Reine des Bois

- Grape Varieties: Syrah 33%, Grenache 33%, Mourvèdre 34%
- Average vine age: 40 years
- Vineyard size: 25 hectares
- Soil type: Clay and silica
- Average production: 15,000 bottles

Tavel rosé has long enjoyed a reputation as France's best pink wine, with a full-bodied, dry and aromatic character very different to that of other French rosés. Whether the reputation is still merited is open to discussion, for the general standard today seems inconsistent and the wines too often lacking in body and typicity. The fault of modern oenological science? One of the finest Tavels, and certainly the best known, is that made by the Bez family on their large property Château d'Aquéria.

Demand from post-Prohibition America Aquéria is an imposing and beautiful 18th-century house surrounded by its vineyard, one of Tavel's largest. It was acquired in the 1920s in a state of neglect by Jean Olivier, who refurbished it and laid the foundations of its fine reputation. Olivier's son-in-law Paul de Bez continued his work after his death, and since 1984 the estate has been run by de Bez's son Vincent. Tavel has been very popular in the United States ever since the 1930s, a curious fact for which Jean Olivier may take all the credit. He, it appears, had a number of friends from New York and Boston who had visited his new estate and much enjoyed the wine. After the repeal of Prohibition in 1933 he sent them consignments, which were much appreciated by all their friends. Orders started coming back thick and fast, and Château d'Aquéria was one of the first French wines to be in regular demand from the newly-reopened market. Demand for it and for Tavel in general has remained firm ever since.

Vinification by the saignée method The Aquéria rosé is made by the *saignée* method, whereby it is macerated for a short period on its skins like a red wine, and run off them as soon as the required colour has been attained. Fermentation then takes place in stainless steel vats at a controlled low temperature of 18-20°C, which preserves aromatic freshness and reduces the risk of oxidation. The 6 grape varieties used are vinified two by two for greater aroma development, then blended together and aged for 6 months before bottling. When Vincent de Bez took charge he decided to block the malolactic fermentation, which changed the style towards crisper, less alcoholic wines from the mid-1980s. The wine nevertheless has all the power and flavour one would hope for from this appellation.

Tavel With 44 hectares of its vineyard producing fruit for its Tavel, the Aquéria production seems positively industrial compared with that of other estates in the region… and yet, paradoxically, here quantity and quality go hand in hand, producing sufficient bottles of this attractive orange-tinted pink wine to satisfy Tavel-lovers around the world. Aquéria's quality lies in its fine balance between its 13° alcohol, its freshness and its depth of flavour, giving a wine which is thirst-quenching yet will complement dishes such as lamb cooked with herbs, ratatouille and oriental food perfectly. This is a rosé which may be enjoyed outside the summer-holiday period!

- Red wine: Lirac
- White wine: Lirac
- Owners:
Vincent & Bruno de Bez
- Wine-maker:
Vincent de Bez
- Combined vineyards:
65 hectares
- Production:
360,000 bottles
- Exports: 35%
- Take-away sales:
8-12 a.m., 2-6 p.m.
- Visits: Yes

Wine selected:
Tavel

- Grape Varieties:
Grenache 45%,
Clairette 20%,
Cinsault 15%,
Mourvèdre 10%,
Bourboulenc 5%,
Syrah 5%
- Average vine age:
30 years
- Vineyard size:
44 hectares
- Soil type: Sand and clay
- Average production:
270,000 bottles

1997

APPELLATION TAVEL CONTROLÉE

Château d'Aqueria

AU CHÂTEAU

MIS EN BOUTEILLE

TAVEL

Jean OLIVIER, S.C.A., Producteur à TAVEL 30126, FRANCE

PRODUIT DE FRANCE

DOMAINE CORNE-LOUP

Vineyard workers fortunately have less to fear these days while out in the vines than they did in the Middle Ages. One part of the village of Tavel was regularly visited by wolves, and a look-out was therefore posted to watch for their arrival and warn everyone with a good loud blast of his horn. Domaine Corne-Loup, which owns vines in the said area, commemorates this important personage with its name, although these days nothing more fearsome than the odd rabbit is likely to way-lay its vineyard hands!

A standard-bearer for the village Jacques Lafond, like his father before him, used to deliver his crop to the local co-operative, but ceased doing so in 1966. After a decade of selling in bulk he started bottling on the property in 1976, and has not looked back since. Today his estate covers 44 hectares, of which 27 are in the Tavel appellation and the rest make principally red and white Côtes-du-Rhône, and also provide a little red Lirac.

One of the standard-bearers of Tavel rosé, producing a wine which is a delight to behold and to taste with its light ruby colour and scintillating, fruity flavour, Corne-Loup is not made any differently to the great majority of Tavels, yet it stands out in any comparative tasting.

The right grape variety for each parcel The difference no doubt lies in a number of factors. Selection of vine varieties and rootstock to the soils, and careful, respectful growing habits play their role. Over the years much care has gone into planting the numerous parcels, which are spread all over the Tavel appellation and present a certain geological diversity; the soils are generally of sand and red clay mixed with calcareous debris, covered with a layer of quartzite *galets roulés* or flat stones. Selecting the right grape variety for each plot is naturally of great importance for the vine's performance and the wine's long-term quality.

Vinification by the saignée method Selection of the raw material and careful vinification are also all-important. The harvest is by hand, which enables a quality control in the vineyard. The grapes are entirely destalked before vatting, which takes place in stainless steel and enamel-lined vats. They are macerated at a cool 16-18°C for 24 hours, to extract just the required degree of colour, and the liquid is then run off the skins and slowly fermented. In common with nearly all producers these days the malolactic fermentation is blocked, in order to preserve the wine's vivacity. The wine is then bottled with no further ado, without any loss of its delicious freshness.

Tavel Corne-Loup is perhaps the darkest-coloured Tavel, a fact which might be explained by the unusually large proportion of black grapes (including 10% of the colour-imparting Syrah) in the mix. It has a fresh aroma of violets and a fine rich flavour of red fruit, very good balance between its alcohol and acidity, and a long, clean finish. Like all rosé it is best drunk young, although this wine loses its fruit and freshness somewhat more slowly than most others. At table, served at 12-14°C, it is perfect with *charcuterie*, a gratin of skate *à la provençale* or rabbit cooked with mustard *à la dijonnaise*.

- Red wines:
Lirac, Côtes-du-Rhône
- White wine:
Côtes-du-Rhône
- Owner: Jacques Lafond
- Wine-maker:
Jacques Lafond
- Oenologist: Noël Rabot
- Combined vineyards: ·
44 hectares
- Production:
226,000 bottles
- Exports: 40%
- Take-away sales: Yes
- Visits:
8-12 a.m., 2-6 p.m.

Wine selected:
Tavel

- Grape Varieties:
Grenache 65%,
Cinsault 15%,
Syrah 10%,
Mourvèdre, Clairette and
Carignan 10%
- Average vine age:
35 years
- Vineyard size:
27 hectares
- Soil type:
Sand, red clay, quartzite
and flat stones
- Average production:
150,000 bottles

PRIEURÉ DE MONTÉZARGUES

Some Tavel rosés, those of roundness and depth, are best drunk with food, while others, the lighter and fruitier in style, are sufficiently delicate and crisp for enjoying on their own. The Tavel made at the Prieuré de Montézargues, a gloriously perfumed, crisp and tasty rosé to equal any in France, sits astride the two styles.

An appeal for royal protection Things are somewhat calmer today at the *prieuré* than they apparently were in the past: a proclamation of Royal Protection dated 1675 refers to "disturbances and damage" caused by soldiers from the nearby garrison of Château Saint-André, who availed themselves of the priory's lands for hunting and pasturing their livestock. The prior, one Sieur Estival, used his connections with the Secretary of State Louvois and successfully sought Louis XIV's protection for the ecclesiastical lands.

The priory's history in fact dates back to at least the 12th century, when it housed monks of the Grandmont order. Today the handsome edifice, lying snugly at the foot of the Montagne Noire and surrounded by its vines, is owned by the Allauzen family. The late Louis Allauzen ran it as a one-man show, selling most of his wine in bulk to the local merchants. Nowadays his children work as a team, refining their methods and carefully crafting their one wine. Needless to say it is now bottled on site—a prerequisite to quality—and finds its way in small quantities as far afield as Japan, Australia and the U.S.A.

Organic viticulture and cool fermentations All possible measures are taken to produce as fine a rosé as the land will permit. Viticulture is as organic as possible, along the *lutte raisonnée* philosophy which requires careful analysis of all the options before resorting to the use of any chemical treatments. Once careful observation has established that it is time to harvest, this is done manually, and on arrival at the vatroom the fruit is tipped into stainless steel tanks for an initial 24 hours of maceration, the temperature maintained at a low level to prevent the onset of fermentation. The juice is then bled off and the remaining fruit gently pressed in a pneumatic Bucher, before all is run into large glass-lined concrete vats to ferment at 18-20°C.

Bottling takes place from spring onwards over the following year, in some 5 stages. While awaiting this operation the wine is kept underground at a cool temperature and its malolactic fermentation blocked, which ensures that the wine retains sufficient freshness and fruitiness.

Tavel The Prieuré de Montézargues Tavel is a delightful medium-deep pink colour with a slightly orange hue. On the palate it is deceptively light—it does not give the impression of containing 13° of alcohol—and fresh, with very attractive blackcurrant and strawberry aromas, and its perfect balance makes the wine irresistible. Excellent aperitif though it might be, it also makes a fine partner for a salad of smoked trout and wild rice.

- Owners:
Allauzen-Lucenet family
- Wine-makers:
Allauzen-Lucenet family
- Oenologist: Noël Rabot
- Combined vineyards:
34 hectares
- Grape Varieties:
Grenache 51%,
Cinsault 15%,
Syrah 9%,
Mourvedre 8%,
Carignan 6%,
Clairette 5%,
Picpoul 3%,
Bourboulenc 3%
- Average vine age:
30 years
- Soil type:
Sand and quartzite stones
- Production:
190,000 bottles
- Exports: 12%
- Take-away sales: Yes
- Visits: By appointment

DOMAINE DES BERNARDINS

The pretty Vaucluse village of Beaumes-de-Venise has its very own vinous speciality, the sweet, aromatic Muscat de Beaumes-de-Venise. A handful of estates make and sell this *vin doux naturel* themselves, while the vast majority of the village's growers deliver their crop of Muscat grapes to the local cooperative. One of the handful, producing an excellent 'old style' Muscat, is the Domaine des Bernardins.

The decline and renaissance of a local tradition Like many villages in the area, Beaumes has made wine since Roman times, and in the 1870s its vineyards, like nearly all others, suffered the ravages of Phylloxera, which almost consigned its long viticultural tradition to history. The production of *vin doux naturel* is thought to date back to the beginning of the 19th century, yet in the post-Phylloxera decades, growers having planted other more profitable and less disease-prone crops, Muscat vines were a rare sight.

It was Louis Castaud of Domaine des Bernardins who first raised the alarm at the gradual disappearance of this village tradition, and thanks to whose efforts the wine won *appellation contrôlée* status in 1943. A *cave coopérative* was founded 13 years later, and small growers could again hope to earn a living from Muscat. The surface area under that variety slowly began to increase…

At Les Bernardins Louis Castaud was eventually succeeded by his son Pierre, who took retirement in 1976 and handed over to his daughter and son-in-law, Jean Maurin. Today their own daughter and her English husband Andrew Hall are progressively taking over responsibilities.

Overripe grapes and halted fermentation Nearly all Muscat de Beaumes-de-Venise is made from the Muscat blanc à petits grains. The grapes are picked when almost overripe, crushed, separated from their skins and then fermented in stainless steel at temperatures ranging from a little more than 20°C to as low as 6°C. Domaine des Bernardins has always been the most traditional of the village's estates, using 25% Muscat noir à petits grains, which gives a fuller body and a more golden colour than the Muscat blanc, and fermenting at a little over 20°C for a month. The fermentation is halted by the addition of alcohol before all the sugar is fermented out, and the wine is then kept in vat for a few months before bottling and sale.

Muscat de Beaumes-de-Venise The Domaine des Bernardins little resembles the run-of-the-mill 'technological' Muscat made today. A fine amber-gold in colour, heavy, rich and rounded on the palate, its grapey aromas are somewhat dominated by its unctuous sweetness, and hints of almond and oxidation are also detectable. It needs several years in bottle to develop its bouquet and attain the ideal balance, and its makers claim it improves for up to 20 years. This Muscat is versatile at table, and proves a well-suited partner for foie gras, Roquefort cheese and even chocolate dishes.

• Red wines:
Côtes-du-Rhône-Villages Beaumes-de-Venise,
Côtes-du-Rhône Les Balmes
• Rosé wine:
Côtes-du-Rhône Les Balmes
• Owners:
M. and Mme. Castaud-Maurin &
M. and Mme. Hall
• Wine-maker:
Andrew Hall
• Combined vineyards:
22 hectares
• Production:
120,000 bottles
• Exports: 15%
• Take-away sales:
9-12 a.m., 2-5 p.m.
(6 p.m. closing in summertime)
• Visits: No

Wine selected:
Muscat de Beaumes-de-Venise

• Grape Varieties:
Muscat blanc à petits grains 75%,
Muscat noir à petits grains 25%
• Average vine age:
25 years
• Vineyard size:
15 hectares
• Soil type:
Sand and limestone
• Average production:
66,000 bottles

1998

que bèn béura ... diéu veìa

PRODUCE OF FRANCE

Muscat
de Beaumes de Venise

VIN DOUX NATUREL

APPELLATION MUSCAT DE BEAUMES DE VENISE CONTROLÉE

Muscat de Beaumes et le Perigoulet
béuraï à la régalade

Lou bon Muscat de Baume de Venise
Alor sé chourlo à la ...

Mireille, Opéra Gounod Air

Mireio, cant ...

DOMAINE des BERNARDINS

MISE D'ORIGINE

CAVE CASTAUD, PROPRIÉTAIRE A BEAUMES-DE-VENISE (VAUCLUSE) FRANCE

Imp. Rullière Libeccio

DOMAINE DE COYEUX

A mong the few estates which produce, bottle and sell their own Muscat de Beaumes-de-Venise, one of the finest, and certainly that with the highest profile thanks to its size and the dynamism of its charming proprietor, is Domaine de Coyeux. Here Yves Nativelle makes a Muscat of beautiful purity, fragrance and elegance, in a modern style very different to that of the more traditional estates.

From business to wine-making Nativelle bought the estate in the late 1970s. His background could hardly have been more different to that of the other growers in the region, coming as he did from a job in Paris working in marketing with Rhône-Poulenc, yet with single-minded determination he set about his new challenge, no doubt aided by having the outsider's perspective and fresh eye. Coyeux at the time was much smaller, and its owner sold his produce to the co-operative. Today this magnificent estate covers 125 hectares, and its wine-making facilities are, naturally, thoroughly modern and well-equipped for their task, which includes making Gigondas and Beaumes-de-Venise red wines.

Exceptional viticultural conditions The vineyard lies in one single block on an elevated plateau at 260 metres, at the feet of the Dentelles de Montmirail. The soil is deep, fertile and rich in oligo-elements, and this fertility, restrained by the altitude, provides exceptional conditions for the development of slow-ripening varieties such as the Muscat. The altitude also greatly enhances the vines' sanitary condition.
Nativelle conducts his vineyard along thoroughly natural lines, keeping it free of weeds by manual labour and using organic soil enrichment. Yields are kept down to around 28 hectolitres per hectare by crop-thinning, and the fruit is gathered by successive passages, in order to enable everything to ripen sufficiently.

Protecting the Muscat's delicate aromas Once the fruit has arrived at the winery it is given a short fermentation of 7-9 days in stainless steel, at a very low temperature of 6-10°C for maximum protection of the Muscat's delicate aromas. Then comes the moment for the *mutage*, the addition of alcohol obtained from the distillation of *marc*, which kills the yeast and gives the wine an alcohol level of 15% by volume, while there remain some 110 grams of unfermented sugar left. Different blendings are then carried out between the vats of fruit of similar ages, similar parcel orientation and similar harvest dates. The definitive blending of these working blends takes place near the end of February, following which the wine is aged for one year in stainless steel and then for 6-18 months in bottle.

Muscat de Beaumes-de-Venise The net result of this rapid, cold fermentation is a brilliant, light-gold wine of supreme aromatic purity and definition and great elegance. Lighter in body, a little less sweet and less complex than more traditionally-made examples, its exquisite freshness and irresistible grapey flavour set it apart. Yves and Catherine Nativelle recommend sipping it alongside foie gras, blue cheese, or desserts such as red fruit gratin, sabayone, pineapple or apple in a warm puff-pastry, sorbets... The list is long!

- Red wines:
Gigondas,
Côtes-du-Rhône-Villages
Beaumes-de-Venise
- Owners:
Yves & Catherine Nativelle
- Oenologist:
Alain Benquet
- Combined vineyards:
70 hectares
- Production:
330,000 bottles
- Exports: 45%
- Take-away sales:
8-12 a.m., 2-6 p.m.
- Visits: By appointment

Wine selected:
Muscat de Beaumes-de-Venise

- Grape Variety:
Muscat blanc à petits grains
- Average vine age:
30 years
- Vineyard size:
50 hectares
- Soil type: Triassic
- Average production:
250,000 bottles

DOMAINE BRESSY-MASSON

The village of Rasteau, lying on an elevation with a fine view over the plain towards the Dentelles de Montmirail, is one of the 16 'named' Côtes-du-Rhône villages, and the source of many a fine, powerful and deeply-flavoured red wine. It also has its own speciality, a *vin doux naturel* bearing the village name, made in either white or red form principally with Grenache grapes. The Bressy family have always made a speciality of this fortified wine, and for a half-century have also made some of the best unfortified wines in the village.

A pioneering family Curiously, women wine-makers are much thinner on the ground in the Rhône Valley than in Bordeaux and Burgundy, yet the highly competent Marie-France Masson, née Bressy, distinguishes herself, aided by her husband Thierry, in perpetuating standards on the family estate, which was founded by her grandfather Marius Bressy with some 10 hectares of vineyard.

Marius was one of the first to make a *vin doux*, starting in 1932, and a few years later he and his son Emile decided to put a quantity aside each year to see how it would age. The wine acquired an unexpected smoothness and a fine, nutty flavour, and they christened their innovation with the Spanish word *rancio*, which loosely means maderized. For decades this was a house speciality, made by no one else. Emile was one of the first to bottle his own wines, starting in 1949, and he acquired a further 20 hectares of land over the years. However in 1976 his untimely death at the age of 65 left his wife, who had not been involved, completely helpless. Marie-France put aside her literary studies to help out, and Thierry, then her fiancé and fresh out of accountancy school, headed for Macon to learn about wine-making.

The vintages succeed each other That all seems long ago now. Marie-France herself attended a wine-making course at the nearby Suze-La-Rousse University, and in the intervening years they have progressively modernized the facilities, investing in a cooling machine, a press, a destemmer... and have fitted out a tasting cellar in which to greet clients.

Today 22 of their 33 hectares are planted with Grenache, and 6 of these are plantings dating back at least to the last war, giving superlative raw material for the *vins doux naturels* and the top wine, named Cuvée Paul Emile, which is generally harvested at 20 hectolitres per hectare. Naturally the Grenache needs balancing with other varieties, and the vineyards include Syrah, Mourvèdre, Carignan and Cinsault, with Viognier, Grenache Blanc and Clairette to make the white wines.

Rasteau Cuvée Paul Emile In a persuasive display of the quality of the Rasteau vineyards and their suitability to the Grenache, the deeply-coloured Cuvée Paul Emile offers up a powerful bouquet of black fruit and a rich, spicy mouthful with a distinctly animal character, with very fine middle-mouth development and finish. It has the tannin necessary for 6-8 years' development, and a few years give it nuances of chocolate, kirsch and even a hint of peppermint. This wine has all the character one could wish for, and makes a fine partner for venison stew.

Côtes-du-Rhône Villages | Rasteau

- Other red wines: Côtes-du-Rhône-Villages Rasteau, Côtes-du-Rhône, Rasteau Vin Doux Naturel Rouge
- White wines: Côtes-du-Rhône, Rasteau Vin Doux Naturel Doré, Rasteau Vin Doux Naturel Rancio
- Owner: Marie-France Masson
- Wine-maker: Thierry Masson
- Oenologist: Nicolas Constantin
- Combined vineyards: 33 hectares
- Production: 200,000 bottles
- Exports: 15%
- Take-away sales: 9 a.m.- 7.30 p.m.
- Visits: Yes

Wine selected:
**Rasteau
Cuvée Paul Emile**

- Grape Varieties: Grenache 60%, Syrah 30%, Mourvèdre 10%
- Average vine age: 80 years
- Vineyard size: 2 hectares
- Soil type: Clay and limestone
- Average production: 8,000 bottles

DOMAINE MARCEL RICHAUD

The village of Cairanne is the source of much delicious wine, and is perhaps the finest of those Côtes du Rhône 'named' villages which do not yet have their own *appellation contrôlée*. Indeed the fact that it does not is scandalous. A taste of Marcel Richaud's wine should convince even the most blinkered I.N.A.O. authority…

A break with family tradition The short, silver-haired and voluble Richaud is not one for following the crowd. He forms definite ideas on things and follows them through, and it is this independence and intelligence as much as anything else which has brought him success. Born into a family who had been members of the cooperative back to his great-grandfather's time, Richaud decided while at school that that way would not be for him, and started making his own wine as soon as his schooldays were over in 1974.

He started off with rented vines, making the wine in a borrowed cellar. Lack of formal training was probably an advantage, for with an obvious feel for his vines and the different qualities that the different parcels of land could give, he gradually progressed in his wine-making, and was soon crafting wines of great purity, complexity and class. As vintage succeeded vintage and the wine sold well he rented more land, then was in a position to buy some himself…

A duty to safeguard typicity Success has not gone to Richaud's head. He finds it unhealthy that good growers are now lauded as artists, and reprehensible that so many, obsessed with earning critical success, lack the courage to make the sort of wine they really like, choosing instead to make highly-extracted, heavily-oaked 'competition' wines. A grower has a moral duty to safeguard the typicity of his region and its wines, in order that the consumer, broaching a bottle far away, can imagine himself back there. He personally keeps a low profile, working hard in his vineyards, for only with intimate experience of them can one understand them, and thus obtain regularity in quality year after year, and progress even in the difficult years.

Delicious from the outset Richaud likes to make wines which are good to drink from the outset, yet which at the same time have the wherewithal to improve in elegance and harmony. Perfect fruit is naturally a prerequisite, harvested only when it is properly ripe, and careful vinification by vineyard-parcel and variety is nothing more than common sense. Unusually in the region, he does not like wood of any kind, and all his wines are made and then aged in cement vats. However, with typical open-mindedness, in early 1999 he was toying with the idea of acquiring some casks to see what they could contribute to the ageing of his top *cuvée*, L'Ebrescade…

Cairanne L'Ebrescade The land where Cairanne and its neighbour Rasteau rub shoulders is great viticultural terrain, and it is here that Richaud's oldest Grenaches grow, which form the basis of his cuvée L'Ebrescade. Supple in the mouth and richly fruity, a blend of plum, liquorice and spice with a subtle tannic structure, this *cuvée* has finesse and elegance in abundance, and is an eloquent demonstration of Marcel Richaud's way of thinking. Just the wine for fillet of beef with *marchand au vin* sauce.

- Other red wines: Côtes-du-Rhône-Villages Cairanne, Côtes-du-Rhône-Villages Cairanne Cuvée Les Estranbords, Côtes-du-Rhône, Vin de Pays
- White wine: Côtes-du-Rhône-Villages Cairanne
- Owner: Marcel Richaud
- Wine-maker: Marcel Richaud
- Oenologist: Bruno Sabatier
- Combined vineyards: 50 hectares
- Production: 160,000 bottles
- Exports: 25%
- Take-away sales: Weekdays, 9-12 a.m., 2-6 p.m.
- Visits: By appointment

Wine selected:
Cairanne L'Ebrescade

- Grape Varieties: Grenache 60%, Syrah/Mourvèdre 40%
- Average vine age: 40 years
- Vineyard size: 4 hectares
- Soil type: Clay and limestone
- Average production: 10,000 bottles

Côtes-du-Rhône Villages | Cairanne

DOMAINE
RICHAUD

PRODUIT DE FRANCE

CUVÉE
l'Ebrescade

1995
Cairanne
Côtes du Rhône Villages
APPELLATION CÔTES DU RHÔNE VILLAGES CONTRÔLÉE
MIS EN BOUTEILLE AU DOMAINE - MARCEL RICHAUD, VIGNERON, F 84290 CAIRANNE FRANCE

N ot for the Alarys a quiet life making good, saleable, easy-drinking Côtes-du-Rhône every year, which the Vaucluse climate indeed permits with not much effort from the grower. This is a family which is always striving for self-improvement, always trying out new ideas and methods in the pursuit of added complexity and personality. L'Oratoire Saint-Martin produces Cairanne and Côtes-du-Rhône of the quality of much more prestigious appellations with far more serious price tags.

Silkworms, Madder and the vine Today Bernard Alary's sons Frédéric and François run L'Oratoire Saint-Martin, which is not to be confused with Domaine Alary, owned by Daniel and Denis Alary, the two being the result of the division of the one original estate in 1983. The Alary family tree attests to the family's presence in the Vaucluse département over 10 generations, during which time they have had a number of occupations. In the second half of the 19th century the great-grandfather bred silkworms for the Cairanne silk factory, and cultivated not the vine but *garance*, the Madder plant which was used for making the red dye which coloured the French army's trousers during the Great War. The invention of nylon and the Army's decision to change the colour of their trousers was a double blow, yet the great-grandfather nevertheless fortunately had his previous occupation of *vigneron* to fall back on.

Improving on a fine reputation The estate's wines were always highly reputed in Bernard Alary's time, yet through their constant pursuit of greater quality Frédéric and François have made great strides. All 25 hectares of vineyard lie in the Cairanne commune. They are worked ecologically, with just very sparing use of organic manure, and all the necessary measures are taken to produce yields compatible with quality wine; indeed the very severe pruning, green harvesting and leaf-stripping have given them a 10-year average production figure of 38 hectolitres per hectare, Cairanne and Côtes-du-Rhône appellations combined, whereas the law allows 42 and 50 hls/ha respectively.

The manually-harvested crop is examined on a sorting table and then transferred by gravity to the open vats of concrete or stainless steel in which the red wines are to ferment. The whites go straight into oak barrels for their vinification. Since 1996 the property has been equipped with a *pigeage* machine mounted on overhead rails, and once the red fermentations are under way, by forcing the cake of solids down into the liquid the brothers have been able to achieve a better extraction of the wines' tannin and colour.

Cairanne Haut-Coustias Recent innovations include a white Viognier wine, and some Muscat à Petits Grains has been planted to blend with this eventually. A *vin de paille* of Marsanne or Clairette is also on the drawing-board. Choosing which of the estate's three Cairanne reds one prefers is not easy, yet the Haut-Coustias, made only in fine years, proclaims its quality loud and clear. Lightly toasted and redolent of leather, spice and liquorice, this is a splendid wine to serve with hare *à la royale*, or a lamb ragout with thyme.

• Other red wines:
Cairanne Réserve
des Seigneurs,
Cairanne Cuvée Prestige,
Côtes-du-Rhône
• White wines:
Cairanne Haut-Coustias,
Côtes-du-Rhône
• Owners:
Frédéric & François Alary
• Wine-makers:
Frédéric & François Alary
• Combined vineyards:
25 hectares
• Production:
100,000 bottles
• Exports: 55%
• Take-away sales: Yes
• Visits:
8-12 a.m., 2-7 p.m.

Wine selected:
Cairanne Haut-Coustias

• Grape Varieties:
Mourvèdre 50%,
Syrah 30%,
Grenache 20%
• Average vine age:
50 years
• Vineyard size:
2 hectares
• Soil type:
Clay and limestone
• Average production:
6,000 bottles

Côtes-du-Rhône Villages | Cairanne

DOMAINE
DE L'ORATOIRE SAINT-MARTIN

HAUT-COUSTIAS

CAIRANNE

CÔTES DU RHÔNE VILLAGES
APPELLATION CÔTES DU RHÔNE VILLAGES CONTRÔLÉE
1996

Alc. 13% by Vol.   750 ml
MIS EN BOUTEILLE AU DOMAINE
F & F ALARY GAEC ST MARTIN - PROPRIÉTAIRES-VIGNERONS A CAIRANNE FRANCE

PRODUCT OF FRANCE

DOMAINE PÉLAQUIÉ

Along with Gigondas, Cairanne and Chusclan, the village of Laudun was one of the four originals to be awarded the new Côtes-du-Rhône-Villages appellation in 1953, with the right to feature its name on the label. Today Laudun and its neighbour Chusclan, both situated in the Gard département on the Rhône's right bank, find themselves somewhat overshadowed by the more famous Vaucluse villages, and nearly all the growers deliver their grapes to the cooperatives. Yet at Laudun there are a handful of estates which make and bottle their own produce, which can be very good... particularly good even, in the case of Domaine Pélaquié.

Joseph Pélaquié's legendary red wines The Pélaquié family have cultivated the vine at Saint-Victor-la-Coste—a stone's throw away, but benefiting from the Laudun appellation—since the 16th century. The village *cave coopérative* was founded by Joseph Pélaquié and others in 1921, and Joseph was famous for his huge red wines, produced, as John Livingstone-Learmonth recounts it in the excellent *The Wines of the Rhône*, by a good month's vatting on the skins and 2-4 years in cask. On his death in 1976 his grandsons Luc and Emmanuel took over responsibilities, and modified the wine-making somewhat to take into account the lighter style demanded by the modern consumer.

Together the two brothers set about expanding the estate, which today covers 78 hectares and includes vineyards in nearby Lirac and Tavel. Luc, whose has been alone at the helm since his brother's premature death, now finds himself with perhaps the highest profile in the Laudun region, for although the appellation's 3 cooperatives between them produce over 95% of its wine, for quality they are not in the same league.

Fine whites in an ocean of reds The quality of Domaine Pélaquié wines lies in the raw material, which is never harvested until perfectly ripe and which is picked by hand, with the exception of the Côtes-du-Rhône generic wines. Destalking is systematic, and stainless steel is the favoured medium for vinification and ageing. The red wines and the rosés are deliciously fruity, elegant and fresh, with commendable depth of flavour. However it is perhaps his white wines which are closest to Luc Pélaquié's heart.

In this region noted for its reds and rosés, Laudun in fact has a reputation for its whites which goes back at least as far as the 17th century. The explanation generally given for the quality of the whites is the soil make-up, which has a higher sand content than the lands east of the Rhône.

Laudun The Pélaquiés have long favoured Clairette as the basis for their white wine, because of its marked perfume. However its other traits are low acidity and high alcohol, and it is therefore best blended with other, complementary varieties, which in the case of Luc Pélaquié's white Laudun means Bourboulenc, Grenache Blanc, Viognier and Roussanne. The resulting wine, pale gold with green glints, is delightfully perfumed and fresh, with sufficient roundness and depth of flavour to justify its presence at table, in the company of most fish or white-meat dishes. This is certainly one of the finer white wines from the southern Rhône Valley.

- Other white wines: Côtes-du-Rhône Viognier, Côtes-du-Rhône
- Red wines: Côtes-du-Rhône-Villages Laudun, Lirac, Côtes-du-Rhône
- Rosé wines: Tavel, Lirac
- Owner: G.F.A. du Grand Vernet
- Wine-maker: Luc Pélaquié
- Oenologist: M. Ganichot
- Combined vineyards: 78 hectares
- Production: 400,000 bottles
- Exports: 20%
- Take-away sales: 9-12 a.m., 2-6 p.m. (closed Sundays)
- Visits: By appointment

Wine selected:
Laudun

- Grape Varieties: Clairette Blanche 55%, Viognier 15%, Bourboulenc 10%, Grenache Blanc 10%, Roussanne 10%
- Average vine age: 20 years
- Vineyard size: 13 hectares
- Soil type: Clay and sand
- Average production: 60,000 bottles

DOMAINE PÉLAQUIÉ

1997

LAUDUN

CÔTES DU RHÔNE VILLAGES
APPELLATION CÔTES DU RHÔNE VILLAGES CONTRÔLÉE

MIS EN BOUTEILLE AU DOMAINE

LUC ET BÉNÉDICTE PÉLAQUIÉ S.C.E.A. SAINT-VICTOR-LA-COSTE 30290 LAUDUN FRANCE • PRODUCE OF FRANCE

For many years the *cave coopérative* of the small village of Sablet was the shop window for the local wines, and rare were the growers who sold their own produce directly to clients. Today that is not the case, for a handful of ambitious estates have stolen the limelight with wine of very good quality which they sell in bottle to a private clientele and to French and foreign retailers and restaurants. The estate which has made the most progress in recent years is undoubtedly Domaine de Piaugier.

From bulk to bottle Piaugier is the property of Jean-Marc and Sophie Autran. Heir to a family viticultural tradition going back several generations, Autran makes his wine in cellars in the centre of Sablet built by his grandfather Alphonse Vautour in 1947. After taking over in 1985, with the help of his father the young man set about adding to the family vineyards and started bottling the estate's produce. The cellar built by Vautour soon became too small, and the two men enlarged it in 1995.

Autran rapidly displayed a sure hand with his pure, fruity and harmonious wines, and the French press were not slow to 'discover' him. Consecration of a sort came in 1990 with his being selected as *Vigneron* of the Year by the magazine *Gault & Millau*.

Raw material of great diversity and quality Autran has a fine estate to exploit: Piaugier comprises 30 hectares of vineyard, of which almost half is appellation Côtes-du-Rhône, and the remainder, with the exception of 3.66 hectares of Gigondas, is Côtes-du-Rhône-Villages Sablet. These vineyards have the great advantage of being very dispersed, and lie over several different types of soil—clay/silt/sand, clay/limestone, sand/gravel—presenting characteristics to suit each of the 6 grape varieties planted. Grenache naturally forms the basis of the wines, with complementary colour, backbone, aroma and freshness being added by Syrah, Mourvèdre, Counoise, Cinsault and Carignan. The vines, planted at a density of 4,000 plants per hectare, are 20-45 years old, which is generally considered to be the prime of life.

The great strides of recent years Vinification of the red wines aims resolutely at the *vin de garde* style. The grapes are neither crushed nor destemmed, and are fermented and macerated at 28-30°C in concrete vats for 1 week (Côtes-du-Rhône) or 3 weeks (Sablet and Gigondas). Subsequent ageing is again in concrete, and bottling is then carried out in one go without filtration.

Besides his red wines Autran makes a delicious white Sablet by skin maceration and vinification in 2-year-old barrel, with *bâtonnage* (lees-stirring) and then fairly rapid bottling. This rich, fat and yet fresh and balanced wine is a conclusive demonstration of the great strides which have been made in recent years.

Sablet Cuvée Montmartel Of the 3 finest parcels in Sablet, the very poor, sandy *lieu-dit* named Montmartel produces perhaps the most distinguished wine. Richly fruity, ample, indeed opulent on the palate and with a very enticing morello cherry, pepper and liquorice flavour, Montmartel improves over a half-dozen years, but is really irresistible at any age! Lamb cutlets *à la provençale*, or even a tajine, make a harmonious accompaniment.

- Other red wines:
Côtes-du-Rhône-Villages Sablet Les Briguières,
C-d-R-V Sablet Ténébi,
C-d-R-V Sablet, Gigondas,
Côtes-du-Rhône
- White wine:
Côtes-du-Rhône-Villages Sablet
- Owner:
Jean-Marc Autran
- Wine-maker:
Jean-Marc Autran
- Combined vineyards:
30 hectares
- Production:
200,000 bottles
- Exports: 80%
- Take-away sales:
9-12 a.m., 2-6 p.m.,
by appt.
- Visits: By appointment

Wine selected:
**Sablet
Cuvée Montmartel**

- Grape Varieties:
Grenache 80%,
Mourvèdre 20%
- Average vine age:
40 years
- Vineyard size:
7 hectares
- Soil type:
Clay, silt and sand
- Average production:
7,000 bottles

DOMAINE RABASSE CHARAVIN

The fine reputation enjoyed by the village of Cairanne has been earned by families such as the Couturiers, growers who live for their land and its vines and devote all their energy and talent to transforming their fruit into the finest wine possible. Rabasse Charavin has long been one of the most reliable names in the Vaucluse, producing a fine range of wines of great character.

Unceasing efforts to ameliorate quality Since 1984 the estate has been run by Corinne Couturier, a woman who excels at her work in what is largely a male-dominated business. Corinne learnt how to make wine from her father Abel, who instilled in her the essential notions of care for the vine and limitation of its yields. The estate's reputation was already established when Abel retired, but Corinne has consolidated it and devoted unceasing efforts to ameliorating the general quality even further; while her methods may by and large be described as traditional, the lady is not averse to trying out new ideas which could give interesting results.

Old vines for greater character Rabasse Charavin is of a very respectable size, covering 68 hectares of which 60 were in production at the end of the 1990s. At the heart of the estate are the Cairanne vineyards, which cover 17 hectares; there are also 8 hectares in the neighbouring village of Rasteau, and the remainder lie around Violès, several kilometres to the south. A noteworthy aspect of most of these vineyards is the high average age of their vines, which has the highly desirable effect of producing less but better-quality fruit, giving wine which is more intensely aromatic and also expresses the character of its *terroir* more forcefully. From the bottom of the range *vin de table*, which includes 50-year-old Carignan, to the Cuvée Estevenas with its centenarian Grenache, there is not one of the 11 wines which could be accused of lacking personality.

Careful, intelligent wine-making The wines' intrinsic quality comes not only from the vineyard sites, but also from rigorous selection of the fruit during picking and on arrival at the winery, and subsequently from careful, intelligent wine-making. The grapes are left on their stems for vinification and lightly crushed before vatting in concrete, and the different varieties and parcels are kept apart until after the malolactic fermentation, in order to be able to assess the finished wines better. The grapes having been left on their stems, *cuvaison* is relatively rapid, lasting 4-8 days, with 2 *remontages* per day to extract colour, aroma and tannin. Then the wines are blended, and the finished products are aged, either in concrete or enamel-lined tanks, and eventually bottled without filtration.

Cairanne Cuvée d'Estevenas A south-facing parcel at the top of clay and limestone slopes bears the fine fruit which is vinified as Cuvée Estevenas, the estate's greatest achievement. Concentrated and exhaling a splendid pepper-and-spice nose, with a spine of fine-quality tannin, Estevenas may be kept for a dozen years, and is best served from a decanter for maximum development of its bouquet, alongside any stewed and well-seasoned red meat.

- Other red wines: Côtes-du-Rhône-Villages Cuvée les Amandiers, C-d-R-V Rasteau, C-d-R-V Cairanne, Côtes-du-Rhône-Villages, Côtes-du-Rhône Cuvée Laure Olivier, Côtes-du-Rhône, Vin de Pays, Vin de Table
- White wine: Côtes-du-Rhône-Villages
- Owner: Domaine Rabasse Charavin Couturier
- Managers: Corinne Couturier & Olivier Plasse
- Wine-makers: Corinne & Laure Couturier-Plasse
- Oenologist: M. Sabatier
- Combined vineyards: 60 hectares
- Production: 225,000 bottles
- Exports: 25%
- Take-away sales: 8-11.30 a.m., 2-6 p.m. (Mon.-Fri.). Weekends (10 a.m.-7 p.m.) at La Maison Vigneronne, Place des Ecoles, Cairanne
- Visits: No

Wine selected:
Cairanne Cuvée d'Estevenas

- Grape Varieties: Grenache 80%, Syrah 20%
- Average vine age: 30-100 years
- Vineyard size: 2.5 hectares
- Soil type: Clay and limestone
- Average production: 8,000 bottles

Several kilometres north of Orange, in the gentle rolling countryside that constitutes the massif d'Uchaux, the cream-coloured buildings which make up Château Saint-Estève d'Uchaux overlook the plain stretching away into the far distance. Saint-Estève has for several decades been at the forefront of local wine-making innovation, earning itself a solid reputation, a faithful clientele and a good number of medals in the process.

The most noble Rhône varieties This estate has been the property of the Français family since 1809. The first century of its existence, we learn from John Livingstone-Learmonth in *The Wines of the Rhône*, was taken up with forestry, sheep-farming and silkworm rearing, and the vine was only planted in its soils at the beginning of the 20th century.
The prime mover behind its progress in the domain of wine-making was Gérard Français-Monier, who in 1953 decided to uproot the 20 hectares of vines that existed at the time and plant afresh an area extended to 60 hectares with the Rhône's most noble varieties: Grenache, Syrah, Cinsault and Mourvèdre for the red wines, Grenache Blanc, Roussanne, Clairette and Bourboulenc for the whites, to which was added in 1981 an experimental hectare of Viognier, which has since been increased threefold. Français-Monier having other unconnected business interests to occupy him, he entrusted the running of the estate totally to his son Marc, who has proved a talented manager and innovative wine-maker.

Modernity in harmony with tradition At Saint-Estève tradition rubs shoulders with modernity in the most relaxed fashion. Here the vines, cultivated naturally and perfumed by the surrounding *garrigue*, are covered over to protect them from the rigours of the local climate when young. Since 1983 the vintage has been partially harvested by machine. The crop is destalked, and in the case of the white wines lightly crushed and then pneumatically pressed; the different white varieties are united and vinification follows, at 17°C in gleaming stainless steel vats with temperature-control equipment, lasting some 10 days. Saint-Estève's famous Viognier wine then enjoys a year's ageing in vat before bottling. As for the black grapes, they are vinified variety by variety and parcel by parcel in stainless steel, and the quality of fruit dictates the type of ageing they undergo. The estate never chaptalizes, nor does it use artificial yeast.

Côtes-du-Rhône-Villages Vieilles Vignes Four red wines are produced, of which the most interesting is the Vieilles Vignes. Demand outstrips supply for this *cuvée*, from the oldest vines and best parcels, aged some 20 months in barrel and vat and bottled with less tampering than the other wines. Deeply fruity, succulent and fairly structured, this splendidly pure wine improves over a dozen years, after which it makes a fine partner for leg of lamb, perfumed with thyme.

- Other red wines:
Côtes-du-Rhône-Villages Grande Réserve, Côtes-du-Rhône Tradition, Côtes-du-Rhône Cuvée Friande
- White wines:
Côtes-du-Rhône Vionysos, Côtes-du-Rhône Cuvée Thérèse, Côtes-du-Rhône
- Rosé wine:
Côtes-du-Rhône
- Owners:
Français-Monier de Saint-Estève family
- Managing Director:
Marc Français
- Wine-maker:
Marc Français
- Combined vineyards:
60 hectares
- Production:
375,000 bottles
- Exports: 30%
- Take-away sales:
Yes, except Sunday
- Visits:
9-12 a.m., 2-6 p.m.

Wine selected:
Côtes-du-Rhône-Villages Vieilles Vignes

- Grape Varieties:
Syrah 60%,
Grenache 40%
- Average vine age:
Over 35 years
- Vineyard size:
4 hectares
- Soil type:
Sand and gravel
- Average production:
20,000 bottles

VIEILLES VIGNES
1995
CHÂTEAU

Saint Estève d'Uchaux

DEPUIS 1809
CÔTES DU RHÔNE VILLAGES
APPELLATION CÔTES DU RHÔNE VILLAGES CONTRÔLÉE

75cl

PRODUCE OF FRANCE

MIS EN BOUTEILLE AU CHÂTEAU

GÉRARD & MARC FRANÇAIS, PROPRIÉTAIRE-RÉCOLTANT
SARL CHATEAU SAINT ESTEVE D'UCHAUX - 84100 UCHAUX - FRANCE

DOMAINE SAINTE-ANNE

The sleepy village of Saint-Gervais forms the western outpost of the Côtes-du-Rhône-Villages region, and is perhaps a name with less of the viticultural cachet of others such as Cairanne, Sablet, Rasteau and others to the east. Yet it gained 'Villages' status in 1974, and is today noteworthy principally because of one estate, the excellent Domaine Sainte-Anne.

Back from the brink of extinction   In truth, Saint-Gervais has just two estates which bottle their own produce, and has a *cave coopérative*, founded in 1924, which puts to good use the fruit of all the other growers of the village. Domaine Saint-Anne, which may be found in the nearby hamlet of Les Cellettes, was part of the estate of the Carthusian monastery of Valbonne until the Revolution, when the monks fled to Spain and their estate was put up for sale. Olives and grain were the monks' principal crops, and there was a flourishing silkworm business. The vine had also been sporadically cultivated in the region since the 17th century.

In the ensuing years the estate was progressively split up, and the hamlet of Les Cellettes was almost completely abandoned by 1920. Only in 1945 were efforts made to revive agriculture there, yet nevertheless by 1965 there were only a handful of hectares under vine.

A move from Burgundy to the Rhône Valley   It was in that year that the Steinmaier family from Burgundy bought 13 hectares of land, which they had to clear and plant. Having got their estate up and running they increased it with successive purchases in the 1970s, bringing it up to its present-day size of 33 hectares, and also acquired the ancient buildings in which the business is now based. In order to cope with the increasing amount of fruit produced, the wine-making facilities have had to be enlarged on three occasions and the bottle cellar capacity correspondingly increased.

With the excellence of the produce the reputation spread inexorably, and as the vineyards have matured the wines have gained in character and style. Sainte-Anne now produces five red wines and two whites, all of impeccable quality, and is perhaps best known for its white Viognier wine, one of the first southern-Rhône examples of its kind, produced from cuttings obtained from Georges Vernay in the early 1980s. Its red wines are arguably better than any others produced on the right bank of the Rhône, the result of careful, respectful viticultural habits, low yields and severe selection of the fruit before vinification.

Côtes-du-Rhône-Villages Notre Dame des Cellettes   The best red of the Sainte-Anne range, the *cuvée* Notre Dame des Cellettes, is a selection of old vines and best-sited vineyards. It is exceptional, given its relatively humble appellation: very dark to behold and glinting violet, it is soft and suave on the palate, concentrated and juicy, with sublime aromas of red fruit, spice and Provençal herbs. A superb, seductive mouthful, it is delicious on its own and is not fussy about its table companions: any red or white meats will do, preferably cooked with garlic and seasoned with the local herbs, and then followed by some Pont l'Evêque.

- Other red wines:
Côtes-du-Rhône-Villages
Saint-Gervais, Côtes-du-
Rhône-Villages, Côtes-du-
Rhône, Côtes-du-Rhône
(Syrah)
- White wines:
Côtes-du-Rhône-Villages,
Côtes-du-Rhône (Viognier)
- Owner:
Steinmaier family
- Wine-maker:
Jean Steinmaier
- Combined vineyards:
33 hectares
- Production:
186,000 bottles
- Exports: 60%
- Take-away sales:
9-11 a.m., 2-6 p.m.
- Visits: By appointment

Wine selected:
**Côtes-du-Rhône-
Villages Notre Dame
des Cellettes**

- Grape Varieties:
Grenache 60%,
Syrah 30%,
Mourvèdre 10%
- Average vine age:
30 years
- Vineyard size:
4 hectares
- Soil type:
Calcareous sandstone
- Average production:
20,000 bottles

DOMAINE LA SOUMADE

The Vaucluse département is not short of powerful, dense, tannic wines which need time to soften up and demonstrate their complexity, but very few match those of André Roméro of Domaine La Soumade for dimension and sheer depth of flavour. Roméro is self-taught and has a feel for extracting all that is best out of his carefully-cultivated grapes; his wines, one could argue, have all the more personality for it.

Two centuries of family tradition La Soumade has been in Roméro's family for 200 years. With the panorama of the Dentelles de Montmirail and the Mont du Ventoux making a splendid backdrop in the distance, the estate's 28 hectares are made up of a number of parcels, which lie on the gently sloping land below the village of Rasteau. The vines are cultivated *à l'ancienne*, the weeds being kept at bay by *labourage* and the soil being enriched only by the occasional organic treatment.

Terrain well suited to Grenache Grenache Noir holds pride of place, as is to be expected, for the land around the village of Rasteau is recognized as singularly suitable for that variety, with Syrah and Mourvèdre playing principal supporting roles. These three together produce the two finest wines of La Soumade, the *cuvées* Prestige and Confiance. Yet a long list of other varieties such as Grenache Blanc, Cinsault, Carignan, Clairette Rose and Blanche, Bourboulenc, Roussanne and Muscardin, give Roméro fine raw material to make his Côtes-du-Rhône-Villages, rosé, and red and golden *Vin Doux Naturel*.

Their owner, an out-and-out claret fan, also has a couple of hectares of Cabernet-Sauvignon and Merlot; these of course are not authorized varieties in the Rhône Valley, and their wine has to be sold as Vin de Pays de la Principauté d'Orange.

Tradition without compromise At the end of a year's attentive viticulture, once optimum ripeness is reached the harvest is carried out by hand, enabling pickers to discard any unripe, rotten or generally substandard fruit. Roméro appreciating the uncompromisingly 'traditional' style, the fruit is left on its stalks for fermentation; after a light crushing the fruit is fermented and macerated in stainless steel vats for 12-15 days, with lots of *pigeage*. Then the wine is transferred to *foudre*, the press-wine is added, and a year's ageing begins.

Rasteau Cuvée Confiance The greatest wine produced at La Soumade is the Cuvée Confiance, a giant of a wine which is only made in the best years. Four-fifths very old Grenache, one-fifth Syrah, it is the product of the very oldest vines on the estate, which, aided by suitable vinification, impart extraordinary depth and aromatic complexity. Almost black and powerfully peppery on the nose, it has a wide flavour spectrum which encompasses primary black fruit, cinnamon and pepper spice, mineral, earthy nuances and, as it ages, gamey flavours. This thick-set character has a tannic structure to match, and does require at least a decade in the cellar! Flavoursome food such as jugged hare is called for!

- Other red wines: Côtes-du-Rhône-Villages Rasteau Cuvée Prestige, Côtes-du-Rhône, Vin de Pays de la Principauté d'Orange, Rasteau Vin Doux Naturel
- White wine: Rasteau Vin Doux Naturel
- Owner: André Roméro
- Wine-maker: André Roméro
- Oenologist: Nicolas Constantin
- Combined vineyards: 28 hectares
- Production: 133,000 bottles
- Exports: 65%
- Take-away sales: 8.00-11.30 a.m., 2.00-6.00 p.m.
- Visits: Yes

Wine selected:
**Rasteau
Cuvée Confiance**

- Grape Varieties: Grenache 80%, Syrah 10%, Mourvèdre 10%
- Average vine age: 40-95 years
- Vineyard size: 5 hectares
- Soil type: Clay and limestone
- Average production: 10,000 bottles

Domaine la Soumade

Rasteau

Côtes du Rhône Villages

APPELLATION CÔTES DU RHÔNE VILLAGES CONTRÔLÉE

Mis en bouteille au domaine

Romero André propriétaire récoltant à Rasteau - Vaucluse

Récolte 1996   PRODUCT OF FRANCE   Cuvée Confiance

The vast 45,000-hectare appellation Côtes-du-Rhône produces wines of all qualities, from the light, fruity, carbonic-maceration liquids to far more serious beverages. Perhaps the most serious of them all, a great wine which proves just what is possible if one is determined enough, is the Reynaud family's Château de Fonsalette.

Louis Reynaud's second estate The Reynaud dynasty is of course better known to Rhône-wine aficionados as owner of the great Châteauneuf-du-Pape, Château Rayas. Louis Reynaud purchased the 130-hectare Château de Fonsalette, at Lagarde-Paréol, in 1945.

At the time there were very few vines, and during the decade after the acquisition Reynaud did much experimentation with different varieties to see exactly which worked best in Fonsalette's soil. Pride of place, unsurprisingly, went to Grenache Noir, with Cinsault and Syrah being chosen to play the supporting roles. White grapes were also planted, Reynaud opting for Grenache Blanc, Marsanne, Clairette and Chardonnay. In all 12 hectares were planted, and the château remained surrounded on three sides by its huge park. The wines are made at Château Rayas, in more or less the same manner as their big brother and from yields only a little more generous.

Jacques Reynaud duly took over after his father's death in 1978, and during his lifetime made four different wines: a white Côtes-du-Rhône, never reputed for regularity but sublimely rich and complex in the best vintages; the red Fonsalette Côtes-du-Rhône; a red 100% Syrah wine; and a lighter red wine named La Pialade. Since his death in 1997 his nephew Emmanuel Reynaud has taken on the responsibility of producing these wines.

Grand wines from a humble appellation The two principle Fonsalette red wines have absolutely nothing in common with the average run-of-the-mill Côtes-du-Rhône, and can proudly hold their heads high in the company of the Rhône Valley's finest. The Cuvée Syrah is made from what is left over of that variety after the Fonsalette has been blended; curiously there is even more demand for it than for the blended wine, and it is as good as most Hermitage. It should not be approached until it has had half-a-dozen years in bottle, at which stage it still has its sumptuous rich blackcurrant flavour yet has shrugged of its tannic structure to a degree. Better vintages will nevertheless keep for far longer. The third red, Pialade, does not have the same ambition, being made up of the other leftovers.

Côtes-du-Rhône The 'standard' Château de Fonsalette is a splendid wine, with a rich, intense, spicy flavour, substantial body and an impressive structure. The grapes are picked, as they are for Château Rayas, on the point of overripeness, which, combined with the low yields and the great age of the vines makes for an extraordinary Côtes-du-Rhône, with great potential for improvement in bottle. The magnificent 1989 vintage, for example, after 10 years was developing an amber hue and opening up nicely, yet was still some way from full maturity. Fonsalette, which makes a fine partner for game pie, naturally costs far more than other Côtes-du-Rhônes, but is not expensive for what it is—a great wine.

Côtes-du-Rhône | Lagarde-Paréol

- Other red wines: Côtes-du-Rhône Cuvée Syrah, Côtes-du-Rhône La Pialade
- White wine: Côtes-du-Rhône
- Owner: Reynaud family
- Wine-maker: Emmanuel Reynaud
- Combined vineyards: 12 hectares
- Production: 32,000 bottles
- Exports: 70%
- Take-away sales: No
- Visits: No

Wine selected:
Côtes-du-Rhône

- Grape Varieties: Grenache 50%, Cinsault 35%, Syrah 15%
- Average vine age: 15 and 70 years
- Vineyard size: 10.5 hectares
- Soil type: Clay and limestone
- Average production: 28,000 bottles

DOMAINE GRAMENON

I n these days of oenology diplomas and high-tech vinification equipment, it would be interesting to see who could still make good wine if just left with his vines, a pair of secateurs and a cellar equipped as in days long gone by. The late Philippe Laurent would have been a sure-fire candidate for the gold medal. That was the way he worked while he was alive, and is the way his widow Michele continues to work. The Laurent wines are of great quality and character, yet simply bear—it is difficult to believe it when savouring them—the modest Côtes-du-Rhône appellation.

Putting a simple idea into practice Domaine Gramenon lies in the heart of the Drôme Provençale region, between Grignan and Nyons, at some 300 metres altitude. The estate covered 24 hectares until 1999, when the Laurents acquired a second estate which they named Les Hauts de Gramenon, which brought the total vineyard area up to 40 hectares. With wine-lovers more and more appreciative of all that is made naturally, its success is no surprise. The first wines made were of the 1990 vintage, yet the estate is no longer a secret to serious Rhône-wine lovers, and its produce is avidly sought out by top restaurants and retailers for their lists "Le Vin en Liberté", branded on the corks, and "Vin de Raisin", printed on the stationary, sum up the Laurent philosophy. Viticultural and wine-making methods are based on the knowledge that the vine, unsoiled by any artificial treatments, really can produce excellent, healthy fruit, as long as its natural productivity is curbed... and that there is no reason why this should not make superbly natural wine, as long as man does not tamper and intervene. It is simple enough as ideas go, yet numerous *vignerons* do not dare work without a safety net at every turn, to the inevitable detriment of their produce.

Natural wines without artificial additives Low yields and very old vines then are the cornerstone of Gramenon's reputation. If there is replanting to be done, when possible the grafting of the plant onto its Phylloxera-resistant rootstock is done on the estate, a time-consuming and tricky operation. When it comes to making the wine, Michele assesses the year's crop and treats it as necessary—routine is out at Gramenon. The deliciously ripe fruit, carefully harvested by hand and checked for quality, may be a little or almost completely destemmed, and is fermented without any additives: musts are neither chaptalized nor acidified, nor is SO2 used. Fermentations are carried out by the fruit's own yeast, and after long ageing in old wood the wines are bottled with neither fining nor filtration. Throughout the process all movement of must and wine is by gravity, to protect its aromas.

Côtes-du-Rhône Ceps Centenaires "La Mémé" The most concentrated and complex of the red wines which emerge from the Gramenon cellars is "La Mémé", made from a plot of centenarian Grenache plants. This thick, opulent and rich nectar, pure and powerful, has a kirsch-type flavour which develops a smokiness with age which is memorable. A loin of lamb, grilled over dead vine wood, would accord it all the respect its venerable vines deserve!

- Other red wines: Côtes-du-Rhône Poignée de Raisins, C-d-R Le Gramenon, C-d-R Syrah "Sierra du Sud", C-d-R Les Laurentides, C-d-R La Sagesse
- White wines: Côtes-du-Rhône, C-d-R Viognier "Vie, on y est..."
- Owner: Michèle Aubery Laurent
- Wine-maker: Michèle Aubery Laurent
- Combined vineyards: 40 hectares
- Production: 240,000 bottles
- Exports: 40%
- Take-away sales: By appointment
- Visits: No

Wine selected:
Côtes-du-Rhône Ceps Centenaires "La Mémé"

- Grape Variety: Grenache
- Average vine age: 100+ years
- Vineyard size: 2 hectares
- Soil type: Clay and limestone
- Average production: 5,000 bottles

PRODUCERS

The addresses and telephone numbers of the sales outlets referred to here by their initials are given in the separate Sales Outlets list.

Prices indicated correspond to the specific wine photographed, and are those asked at the property, except in cases where there are no on-site sales, in which case they represent the average price charged by sales outlets. The star notations represent the following price brackets:

*	Less than 60 F.
**	60 F. - 120 F.
***	120 F. - 200 F.
****	200 F. - 300 F.
*****	In excess of 300 F.

CÔTE-RÔTIE

Domaine Bernard Burgaud
Le Champin – 69420 Ampuis
Tel. 04 74 56 11 86
From Ampuis take the road towards Givors, which passes through the hamlet of Le Champin. Domaine Burgaud is well indicated.
Sales Outlets: CA, CMV, CR, LGC, LCI, RM
Price: **

Domaine Clusel-Roch
15, route du Lacat – Vérenay
69420 Ampuis
Tel. 04 74 56 15 95
If heading north on the RN86 from Ampuis, once in the hamlet of Verenay take the Route du Lacat on the left. Domaine Clusel-Roch is signposted, some 300 metres along.
Sales Outlets: JUV, CDV, LG, CMV, EV, IM, RM
Price: ***

Maison E. Guigal
Route Nationale – 69420 Ampuis
Tel. 04 74 56 10 22
The Guigal offices and cellars lie on the main road at the southern end of Ampuis.
Sales Outlets: CA, CAP, CLT, CMV, CM, MIL, CH, CR, EV, LGC, LCI, PER, RM, CT
Price: *****

Domaine Gilles Barge
8, boulevard des Allées
69420 Ampuis
Tel. 04 74 56 13 90
Domaine Gilles Barge is situated opposite the Ampuis church.
Sales Outlets: CA, CAP
Price: ***

Domaine J. Vidal-Fleury
19, route de la Roche
69420 Ampuis
Tel. 04 74 56 10 18
Vidal-Fleury lies on the RN86 on the northern edge of Ampuis.
Sales Outlets: MVL, RM
Price: ***

Domaine Jamet
Le Vallin – 69420 Ampuis
Tel. 04 74 56 12 57
Follow the RN86 northwards from the Ampuis church for some 200 metres and take the road on the left. The Jamet estate is 4 kms from Ampuis, and is signposted.
Sales Outlets: CA, CAC, CMV, MIL, CR, CDC, C41, RM
Price: **

Domaine Jasmin
14, rue des Maraîchers
69420 Ampuis
Tel. 04 74 56 11 41
The Jasmin cellars are 100 metres from the Ampuis church.
Sales Outlets: LFF, CA, CMV, MIL, C41, LGC, PER, CT
Price: **

Domaine Jean-Michel Gerin
19, rue de Montmain – Vérenay
69420 Ampuis
Tel. 04 74 56 16 56
If heading north on the RN86, once in the hamlet of Verenay take the Route du Lacat on the left. Rue de Montmain is 100 metres along on the left-hand side.
Sales Outlets: CMV, RM, CAC, CE, CR, C41, VTQ
Price: ****

Domaine Joël Champet
12, chemin de la Viaillère
Vérenay – 69420 Ampuis
Tel. 04 74 56 14 86
Head north from Ampuis to Verenay and take the first turning on the left. Chemin de la Viaillère is a little way along on the left-hand side.
Price: **

Domaine René Rostaing
1, Petite Rue du Port
69420 Ampuis
Tel. 04 74 56 12 00
Follow the first road north of the church down to the Château d'Ampuis and turn right. Rostaing's establishment is on the corner.
Sales Outlets: CA, CMV, MIL, DMC, LGC, PER
Price: ***

CONDRIEU

Domaine André Perret
Verlieu – 42410 Chavanay
Tel. 04 74 87 24 74
Perret's establishment lies on the RN86, 200 metres past the church as one heads up to Condrieu.
Sales Outlets: JUV, CA, CAC, CDC, LGC, RM, LFF
Price: ***

Domaine François Villard
Montjoux
42410 Saint-Michel-sur-Rhône
Tel. 04 74 56 83 60
Drive up to and through Saint-Michel and continue for 200 metres. A large new building just after the fork in the road houses Domaine François Villard.
Sales Outlets: RM, CAC, LGC
Price: ***

Domaine Georges Vernay
1, route Nationale
69420 Condrieu
Tel. 04 74 59 52 22
Domaine Vernay is situated at the northern end of Condrieu, on the N86. There is a car park for visitors.
Sales Outlets: CA, CE, CMV, CM, IM, LCI, PER
Price: ***/****

Domaine Robert Niero
20, rue Cuvillière
69420 Condrieu
Tel. 04 74 59 84 38
Follow Rue Cuvillière from the Condrieu church northwards. The Niero estate is indicated.
Sales Outlets: JUV, RM
Price: ***

Domaine Yves Cuilleron
Verlieu – 42410 Chavanay
Tel. 04 74 87 02 37
Yves Cuilleron's cellars lie next to the Verlieu church.
Sales Outlets: CMV, RM, CA, CAC, LGC
Price: ***

CHÂTEAU-GRILLET

Château-Grillet
42410 Vérin
Tel. 04 74 59 51 56
Turn left off the RN86 (there is a small sign), pass under the bridge and follow the road uphill for 100 metres. Château Grillet is on the right-hand side.
Sales Outlets: CA, CMV, CM, MIL, EV, LG, LCI, PER, RM, CT
Price: ****

HERMITAGE

Domaine Bernard Faurie
27, avenue Hélène-de-Tournon
07300 Tournon-sur-Rhône
Tel. 04 75 08 55 09
Avenue Hélène de Tournon leads off Avenue du 8 Mai 1945. Faurie's house is opposite the phone booth.
Price: ***

Maison Delas Frères
Z.A. de l'Olivet
07300 Saint-Jean-de-Muzols
Tel. 04 75 08 60 30
From Tournon follow the RN86 northwards towards Saint-Jean-de-Muzols. Maison Delas is very well signposted from the main road.
Sales Outlets: CE, CH, C41, IM, LG, LV, VIN
Price: ***

Domaine Jean-Louis Chave
37, avenue de Saint-Joseph
07300 Mauves
Tel. 04 75 08 24 63
Sales Outlets: BAD, CA, CLT, CMV, MIL, CH, CR, CDC, EV, LGC, LCI, PER, LFF, CT
Price: ***

Maison M. Chapoutier
18, avenue du Docteur-Paul-Durand – BP 38
26601 Tain-l'Hermitage
Tel. 04 75 08 28 65
Internet:
http://www.chapoutier.com
Maison Chapoutier is 50 metres from the Tain railway station.
Sales Outlets: BAD, CA, CAP, CAC, CLT, CMV, CH, CR, EV, IM, LG, LCI, LV, MVL, PER, RM
Price: ***

Domaine Marc Sorrel
128 bis, avenue Jean-Jaurès
26600 Tain-l'Hermitage
Tel. 04 75 07 10 07
From the church of Tain head towards the RN7 and turn right. The cellars are situated some 200 metres along on the right-hand side.
Sales Outlets: DMC, CA, LGC, IM, LG, LCI, PER
Price: ***

Maison Paul Jaboulet Aîné
Les Jalets – RN7
La Roche-de-Glun
26600 Tain-l'Hermitage
Tel. 04 75 84 68 93
The Jaboulet building lies on the RN7 a few kilometres south of Tain, on the right-hand side as one drives south.
Sales Outlets: CA, CAC, CE, CLT, CMV, MIL, CH, CR, DMC, EV, IM, LG, MVL, PER, RM, CT, RB
Price: ****/*****

Maison Tardieu-Laurent
Chemin de la Marquette
84360 Lauris
Tel. 04 90 08 32 07
Sales Outlets: DUB, LGC
Price: ****

Domaine de Vallouit
24, avenue Désiré-Valette
26240 Saint-Vallier
Tel. 04 75 23 10 11
The De Vallouit premises are 30 metres from the Syndicat d'Initiative.
Sales Outlets: CR, EV, otherwise the De Vallouit shop at 78, bd. des Allées, 69420 Ampuis (Tel. 04 74 56 12 33).
Price: ***

CROZES-HERMITAGE

Domaine Alain Graillot
Les Chênes Verts
26600 Pont-de-l'Isère
Tel. 04 75 84 67 52
Sales Outlets: JUV, CA, CAC, CLT, CMV, CM, MIL, CH, CR, CDC, C41, LCI, LGC, MVL, PER, LFF, CT
Price: **

Domaine Bernard Chave
La Burge – 26600 Mercurol
Tel. 04 75 07 42 11
From Tain l'Hermitage take the D532 towards Romans. The Chave estate is on the road on the left leading to Mercurol just after the motorway.
Sales Outlets: MVL
Price: *

Domaine Combier
RN7 – 26600 Pont-de-l'Isère
Tel. 04 75 84 61 56
Domaine Combier lies on the RN7 between Pont de l'Isère and Tain.
Sales Outlets: CA, LG, CT, CMV, CAC, CE, CH, LGC, IM, LCI, VTQ
Price: **

Domaine Étienne Pochon
Château Curson
26600 Chanos-Curson
Tel. 04 75 07 34 60
At the entry to the village of Curson turn left off the RD532 and follow the signs to Château Curson.
Sales Outlets: LGC, RM
Price: **

Domaine du Pavillon
Les Châssis – 26600 Mercurol
Tel. 04 75 08 24 47
The estate lies next to the Salle des Fêtes of Les Chassis, on the N7 some 800 metres north of the Paul Jaboulet Aîné premises.
Sales Outlets: LFF
Price: *

Domaine des Remizières
Route de Romans
26600 Mercurol
Tel. 04 75 07 44 28
From Tain l'Hermitage take the D532 towards Romans. Cave Desmeure is on the left-hand side of the road.
Sales Outlets: CE, CH
Price: **

SAINT-JOSEPH

Domaine Bernard Gripa
5, avenue Ozier – 07300 Mauves
Tel. 04 75 08 14 96
Bernard Gripa's establishment lies on the main street in the centre of the village of Mauves.
Sales Outlets: CA, CMV, CR, LGC, MVL, CT
Price: **

Domaine Jean-Louis Grippat
La Sauva – 07300 Tournon
Tel. 04 75 08 15 51
Sales Outlets: CA, CH, EV, LGC, PER, RM
Price: **

Domaine Philippe Faury
La Ribaudy – 42410 Chavanay
Tel. 04 74 87 26 00
The road to La Ribaudy leads off the main road, opposite the Tabac.
Sales Outlets: RM
Price: *

Domaine Pierre Coursodon
3, place du Marché
07300 Mauves
Tel. 04 75 08 29 27
Place du Marché is at the centre of Mauves
Sales Outlets: PER
Price: **

Domaine Pierre Gaillard
42520 Malleval
Tel. 04 74 87 13 10
From Malleval take the road to Pélussin, and after 2 kms take the left-hand turn towards Martel. From that village the estate is signposted.
Sales Outlets: CA, CDV, CMV, CR, DMC, JUV, IM, LG, RM, RB
Price: *

CORNAS

Domaine Alain Voge
4, rue de l'Équerre
07130 Cornas
Tel. 04 75 40 32 04
From Cornas's church turn southwards along Grande Rue, then take Rue du Midi, the second on the left. From there signs direct one to Domaine Voge.
Sales Outlets: CA, CMV, CM, MIL, EV, PER, RM
Price: ***

Domaine Auguste Clape
146, route Nationale
07130 Cornas
Tel. 04 75 40 33 64
Domaine Clape is on the main road passing through the village of Cornas, opposite Restaurant Ollier.
Sales Outlets: CA, CMV, JUV, LFF, CDC, LGC, C41, VIN, CT
Price: ***

Domaine Jacques Leménicier
20, impasse des Granges
07130 Cornas
Tel. 04 75 40 49 54

Turn left (if heading towards Saint-Péray) off the main road down either Rue des Lavandes or Rue des Geais. Leménicier's premises are just over the railway line on the right-hand side.
Sales Outlets: CH
Price: **

Domaine Jean-Luc Colombo
Rue Pied-la-Vigne
07130 Cornas
Tel. 04 75 40 24 47
Rue Pied La Vigne leads northwards from Cornas's church. Domaine Colombo is on the left.
Sales Outlets: CE, CM, CR, C41
Price: ****

Domaine Robert Michel
19, Grande Rue
07130 Cornas
Tel. 04 75 40 38 70
From the church head a few metres along Grande Rue. The Michel cellars are on the left-hand side.
Sales Outlets: CA, LGC, RM
Price: **

Domaine Thierry Allemand
22, impasse des Granges
07130 Cornas
Tel. 04 75 81 06 50
Allemand's establishment is on the RN86, opposite the restaurant Ollier.
Sales Outlets: CDC, LFF, CA
Price: ***

SAINT-PÉRAY

Domaine Chaboud
21, rue Ferdinand-Malet
07130 Saint-Péray
Tel. 04 75 40 31 63
The Chaboud establishment is on the main street, which leads out of town in the Le Puy direction.
Price: *

Domaine Jean Lionnet
48, rue Pied-la-Vigne
07130 Cornas
Tel. 04 75 40 36 01
Rue Pied La Vigne leads northwards from Cornas's church.
Sales Outlets: CH, JUV
Price: *

CHÂTEAUNEUF-DU-PAPE

Château de Beaucastel
Chemin de Beaucastel
84350 Courthézon
Tel. 04 90 70 41 00
Internet: www.vinternet.fr/Perrin
Château de Beaucastel lies next to the A7 motorway. Take the exit no. 22 marked 'Orange Sud'.
Sales Outlets: FIC, CA, RB, BAD, CAC, CE, CLT, CMV, CM, MIL, CH, CR, EV, C41, LGC, IM, LCI, PER, RM, VTQ, CT
Price: *****

Domaine de Beaurenard
Paul Coulon & Fils
10, route de Sorgues
84230 Châteauneuf-du-Pape
Tel. 04 90 83 71 79
Internet: http://www.beaurenard.enprovence.com/
Head down Avenue Pierre de Luxembourg, in the Sorgues direction. Domaine de Beaurenard is on the right-hand side.
Sales Outlets: CAP, PER
Price: **

Bosquet des Papes
Route d'Orange
84230 Châteauneuf-du-Pape
Tel. 04 90 83 72 33
From the church follow Rue Porte Rouge until you get to Route d'Orange. The Boiron estate is 300 metres along on the right-hand side.
Sales Outlets: PER
Price: **

Les Cailloux
6, chemin du Bois-de-la-Ville
84230 Châteauneuf-du-Pape
Tel. 04 90 83 72 62
Sales Outlets: REF, CDC, PER
Price: **

Domaine Font de Michelle
84370 Bédarrides
Tel. 04 90 33 00 22

Leave Bédarrides in the Orange direction. At the RN7 crossroads continue on through the lights and head on for 50 metres, then take the road on the right, following the signposts, which leads up to the estate.
Sales Outlets: PER
Price: ***

Château Fortia
84230 Châteauneuf-du-Pape
Tel. 04 90 83 72 25
Leave Châteauneuf-du-Pape by the Sorgues road. The path leading up to Château Fortia is on the left-hand side, just outside the village. Drive slowly, it is easy to miss!
Sales Outlets: CT
Price: **

Château de la Gardine
84230 Châteauneuf-du-Pape
Tel. 04 90 83 73 20
From Châteauneuf-du-Pape take the D17 towards Roquemaure. The road leading up to La Gardine is some 1.5 kms along, on the right
Sales Outlets: CR
Price: ****

Domaine Grand Veneur
Route de Châteauneuf-du-Pape
84100 Orange
Tel. 04 90 34 68 70
From Orange head south towards Châteauneuf-du-Pape on the D68. Grand Veneur is on the right-hand side, well signposted.
Price: ***

Domaine de la Janasse
27, chemin du Moulin
84350 Courthézon
Tel. 04 90 70 86 29
Domaine de la Janasse lies at the southern end of Courthézon, next to the RN7.
Sales Outlets: CE, CMV, LG, CDV, CMV, JUV, LGC, IM
Price: **

Domaine Jean Deydier & Fils
Avenue Saint-Joseph
84230 Châteauneuf-du-Pape
Tel. 04 90 83 71 74
Follow Avenue Saint-Joseph out of Châteauneuf-du-Pape in the Roquemaure direction. Domaine Jean Deydier & Fils is on the right-hand side.
Price: **

Domaine de Marcoux
Chemin de la Gironde
84100 Orange
Tel. 04 90 34 67 43
Leave Châteauneuf-du-Pape by the D68 towards Orange. Turn right at the second junction and follow the signs.
Sales Outlets: CLT, MIL, PER, CT
Price: ***

Domaine de Monpertuis
Vignobles Paul Jeune
14, chemin des Garrigues – BP 48
84230 Châteauneuf-du-Pape
Tel. 04 90 83 73 87
The Monpertuis cellars are on the left-hand side of Avenue Saint-Joseph, which leads out of Châteauneuf-du-Pape in the Roquemaure direction.
Sales Outlets: LV
Price: ***

Clos du Mont-Olivet
15, avenue Saint-Joseph
84230 Châteauneuf-du-Pape
Tel. 04 90 83 72 46
Follow Avenue Saint-Joseph out of Châteauneuf-du-Pape in the Roquemaure direction. The Mont-Olivet cellars are on the left-hand side.
Sales Outlets: REF, PER
Price: **

Château Mont-Redon
84230 Châteauneuf-du-Pape
Tel. 04 90 83 72 75
Leave Châteauneuf-du-Pape by the D68 towards Orange. Mont-Redon lies 5 kms out of the village, and is indicated by a large hoarding.
Sales Outlets: MIL, EV, RM, VIN
Price: **

Château La Nerthe
Route de Sorgues
84230 Châteauneuf-du-Pape
Tel. 04 90 83 70 11
Château La Nerthe lies halfway between Châteauneuf-du-Pape and Sorgues, on the left-hand side as one goes south. It is well signposted.
Sales Outlets: IM, LG, RM
Price: ***

Clos des Papes
13, avenue Pierre-de-Luxembourg
84230 Châteauneuf-du-Pape
Tel. 04 90 83 70 13
From the centre of town head for the Bédarrides-Sorgues crossroads, and turn right in the Sorgues direction. Clos des Papes is 300 metres along on the left-hand side.
Sales Outlets: CA
Price: **

Domaine du Pégau
Avenue Impériale
84230 Châteauneuf-du-Pape
Tel. 04 90 83 72 70
Cave Paul Féraud is 200 metres along Avenue Impériale on the left-hand side as one heads north out of Châteauneuf-du-Pape.
Sales Outlets: C41, LG, CA, MIL, PER, RM
Price: **

Château Rayas
Route de Courthézon
84230 Châteauneuf-du-Pape
Tel. 04 90 83 73 09
Sales Outlets: CA, LFF, CAC, CLT, CMV, CM, MIL, CR, EV, LGC, LCI, VIN, CT
Price: ***/****

Domaine de la Vieille Julienne
Le Grès – 84100 Orange
Tél. : 04 90 34 20 10
Tel. 04 90 34 20 10
Follow the D68 northwards from Châteauneuf-du-Pape in the Orange direction. At the intersection with the D72 turn left; La Vieille Julienne is 1 km along the road.
Sales Outlets: CAC, PER
Price: ***

Domaine du Vieux Télégraphe
3, route de Châteauneuf-du-Pape – 84370 Bédarrides
Tel. 04 90 33 00 31
Domaine du Vieux Télégraphe lies off the Châteauneuf-du-Pape-Bédarrides road.
Sales Outlets: CAC, CLT, CMV, CM, CDC, EV, LCI, PER, LFF
Price: ***

GIGONDAS

Domaine du Cayron
84190 Gigondas
Tel. 04 90 65 87 46
Domaine du Cayron is on the left-hand side as one drives into the centre of the village.
Sales Outlets: CG
Price: *

Domaine Les Goubert
84190 Gigondas
Tel. 04 90 65 86 38
If heading southwards on the D7 from Sablet, do not turn left into the village of Gigondas, but take the small road on the right just after the Vignerons de Gigondas Cooperative. Les Goubert is the second property on the left.
Sales Outlets: CA, MIL, LGC, CG, VTQ
Price: ***

Domaine Raspail-Ay
Le Colombier – 84190 Gigondas
Tel. 04 90 65 83 01
The estate lies below the village, beside the D7.
Sales Outlets: CA, CDC, CR, LGC, CG, PER
Price: *

Château de Saint-Cosme
84190 Gigondas
Tel. 04 90 65 80 80
When leaving the village of Gigondas take the Route des Dentelles de Montmirail. Saint-Cosme is well signposted.
Sales Outlets: CT, CG
Price: **

Domaine Saint-Gayan
84190 Gigondas
Tel. 04 90 65 86 33
Follow the D7 northwards towards Sablet. Saint-Gayan is at the northerly limit of the Gigondas appellation.
Sales Outlets: JUV, CH, C41, CG, RM, VIN
Price: *

Domaine Santa Duc
Les Hautes Garrigues
84190 Gigondas
Tel. 04 90 65 84 49
The estate lies off the D80, between the D7 and the D8.
Sales Outlets: CDC, C41, CG
Price: ***

Château du Trignon
84190 Gigondas
Tel. 04 90 46 90 27
From Gigondas head towards Sablet. Before you enter the village negociate the two bends in the road and then take the first left. Follow the signposts to Château du Trignon.
Sales Outlets: RB, CG, PER
Price: **

VACQUEYRAS

Domaine La Fourmone
Route de Bollène
84190 Vacqueyras
Tel. 04 90 65 86 05
The estate lies on the Bollène road, halfway between Vacqueyras and Gigondas.
Price: *

Domaine La Garrigue
84190 Vacqueyras
Tel. 04 90 65 84 60
From the Vacqueyras fire station turn left, then turn right 50 metres on and follow the Route des Abreuvoirs for 2.5 kms.
Sales Outlets: EV
Price: *

Château des Tours
Quartier des Sablons
84260 Sarrians
Tel. 04 90 65 41 75
From Jonquières take the D950 towards Sarrians. Take the second turning on the left 100 metres after crossing the Ouvèze. The way to Château des Tours is indicated from then on.
Sales Outlets: CA, LFF, CAC, CMV, CR, C41, LGC, VIN
Price: **

LIRAC

Domaine de la Mordorée
Chemin des Oliviers
30126 Tavel
Tel. 04 66 50 00 75
From Tavel's church take the Avignon road. Take the first turning left, then left again. Mordorée is on the left-hand side.
Sales Outlets: NIC, CA, VTQ
Price: *

TAVEL

Château d'Aquéria
30126 Tavel
Tel. 04 66 50 04 56
From Tavel take the D4 towards Avignon. Cross over the D976, and continue for 800 metres. The entry to the estate is on the left-hand side, between two large trees.
Sales Outlets: CDV, CA, CAC, CMV, CR, PER
Price: *

Domaine Corne-Loup
Rue Mireille – 30126 Tavel
Tel. 04 66 50 34 37
The estate lies at the entrance of the village if coming from the Nimes-Avignon-Orange direction.
Sales Outlets: C41
Price: *

Prieuré de Montézargues
30126 Tavel
Tel. 04 66 50 04 48
Leave Tavel by the D4 towards Avignon, and turn right onto the D26 towards Rochefort-du-Gard. Turn left at the first junction,

then on the D976 turn left at the second junction towards Avignon. The earth track leading to the estate is immediately afterwards on the left.
Sales Outlets: CH, C41
Price: *

MUSCAT DE BEAUMES-DE-VENISE

Domaine des Bernardins
Cave Castaud
84190 Beaumes-de-Venise
Tel. 04 90 62 94 13
From the centre of the village take the road towards Lafare. Cave Castaud is 100 metres along on the right-hand side.
Sales Outlets: CT, LFF, CR, CA, CMV, PER
Price: *

Domaine de Coyeux
84190 Beaumes-de-Venise
Tel. 04 90 12 42 42
From Beaumes follow the D90 towards Lafare. The turning on the left-hand side leading towards Coyeux is signposted.
Sales Outlets: CMV, CDC, EV
Price: **

CÔTES-DU-RHÔNE VILLAGES

Domaine Bressy-Masson
Route d'Orange – 84110 Rasteau
Tel. 04 90 46 10 45
The estate lies on the D975 opposite Domaine La Soumade, a couple of kilometres outside the village.
Sales Outlets: NIC, EV
Price: *

Domaine Marcel Richaud
Route de Rasteau
84290 Cairanne
Tel. 04 90 30 85 25
At the roundabout at the edge of the village take the Vaison-la-Romaine direction. Marcel Richaud's premises are a few metres along on the left-hand side.
Sales Outlets: CA, CDC, CDV, JUV, CAC, CMV, LGC, LCI
Price: *

Domaine de l'Oratoire Saint-Martin
Route de Saint-Roman
84290 Cairanne
Tel. 04 90 30 82 07
From Cairanne take the road towards Saint Roman de Malegarde, and follow it for 500 metres.
Sales Outlets: LFF, LCI, VTQ
Price: **

Domaine Pélaquié
7, rue du Vernet
30290 Saint-Victor-la-Coste
Tel. 04 66 50 06 04
Take the Saint-Laurent-des-Arbres direction. Once past the stadium take the first left and follow the signs.
Sales Outlets: C41, EV
Price: *

Domaine de Piaugier
84110 Sablet
Tel. 04 90 46 96 49
Domaine de Piaugier lies on the main road through Sablet, behind the Post Office.
Sales Outlets: CDC, LGC, MVL, PER
Price: *

Domaine Rabasse Charavin
La Font d'Estevenas
84290 Cairanne
Tel. 04 90 30 70 05

Follow the Rasteau road for 2 kilometres, then take the road on the left by the bus shelter.
Sales Outlets: JUV, MVL, CR, EV, C41, VIN
Price: *

Château Saint-Estève d'Uchaux
Route de Sérignan
Tel. 04 90 40 62 38
Château Saint-Estève d'Uchaux lies off the D172, which runs from Piolenc to Sérignan-du-Comtat, several kilometres from the latter.
Sales Outlets: EV, PER
Price: **

Domaine Sainte-Anne
Les Cellettes - 30200 Saint-Gervais
If arriving from Bagnols, take the turning on the left at the entry to the village and follow it for 3 kilometres.
Sales Outlets: LFF
Price: *

Domaine La Soumade
84110 Rasteau
Tel. 04 90 46 11 26
The estate lies on the D975, a couple of kilometres outside the village.
Sales Outlets: CAC
Price: **

CÔTES-DU-RHÔNE

Château de Fonsalette
84290 Lagarde-Paréol
Tel. 04 90 83 73 09
Sales Outlets: CA, LFF, CM, CAC, CLT, CMV, CM, MIL, LCI
Price: ***

Domaine Gramenon
26770 Montbrison-sur-Lez
Tel. 04 75 53 57 08
Domaine Gramenon is on the Valréas road.
Sales Outlets: CA, PER, CR, EV, C41, LGC, LCI
Price: **

SALES OUTLETS

BAD : Badie
62, allée de Tourny
33000 Bordeaux
Tél. : 05 56 52 23 72

CA : Caves Augé
116, boulevard Haussmann
75008 Paris
Tél. : 01 45 22 16 97

CAC : La Cave d'à Côté
5 et 7, rue Pleney – 69001 Lyon
Tél. : 04 78 39 93 20

CAP : La Cave d'Annie Paule
9, rue de l'Hôpital-Militaire
59800 Lille
Tél. : 03 20 54 74 83

CDC : La Cave du Château
17, rue Raymond-du-Temple
94300 Vincennes
Tél. : 01 43 28 17 50

CDV : Le Chemin des Vignes
113 bis, avenue de Verdun
92130 Issy-les-Moulineaux
Tél. : 01 46 38 11 66

CE : Caves Estève
10, rue de la Cerisaie
75004 Paris
Tél. : 01 42 72 33 05

CG : Caveau du Gigondas
Place de la Mairie
84190 Gigondas
Tél. : 04 90 65 82 29

CH : Compagnie de l'Hermitage
7, place Taurobole
26600 Tain-l'Hermitage
Tél. : 04 75 08 19 70

CLT : Caveau de la Tour
7, place de la République
21190 Meursault
Tél. : 03 80 21 66 66

CM : La Cave à Millésimes
180, rue Lecourbe – 75015 Paris
Tél. : 01 48 28 22 62
Minitel : 3615 Alacavamil

CMV : La Cave Malleval
11, rue Émile-Zola – 69002 Lyon
Tél. : 04 78 42 02 07

CR : Caves Royales
6, rue Royale – 78000 Versailles
Tél. : 01 39 50 14 10

CT : Les Caves Taillevent
199, rue du Faubourg-Saint-Honoré – 75008 Paris
Tél. : 01 45 61 14 09

C41 : Les Caves du 41
41, rue Émile-Jamais
30900 Nîmes
Tél. : 04 66 36 20 36

DMC : Domaines, Maisons et Châteaux
29, rue de Saussure
75017 Paris
Tél. : 01 44 40 05 49

DUB : Maison F. Dubecq
32, rue de la Mothe
33800 Bordeaux
Tél. : 05 56 92 09 16

EV : Enclave Vinothèque
11, avenue Charles-de-Gaulle
84600 Valréas
Tél. : 04 90 35 17 96

FIC : Ficofi
16-20, rue des Menus
92100 Boulogne-Billancourt
Tél. : 01 41 31 70 00

IM : Inno Montparnasse
35, rue du Départ – 75014 Paris
Tél. : 01 43 20 69 30

JUV : Juveniles
47, rue de Richelieu
75001 Paris
Tél. : 01 42 97 46 49

LCI : La Cave de l'Ill
6, rue de l'Ill – 68350 Brunstatt
Tél. : 03 89 06 01 06

LFF : Legrand Filles & Fils
1, rue de la Banque
75002 Paris
Tél. : 01 42 60 07 12

LG : Lafayette Gourmet
48, boulevard Haussmann
75009 Paris
Tél. : 01 42 81 25 61

LGC : Les Grandes Caves
76, boulevard Jean-Jaurès
92110 Clichy
Tél. : 01 47 37 87 13

LV : Le Vintage
1, cours Anatole-France
51100 Reims
Tél. : 03 26 40 40 82

MIL : Millésimes
Verger d'Entreprises de la Capelette – 13520 Maussane
Tél. : 04 90 54 49 45

MVL : Maison des Vins de Lyon
73, avenue du Point-du-Jour
69005 Lyon
Tél. : 04 72 38 25 88

NIC : Ets Nicolas (head office)
2, rue Courson – 94320 Thiais
Tél. : 01 41 73 81 81

PER : Les Marchés aux Vins Pérardel
• Avenue Charles-de-Gaulle
21200 Beaune
Tél. : 03 80 24 08 09
• 3, place Léon-Bourgeois
51100 Reims
Tél. : 03 26 40 12 12
• 51460 L'Épine
Tél. : 03 26 66 96 83
• 22, rue Lasalle – 57000 Metz
Tél. : 03 87 76 10 11
• Rue Marcel-Doret
62100 Calais
Tél. : 03 21 97 21 22
• 19, rue de Wissembourg
67000 Strasbourg
Tél. : 03 88 23 50 75

RB : Le Repaire de Bacchus (head office)
31, avenue de l'Opéra
75001 Paris
Tél. : 01 53 29 97 97

REF : Cave Reflets
3, chemin du Bois-de-la-Ville
84230 Châteauneuf-du-Pape
Tél. : 04 90 83 71 07

RM : Rhône Millésimes (La Bouteillerie)
42, Grande Rue – BP 27
69420 Condrieu
Tél. : 04 74 59 84 96

VIN : La Vinothèque
9, rue Pointin – 80000 Amiens
Tél. : 03 22 91 44 31
Minitel : 3615 Alavinotheque

VTQ : La Vinothèque
16, rue Michelet – 37000 Tours
Tél. : 02 47 64 75 27

BIBLIOGRAPHY

Clive Coates M.W.
The Vine (monthly)
Clive Coates M.W., London, various editions

J.-P. Dezavelle and E. Zipper
L'Encyclopédie de la cuisine
SAEP, Colmar, 1995

Roger Dion
Histoire de la vigne et du vin en France
Flammarion, Paris, 1977

Michel Dovaz
Châteauneuf-du-Pape
(Collection « Le Grand Bernard des Vins de France »)
Jacques Legrand, Boulogne, 1992

Hugh Johnson
Wine Companion (2nd edition)
Mitchell Beazley, London, 1987

John Livingstone-Learmonth
The Wines of the Rhône
(3rd edition)
Faber and Faber, London, 1992

Remington Norman
Rhône Renaissance
Mitchell Beazley, London, 1995

Robert Parker
Les Vins de la vallée du Rhône
Solar, Paris, 1998

Jacques Puisais
Le Goût juste
Flammarion, Paris, 1985

La Revue du Vin de France
Revue du Vin de France SA,
Levallois-Perret, various editions

Acknowledgement

The author would like to express his gratitude to all the growers and estate-managers
for the warm welcome and hospitality extended to him during the preparation of this book,
for the time devoted to answering his questions, and for very kindly providing him
with the necessary documentation and a bottle to be photographed.
His warm thanks also go to Tim Johnston of Juvenile's Wine Bar in Paris for his valuable advice.

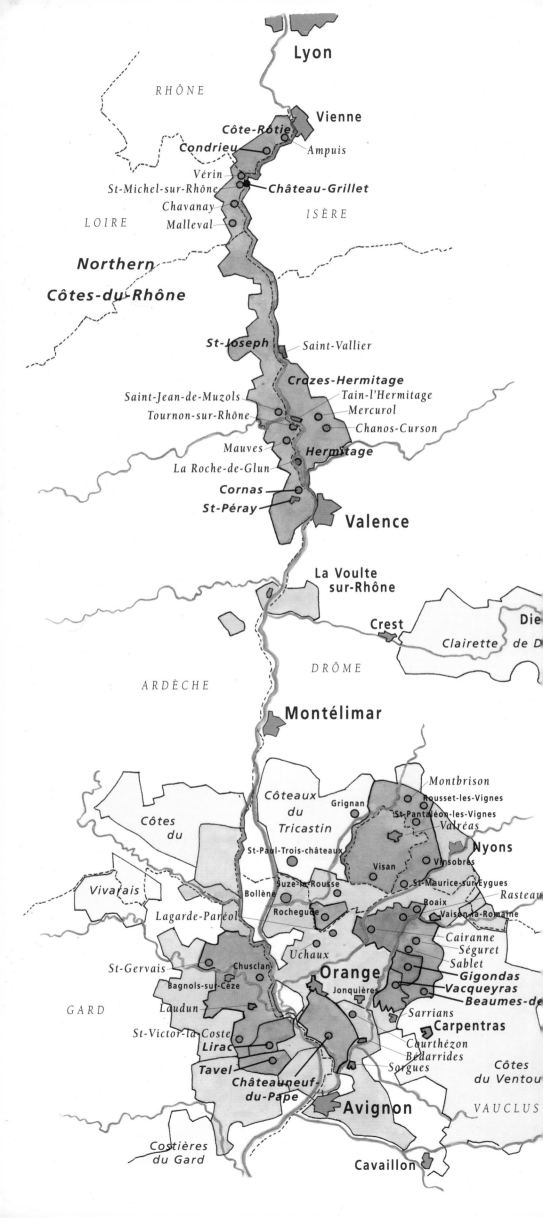